Liberating Eschatology

Liberating Eschatology

Essays in Honor of Letty M. Russell

Margaret A. Farley and Serene Jones, editors

Westminster John Knox Press
Louisville, Kentucky

Book design by Sharon Adams
Cover design by Pam Poll
Cover art: The Gate, *gouache on paper by Shepard Parsons*

First edition
Published by Westminster John Knox Press
Louisville, Kentucky

This book is printed on acid-free paper that meets the American National
Standards Institute Z39.48 standard. ∞

PRINTED IN THE UNITED STATES OF AMERICA
99 00 01 02 03 04 05 06 07 08 — 10 9 8 7 6 5 4 3 2 1

Library of Congress Cataloging-in-Publication Data

Liberating eschatology : essays in honor of Letty M. Russell / edited
    by Margaret Farley and Serene Jones.
        p.   cm.
    Includes bibliographical references and index.
    ISBN 0-664-25788-7 (alk. paper)
    1. Eschatology.   2. Hope—Religious aspects—Christianity.
    I. Russell, Letty M.   II. Farley, Margaret A.   III. Jones, Serene, 1959– .
BT823.L53   1999
236—dc21   99-23656

CONTENTS

INTRODUCTION

Serene Jones and Margaret A. Farley

Most students arrive at Yale Divinity School never having heard of a "shalom meal." If they are lucky, however, they soon find themselves in Letty Russell's liberation theology seminars or feminist theology classes. At the end of each semester, she invites the class to her house to enjoy an evening of potluck feasting and song. In Letty's cozy home, nestled in the tidal marshes of Long Island Sound, her students play games and laugh heartily, sing songs and tell stories, eat and drink abundantly, and in all this offer praise to the God whose hospitality embraces us all.

These evenings are particularly remarkable because they are preceded by a semester of classroom sessions that are far from celebratory. Even though Letty's teaching models a form of hospitality throughout—from the collective provision of coffee and cookies to the organized weekly display of relevant books—nonetheless the classes are not likely to be described in festive terms. From the beginning of her time at Yale, Letty has taken on topics that other teachers avoid, such as feminist hermeneutics, gay and lesbian theology, third-world theology, critical ecclesiology, and racism. Her method of teaching these topics is demanding, not because of a long reading list (which she has) but because she requires that students talk honestly and often heatedly about their experiences with the topics at hand. She encourages truth telling and confrontation just as she encourages the constant sharpening of the students' tools of theological and social analysis. Because of this engaging form of pedagogy, students shed many tears in her classes as they relate stories of the oppressions they suffer because of their race, gender, sexuality, or class. Students shed tears as well when they begin to realize that they are implicated as oppressors, and that they must take responsibility for their privilege. Given this emotional and conflict-ridden atmosphere of hard truth telling, students are sometimes surprised by the celebratory mood of the shalom meal they share at the end of the semester. After enduring twelve weeks of intense struggle with issues such as white privilege and its implication in the harms of racism, students suddenly find themselves sitting together on the floor of her home. Here they join together in eating, singing silly songs, and creating skits filled with humor and hope. And if the evening goes as Letty has planned, they soon discover that in the midst of their struggles, a "community" has been formed.

They discover the beginnings of lifelong friendships that will sustain them in the years ahead, and, even more important, they discover that they are individually and collectively equipped with the tools they need to carry on this struggle in the many contexts of their future ministries. All this is cause for much celebration, and Letty's shalom meals allow her students to experience it.

As Letty always reminds her students in the midst of the party, what they are experiencing is just a brief glimpse of God's gift of shalom to all creation. The joyous meal offers a preview of the New Creation that God, in Jesus Christ, has promised to all. Her parties are thus a small but powerful enactment of the "liberating eschaton" that stretches before all humanity. This glimpse of God's future is liberating, Letty reminds them, because here people gather at a round table where no one is excluded, where power is shared, where multiple gifts are celebrated, and where those who have been historically marginalized are welcomed to the seats of honor. In this way, the shalom meal is a vision of a liberating eschatology—an eschatology that includes the liberation of all persons. It is also a liberating of eschatology because, she explains, when the marginal are invited to the table, the vision of the eschaton they bring is often different from the consumerist eschatology the dominant culture generates. In this sense, the shalom meal enacts a liberating of eschatology from its servitude to the forces of oppression just as it also enacts the liberation eschatology that is promised to all.

The essays collected in this book are written by fellow theologians who for many years have shared this vision with Letty. They are theologians who have gathered with her around many different kinds of tables and at a variety of liberation parties. They represent tables located in communities ranging from East Harlem and Germany to China and Costa Rica. They also represent tables shaped by disciplinary backgrounds ranging from feminist theology to biblical studies and social ethics. These essays are written by scholars who share with Letty a commitment not only to the rigors of theological education but, more important, to an activism that seeks God's shalom in everyday lives of people of faith. In this sense, the essays represent the visions of a generation of scholars who embrace, along with Letty, a "liberation eschatology" and a "liberation of eschatology."

As the essays gathered here demonstrate, Letty Russell's contribution to Christian theology over the last thirty years has been monumental. She has educated generations of students who are now transforming our churches and our society at many levels. Her teaching has primarily been in the classrooms of Yale Divinity School (YDS), where she has not only taught students the complexities of Christian theology from a liberation perspective but advised and shaped the leadership of student groups such as the Women's Center, the Black Seminarians, the Coalition (a gay, lesbian, bisexual, transgendered, and straight group), and the Social Action Committee. She has also taught liberation theology "on the road" as she has led groups of YDS students on travel seminars to such countries as South Africa, South Korea, and Chile. Her teaching further has found more permanent roots in these international contexts through her ongoing work with such groups and projects as the Ecumenical Association of Third World Theologians (EATWOT), the Faith and Order Commission of the World Council of Churches, and the newly designed San Francisco Theological Seminary International Feminist Doctor of Ministry Program.

Letty Russell's contribution to contemporary theology extends far beyond her teaching. During her years at Yale, she has written numerous books that now populate the shelves of pastors' libraries and lay people's living rooms and are carried in the backpacks and purses of many awakening feminists, young and old. It is through these widely read texts that Letty has bequeathed to the theological academy an important legacy of thought. Her theological contributions are of several sorts.

Letty Russell is perhaps best known for her uncanny ability to articulate a vision of the church that is radical in its feminist-liberationist critique but that nonetheless remains anchored in the historic traditions and communities of the Christian church. As Letty has described it, she offers her readers a theology that speaks to those who have good reason to walk away from the church but who, instead, have decided to walk with the church, in love and justice. In doing this, she has provided North American Protestant churches with a Christian feminist ecclesiology that has drawn on both her adeptness at conceptualizing doctrine and her lively pragmatic ability to speak a prophetic word that captures the hearts of readers in many walks of life. In the twentieth-century North American theological guild, she remains one of the few theologians who have been able to speak to common church folks about hard theological issues in a language that refuses to forfeit complexity for superficial but inadequate intelligibility. In doing so, she has given us a genre that lives and breathes the very theology it describes.

Letty Russell's theological bringing together of prophetic critique and historical tradition is nowhere better illustrated than in the use of scripture in her writings. In addition to editing the groundbreaking text *Feminist Interpretation of the Bible,* she has spent years crafting theological arguments that return again and again to the rich texture of the biblical text for substance and vision. In an age when progressive theologians threaten to leave the Bible behind and conservative theologians threaten to turn it into a simplistic fact sheet, Letty manages to march steadily forward down a middle path of biblical hermeneutics that finds in the Bible the voice of a God who speaks to every new generation of persons in search of faithful liberation. For Letty, the Bible is therefore not only a text of terror but also a text of emancipatory hope. And she invites her readers to join her in the imaginative world of scripture, where together they struggle arduously and productively to understand God's New Creation. The promise is that in this struggle with the scripture's "dangerous memory of the future" we will find, with the guidance of the Spirit, the liberating eschatology that comes to each generation anew.

Another striking dimension of Letty Russell's writing is the richness of its own theological texture. In weaving together social analysis, prophetic critique, doctrinal reflection, and scriptural exegesis, Letty gives her readers theological writings that are certain to stand the test of time. Students have found that, when they return to her work years after graduation, her books contain not only the old inspiring sayings that invigorated them in seminary but new and unexpected surprises of theological meaning and possibility.

Nowhere is this more obvious than in the version of Christian feminism Letty has given her readers since her earliest books. When she began writing theology more than thirty years ago, Letty immediately focused on the importance of women affirming their identity as women and creating communities of resistance with other women. In this way she asserted the theological importance of creating communities bound together by shared identity, and she did this long before identity politics hit the scene of feminist theory. Similarly, from her earliest writings to the present, Letty not only has beckoned her reader to celebrate shared identities but has pushed women to acknowledge and celebrate the differences that mark their lives, differences in which God delights. As such, before postmodern invocation of "difference" became a catchall word in feminist theory, Letty was pushing us to respect and attend to the differing borders and edges that mark women's varied identities and life experiences.

Likewise, since her early writings Letty has argued that both women's sameness and differences need to be analyzed in terms of the relations of power that run through them. Thus, before the cultural theories of power hit the scene, Letty was teaching her students to do theological power-analysis of their institutional locations and their culturally mediated relations. As yet another example of her foresight, Letty has for years been articulating a theological vision in which, finally, it is our shared hope for the future, and not just our individual identities or differences, that defines the truly emancipatory character of Christian community. This vision, she argues, is what finally empowers us to struggle for justice and to embody the already/not yet of God's promise.

Hence, long before present-day feminist political theorists began to rediscover the importance of such themes as "community" and "hope," Letty Russell was crafting a theological vision driven by communal eschatological impulses that run deep and strong. In all these ways, Letty Russell's theology offers not only to the church but to the academy and to society a vision of political community that is unabashedly theological in character while also being incontestably pertinent to pressing public concerns. While today many theologians are struggling to find a public voice, it is important to recall that in her own steady and nonflamboyant manner, Letty has spoken in this voice for years.

THE SHAPE OF THIS BOOK

The sixteen theologians, ethicists, and biblical scholars who have contributed essays to this book are colleagues who have in some way participated in one or more of the many theological projects that Letty has organized or at least worked hard to support. Though these essays were not written collaboratively (that is, they were not mutually developed and critiqued as the book was put together), they nonetheless represent a remarkable conversation. Common threads run through them, and common questions emerge repeatedly. In part, this is explained by the unifying theme that they all address—liberating eschatology. But this is also a shared conversation that comes close to representing a community of scholars in which voices are different but commitments converge. Contexts, specialized learning, personal histories vary widely, but concerns for justice in the world and the well-being of all creation make for shared goals and a search for viable strategies.

It does not stretch the imagination too far to think of the authors of this book gathered around a table, conversing, disagreeing, struggling for shared insight even as they offer their own. They refer repeatedly to one another's work, at times critically and at times appreciatively. The same is true of their response to Letty Russell's writings—a response that can be as strongly critical as it is appreciative and genuinely grateful. Some of the essays approach the theme of eschatology explicitly, some implicitly, but all are exploring the parameters of human and Christian hope. To see these scholars as conversants around a table has provided us with the structure of the book, built from the contributions rather than preliminarily imposed on them, following coherent trains of thought from beginning to end.

It is not surprising that such a conversation begins (Part 1) with reflections about Letty Russell's own work, past and present. J. Shannon Clarkson traces the transformative goals and strategies of a lifetime of practice and thought concentrated in translation, education, and liberation. Rosemary Radford Ruether situates Letty Russell's theological commitments and achievements in the historical context of American Protestant Christianity, identifying both the influences of historical location and the distinctiveness of Letty's contributions to feminist liberation theology. Ruether draws important parallels between the rise of feminist and abolitionist (later Civil Rights) movements and movements in both the nineteenth and twentieth centuries for changes in women's participation in the ministry of the churches. Within this history, she locates Letty as both a pioneer and a still-prophetic voice. M. Shawn Copeland focuses on the method that characterizes Letty's theology, probing her preoccupation with the eschatological, her search not only for a "usable past" in the tradition but a "usable future." Thinking "from the other end," this theology (and the praxis that nourishes it and is its fruit) is finally, in Copeland's view, a "churchly" feminist liberation theology.

It is also not surprising that a table conversation such as this one would move to the telling of stories (Part 2). Phyllis Trible begins with an invitation to the table offered to a variety of biblical characters. From Hosea to Huldah, Miriam to Jeremiah, many from ancient Israel are asked to join the conversation, tell their stories, and perhaps adjudicate their sometimes contradictory ideals, forged out of vastly different experiences. Next, Katharine Doob Sakenfeld brings Ruth to the table, trying to find out if there is a "household of freedom" in the patriarchal community that shaped Ruth's story. She puts Ruth in conversation with not only North Atlantic twentieth-century women but Asian Christian women, and the results are both important and surprising. The prophet Ezekiel comes too, brought by Elsa Tamez. Tamez wants to hear how the dreams of persons in exile can include hope for the future, how prophets can speak of Jubilee when all around them is evidence of intractable, systemic "anti-Jubilee."

Katie G. Cannon calls on Zora Neale Hurston to tell the story of Ruby McCollum, a "paradigmatic narrative of injustice." This is a tale of great woe, but also of transformative hope. To repeat it is to place in relief the mid-twentieth-century strategies for mobilizing Black resistance to racial and sexual injustice. A part of the same struggle marks the experience of Martin Luther King Jr., and Malcolm X, for whom the city is either a dream or a nightmare, a symbol of hope or a symbol of despair for poor people. James H. Cone narrates and analyzes the very different stories of these two men. Their lives and ministries diverge yet converge, each seeking finally a "way out of hell *now*" for the Black urban poor.

The final story is Mercy Amba Oduyoye's—her own story as a childless woman in Africa. Neither African religions nor Christian churches offered her an adequate eschatology for understanding childless marriage. Searching to transform her (and others') experience of the "child factor," she discovers the power of her own naming and the creative command of God.

The next phase of the conversation is "work" (Part 3). Of course, it has all been work, in the sense in which Letty Russell insists on calling breakout groups (that is, the small groups formed within a large class) in her classes "work" groups, not merely "discussion" groups. Just as every conversant brings a story, so each participates in the work of discernment, analysis, identification of method, deconstruction and construction of theories, and strategizing of practice. Here to help are a biblical scholar and two theological ethicists. Elisabeth Schüssler Fiorenza argues for an "analytic of kyriarchy" in addressing historical Jesus research and in all feminist theological constructions. Only thus is it possible, she believes, to take critical account of multiplicative inter-structured oppressions, including those that have fostered anti-Judaism and White supremacy. The Jesus movement can then be seen as an emancipatory movement, a *basileia* movement whose vision of God's commonweal can be followed. Kwok Pui-lan, for her part, enters the current debates about women, nature, embodiment, and eschatological hope. Critiquing the various strands of feminist theological anthropology, she proposes a new beginning—not with theories but with the concrete bodies of women who have experienced conquest, slavery, colonization. What hope can rise from these experiences? How can the "tender web of life hold"? There are ways, she maintains, for advancing toward what Letty Russell calls the "mending of creation." In all these struggles, for adequate theory as well as for effective action, Beverly Wildung Harrison charges that some forms of feminist theory will be counterproductive. If liberationist assumptions of "practice as politics" are not kept alive in postmodernist feminist discourses, the goals of a feminism anchored in a movement will be lost. Joining the conversation with Letty Russell and other senior scholars, Harrison opposes neoliberalism and any new claims for "orthodoxy," even those proposed by feminists. This does not mean, however, that we have no clues to the meaning of authentic freedom.

Finally, the conversation moves to more explicitly systematic discussions of eschatology (Part 4). Perhaps only now is it possible to critique and construct a viable eschatology that is liberated and liberating. Participants join in from different perspectives and with different resources. Sharon H. Ringe offers an interpretation of the Fourth Gospel in which she finds no final, eschatological Word of God but an "ultimate" one in the word of God's love for all the world. The notion of "liberating eschatology" provides a lens onto this Gospel, primarily by allowing a focus on the Spirit of truth, the Paraclete who is comforter and advocate and whose engagement with us moves into time beyond the earthly life of Jesus into the future forever. Here is the Word made flesh, in communities whose hope and whose action is for justice and peace.

Jürgen Moltmann has been the theologian par excellence of eschatology. Here he continues his long-standing insistence on the connection between "last things" and "first things," between the end of the systems of this world and the beginning of a new order. Opposing both conservative eschatologies of apocalyptic "delay" and progressive eschatologies of "after history" millenialism, Moltmann argues for a movement now toward a human future that is made possible because it is embraced in God's future. We have anticipatory knowledge of what this future looks like in history, and we have insights into what we must do to bring about what we nonetheless also "expect." Joan M.

Martin provides concrete examples of this sort of eschatology in her render-ing of Black womanist "apocalyptic sensibilities" conjoined with "eschatolog-ical hopes." Hopes are shaped and reshaped, through sacred sources and ongoing experience, and the symbols of hope and despair are held in tension even as they wage battle against each other. The conversation, for now, ends resoundingly with Ada María Isasi-Díaz allowing the voices of Latinas and of *mujerista* theology to unfold further the meaning of prophetic eschatology. *Mujerista* narratives can, she maintains, give shape to our hopes and hope to our prophecies.

Of course, this conversation cannot end. For one thing, so many others need to be around this table—others who have worked with Letty Russell and who have already been part of an ongoing search for a usable future. Among them are many who do not stand in the Christian tradition, either because they stand within other religious traditions or because they have found it necessary to leave all religious traditions behind. Letty's work with students and col-leagues has long included collaboration with Jewish, Muslim, Hindu, Shinto, Buddhist, and Native American scholars and with representatives of the many other religions of Africa and the various parts of Asia. She is also in conver-sation with post-Christian feminists who have found life in Goddess tradi-tions. All these voices belong at this very large table—not only for Letty's sake but for the sake of all of us who need deeper understandings of our reasons for hope.

Moreover, it is not as if this brief conversation has identified all the ques-tions feminists and liberationists have about religious hope. For all the em-phasis here on a this-worldly eschatology, Carol Christ's challenge to a Christian affirmation of an unlimited future may still prod us to further in-sights.[1] For all the concern voiced at this table for a hope that is "hope for us" and not only "hope for me," Rosemary Ruether's concern for an ecological hope may yet leave us with questions of human and even personal immortal-ity.[2] For all the acquiescence to what Elizabeth Johnson calls the "apophatic character of contemporary belief,"[3] we may still ask about the nature of what God's future holds for ours. The opposite of "pie in the sky" illusion is not de-spair of any new possibility. To hope is to believe that what looks like a closed and settled fate is not really so. Without hope in a change that can lessen suf-fering or alter its meaning or provide us with power to resist it, we are crushed and cannot live. If it is a mistake to hope in another world but not in this one, is it also a mistake to hope only in this world and not in another, when the "other" may finally be one with this world transformed? To some extent, hope is always for things unseen, but it also sees in some way that in which it hopes. Far from eliminating the need for moral discernment and action, this kind of hope makes it possible. It is this hope that sustains our presence at this table and that compels us to liberate our eschatology.

We must not end without acknowledging that there are others who have indeed participated at this table but whose names have not yet been heard by all. These include Kristin Brantman, Kalbryn McLean, and Shelley Rambo, who have assisted us along the way with expert and gracious editorial and clerical contributions. They also include Jann Cather Weaver, whose help with the final "recording" of this conversation has been invaluable. J. Shannon Clarkson, whose voice has already been heard, deserves special gratitude for a variety of forms of assistance in concretizing this project. We are happy to introduce to the feminist publishing world the artwork of Shepard Parsons, whose painting graces our cover. And finally, we are extremely grateful to Stephanie Egnotovich, the executive editor of Westminster John Knox Press, who has enthusiastically and patiently facilitated this conversation through to print.

It would be safe to say that no contributors to a book such as this have been more delighted to honor a colleague and to continue with her their critical dialogue. We all owe Letty Russell a debt of gratitude, and we all count on sustaining our colleagueship into a usable future.

NOTES

1. See Carol Christ, *Laughter of Aphrodite: Reflections on a Journey to the Goddess* (San Francisco: Harper & Row, 1987), esp. p. 214. See also Rita Nakashima Brock, *Journeys of the Heart: A Christology of Erotic Power* (New York: Crossroad, 1988), esp. p. 91.
2. See Rosemary Radford Ruether, *Gaia and God: An Ecofeminist Theology of Earth Healing* (San Francisco: HarperCollins, 1992), pp. 250–53.
3. Elizabeth A. Johnson, *Friends of God and Prophets: A Feminist Theological Reading of the Communion of Saints* (New York: Continuum, 1998), p. 245.

CONTRIBUTORS

Katie G. Cannon is associate professor of religion at Temple University in Philadelphia, Pennsylvania.

J. Shannon Clarkson is currently working as an educational consultant and editor for the Bible Translation and Utilization Committee of the National Council of the Churches of Christ in the U.S.A. and for the Women's Division of the United Methodist Church.

James H. Cone is the Charles Briggs Distinguished Professor of Systematic Theology at Union Theological Seminary in New York City.

M. Shawn Copeland is associate professor of systematic theology at Marquette University in Milwaukee, Wisconsin.

Margaret A. Farley is the Gilbert L. Stark Professor of Christian Ethics at Yale University Divinity School in New Haven, Connecticut.

Elisabeth Schüssler Fiorenza is the Krister Stendahl Professor of Scripture and Interpretation at Harvard Divinity School in Cambridge, Massachusetts.

Beverly Wildung Harrison is the Carolyn Williams Beaird Professor of Christian Social Ethics Emerita at Union Theological Seminary in New York City. She currently lives and works in western North Carolina.

Ada María Isasi-Díaz, born and raised in Cuba, is professor of ethics and theology at Drew University in Madison, New Jersey.

Serene Jones is associate professor of systematic theology at Yale Divinity School in New Haven, Connecticut.

Kwok Pui-lan is the William F. Cole Professor of Christian Theology and Spirituality at Episcopal Divinity School in Cambridge, Massachusetts.

Joan M. Martin is a Presbyterian minister and the William R. Rankin Associate Professor in Christian Ethics at Episcopal Divinity School in Cambridge, Massachusetts.

Jürgen Moltmann is professor emeritus of systematic theology on the Protestant faculty of the University of Tübingen in Germany.

Mercy Amba Oduyoye is currently the director of the Institute for Women in Religion and Culture in Accra, Ghana, West Africa.

Sharon H. Ringe is professor of New Testament at Wesley Seminary in Washington, D.C., and adjunct professor of biblical studies at the Universidad Biblica Latinoamericana.

Rosemary Radford Ruether is the Georgia Harkness Professor of Applied Theology at Garrett-Evangelical Theological Seminary and a member of the graduate faculty of Northwestern University in Evanston, Illinois.

Katharine Doob Sakenfeld is W. A. Eisenberger Professor of Old Testament Literature and Exegesis at Princeton Theological Seminary in Princeton, New Jersey.

Elsa Tamez is professor of theology at the Seminario Biblico Latinoamericano in San José, Costa Rica.

Phyllis Trible is professor of biblical studies at Wake Forest University Divinity School in Winston-Salem, North Carolina, and Baldwin Professor of Sacred Literature Emerita at Union Theological Seminary in New York City.

PART 1

LIBERATING THE TABLE:
THEOLOGY AND THE PRAXIS OF LETTY M. RUSSELL

1

TRANSLATION, EDUCATION, AND LIBERATION

A Retrospective

J. Shannon Clarkson

On reading the title of this essay, the reader may well wonder why the term *translation* is grouped with *education* and *liberation*. In particular, one may wonder why such a word is used in an essay that is, in part, a retrospective of the life and work of Letty M. Russell. However, the three terms become intertwined as they describe the efforts of one engaged in transformational education working toward the eschatological task of mending God's creation. And although *translation* may seem the odd one out, in practice the task of the transformative educator begins with translation, and this is particularly true for a feminist. Traditionally, translation has indicated the interpretive move from one language to another. For feminists, however, the first step in any encounter is always to analyze the contents of the engagement: the context; the active biases; the agenda, both hidden and revealed. To do this analysis, one must carefully examine the language of the situation and translate as necessary.

Living with Letty Russell since 1976 has enabled me to see how she has refined her translation skills, in addition to allowing me to observe her considerable gifts as an educator and liberation theologian. The original title for this essay was "Organizing for the Future." Certainly, anyone familiar with Letty's life and work is aware that she is a consummate organizer. Whether she is arranging her notes for a manuscript, strategizing for her latest justice work, or counting out plastic "silverware" for a shalom meal in her home, she will not rest until the work is finished. Her writing of nine books and editing of seven others in the midst of teaching and engaging in work for the church locally, nationally, and globally are a witness to her determination to "do the work" and complete it.

Beginning with her ministry in the East Harlem Protestant Parish in New York City, where she worked from 1952 to 1968, organization was a key component of her work. As the pastor of the Presbyterian Church of the

Ascension, she organized the staff (including the Spanish-speaking janitor, the organist, and all the student interns from Union Theological Seminary) into a team that met every weekday morning for worship and to discuss the tasks for the day. On Mondays they followed worship with a Bible study, which was the focus in the parish for that week. On Wednesdays they went into the parishioners' homes and met in small groups for Bible study in the evening. On Thursday, after worship, the team members reported what they had learned. Letty, as the pastor, incorporated their discoveries into her sermon for the week. Each quarter she prepared a Bible-study booklet, *Daily Bible Reading,* which was published and given to each family in the congregation. Illustrations in the booklet were by Joseph Papin, a New York artist, who included as many drawings of life in East Harlem as of life in biblical times. Although each family had its own copy, the intention was for the family to engage in group study with its neighbors, not to use it for private meditation. "No attempt is made to water the lectionary down to simple verses and poetic thought, which can be read for one minute before jumping into bed."[1]

TRANSLATION

Letty's work in translation began in those days in East Harlem, when she took her knowledge of Greek and Hebrew, which she had learned as a biblical history and philosophy major at Wellesley College and then as a student at Harvard Divinity School, and used it to help interpret the word to those whom she was serving. For her, the "word" is living word and thus not confined to a particular grammar or lexicon. This understanding enabled her easily to join the effort in the early 1970s to make the scriptures more inclusive. Working with Emily V. Gibbes, the director of the Division of Education and Ministry at the National Council of the Churches of Christ in the U.S.A. (NCC), she began gathering other scholars together to create a volume of articles focused on issues of nonsexist language. The Division of Education and Ministry was charged with the task of preparing materials to enable the church, its leadership, and its members to become a biblically rooted community. In addition, the division held the copyright on the Revised Standard Version (RSV) and hence was charged with guarding that translation as well as preparing future translations. The resulting work of the writers Letty helped gather, *The Liberating Word,*[2] published in 1976, not only suggested nonsexist ways in which the biblical materials may be interpreted but also offered readers the information necessary to guide them in creating worship and study materials that were nonsexist. Although the three additional contributors to *The Liberating Word* were biblical scholars, Letty was not daunted by their expertise but rather encouraged by their knowledge, writing that the language of the church needed to change in order to be faithful to the intent of the gospel to be the good news for all people.

Although both Letty and Emily Gibbes knew in their heart of hearts that an inclusive translation of the scriptures was probably not possible in the foreseeable future, they hoped that their book would at least open the discussion further and that some middle way might be found. In fact, within a year a Task Force on Biblical Translation was appointed by the Division of Education and Ministry to consider the possibilities of how the biblical word might be more inclusive. Three years later, the task force recommended the creation of an Inclusive-Language Lectionary Committee, composed of six men and six women. Their task was to produce a three-volume inclusive-language lectionary, the first volume to appear in 1983. Although the National Council of Churches sanctioned and commissioned this work, a mighty uproar ensued when the first volume was published. In fact, so much hate mail was received, and some of it of such a vitriolic nature, that the FBI had to be called in to protect the members of the translation committee. Of course, danger to life and limb is not new to those who would attempt a new translation of the Bible, for those who would dare to translate the word of God have historically met with considerable difficulty, if not death.

Issues of inclusive language, particularly as related to the documents and worship life of the church, were just emerging into debate in the 1970s. Feminist linguists also began in earnest the discussion related to language in general in the early 1970s. However, more than a decade later the number of articles addressing issues of inclusive language as they related to theological concerns could be numbered on one hand. Yet the work of the NCC was to push the churches into the forefront of the debate, whether they liked it or not.

In 1980, the division authorized the translation committee of the RSV to begin working on a new translation, which would be called the New Revised Standard Version (NRSV).[3] The instructions for the committee mandated that "in references to men and women, masculine-oriented language should be eliminated as far as this can be done without altering passages that reflect the historical situation of ancient patriarchal culture."[4] Dr. Bruce Metzger, chair of the NRSV committee, acknowledged that the bias of earlier translators, together with the general bias of the English language toward the masculine gender, had "often restricted or obscured the meaning of the original text."[5]

As a member of the Bible Translation and Utilization (BTU) Committee of the NCC, I was able to follow the deepening understanding of Dr. Metzger concerning issues of inclusive language. Katharine Sakenfeld, one of the four women members of the NRSV translation committee, confirmed this transformation. Over the nine years of translation, the concerns stretched beyond issues of nonsexist interpretation to a broader understanding of inclusive language, adding concerns about racism, anti-Semitism, discrimination against the handicapped, and homophobia. The editors of the Inclusive Language Lectionary (ILL), too, began to recognize that their singular focus on nonsexist language was insufficient to address the broader concerns of inclusive language. As is often the case when new understandings are emerging, we do not at first encompass the fullest comprehension but gradually move in that direction. The first edition of the ILL neglected to change the word *dumb* to *mute* in the reading for the Third Sunday in Advent's version of Isaiah 35:1–10, which happened to come on the first Sunday I was to use this long-awaited new volume. As I read the text before worship, I knew that I was once again going to have to make my own emendations to the biblical text. Fortunately, the committee members soon saw their omission and changed it before the second edition was published. Subsequently, a revised Year A edition was published in 1986.

As the BTU Committee has worked with Dr. Metzger, we have challenged him to think in the most inclusive ways possible while still being faithful to the text. Before the publication of the NRSV, several members of our committee heard that the phrase "practicing homosexual" was to be introduced into the New Testament text as a substitute for "sexual pervert" in the RSV. Our committee members argued vigorously that to insert a term of twentieth-century coinage that carries with it sociological meanings of the present era into the biblical text of the first century would be truly "unnatural." Our voices were persuasive, and the new phrase was not used; nor was the "sexual pervert" phrase of the RSV employed. A victory!

Knowing that years, perhaps decades remain before an authorized translation of the Bible is published that adequately responds to the concerns voiced by the writers of *The Liberating Word*, the BTU Committee approved the proposal for and subsequent publication of *The New Testament and Psalms: An Inclusive Version*.[6] Although many were not happy at its publication, including publisher Oxford University Press's London office, enough readers were supportive to produce substantial sales.

The debate about issues of inclusive language, begun so enthusiastically in the early 1970s, continues to smolder as churches grapple with policies about the language of worship; adoption of new, inclusive hymnals and worship books; and reformulation of creedal statements. Another NCC committee, the Task Force on Educational Strategies for an Inclusive Church, asked me to create a document that might be used in the churches to introduce issues of inclusive language in a nonthreatening manner. *Language, Thought, and Social Justice*[7] was completed in 1986 and distributed widely to the denominations and through them to the churches. Letty also continues to be asked to help churches and institutions with their efforts to become more inclusive. Most recently, in April 1998, Musimbi Kanyoro, president of the World YWCA, asked her to write a paper that would help the YWCA board think about how their creedal statement might be recast, particularly in terms of the trinitarian God language it uses.

While creating a position paper about the language of a creed certainly is an issue concerning translation, at the same time the matter is one of education. To expect to change persons' attitudes about language without engaging in an educational program designed to further those ends would be to liken linguistic change to that discussed in George Orwell's *1984:* change by command rather than by heart. From her earliest postcollege experiences, Letty has been about the work of education, and it is to that part of her life that we now turn.

EDUCATION

Few people who know Letty remember that her first educational work was in the public schools of Connecticut, where she taught third grade for one year in the little town of Higganum. My favorite story of her time there involves a unit she organized around the popular television series *Howdy Doody.* She had the students create a studio where they produced their own show. As usual, Letty was working at the cutting edge. This was 1952, and although she had no TV, she realized the medium was an important one for her students and so decided to capitalize on their interest by using it as a foil for her lessons. Later, in East Harlem, she continued to use technological skills to involve her students. One enthusiastic presentation of the story of the burning bush was nearly a disaster when the cardboard bush almost caught fire from the blowtorch she was using.

That Letty should have begun her educational ministry in public education is perfectly logical for one who believes that education in a religious context should be no different from education found in the school or factory. The move from the third grade in Higganum to Christian educator in the East Harlem Protestant Parish was educationally not much of a move, though ethnographically it was significant. Letty had always thought of herself as a misfit, so despite the fact that as a white person she was a minority in the parish and as a woman trying to make change she was also an anomaly, she simply moved in and continued to move forward, doing the work of justice as she understood it.

One of her first learnings in East Harlem was that as a Christian educator, trying to make significant changes in the Presbyterian structure in the church was impossible without the proper credentials. Consequently, after three years in the parish, she decided to attend seminary. That the school she chose, Harvard Divinity School, did not yet admit women did not deter her. When Harvard wrote back to her noting this, she countered by saying that they ought to admit women and that, after all, the dean's wife was the former president of Wellesley. Thereafter, Letty and several other women were admitted. In her second year in school, the United Presbyterian Church in the U.S.A. voted to ordain women; if it hadn't, another battle might have ensued on her graduation. Even so, the dons at Harvard had a very protracted final faculty meeting to decide the distribution of honors. The two highest grade-point averages belonged to the two women of the class, and the faculty thought it might damage the self-image of the men if the women received the honors. Fortunately, good sense and scholarly tradition prevailed. However, during Letty's service of ordination at the Church of the Ascension, the preacher, Dr. Paul Lehman, argued in his sermon for forty-five minutes about whether or not women ought to be ordained. The congregation was quite relieved when he finally decided in the affirmative! Ever the believer in the goodness and surety of the eschaton, Letty sailed ahead.

After fourteen years as teacher and pastor in East Harlem, Letty wrote in *Christian Education in Mission:*

> When you begin to look at things in terms of how God's grace might be operative in and through them, you soon find: that Christian education is not just a stumbling block, but an opportunity to participate in Christ's invitation to join in God's mission; that peer-group behavior of youth and adults in American culture is not just a denial of individual freedom, but an opportunity to work in terms of meaningful community life; that out-of-date structures of church life are not just a sign of the death of the church, but an opportunity to seek new structures more relevant to the modern world and more faithful to God's calling to witness to [God's] love for that world. In short, you find with Paul that you can "give thanks in all circumstances; for this is the will of God in Christ Jesus for you" (I Thess. 5:18).[8]

As a Christian educator, Letty was committed to the work of the whole church. She found she needed "officially" to be the pastor of the parish, but her purpose in becoming such was that the laity could do the work of ministry unimpeded by hierarchical denominational bureaucracy. For her, all ministry was educational. Until the 1980s, if not still, the work of Christian education was deemed "women's work" by most, and in the U.S. context that means such work is devalued. When I continued using the title "Minister of Education" in my co-pastorate, people had difficulty accepting that I was actually a minister equal in authority with my co-pastor.

Not only was Letty interested in creating a liberating alternative to educational ministry, but she was also quite attuned to the latest theories in secular education. She found that three changes in particular were important to her work. Even though she writes of those changes as they impacted on her work in the late 1960s, those very issues continue to call for change in both secular and religious education, and she herself persists in working toward those goals.

The first issue concerns the revelation that we are called to educate for a world of change. Change is so rapid that it is no longer possible to offer people the information they will need for the future. Rather, we need to see that people have the ability to function in a world of rapid technological change, and that they are able to change with that world.

Second, the way in which knowledge has always been understood is beginning to change. Old ideas about the structure of knowledge continue to give way to newer thoughts about constructivist and transformational education. Learning is no longer to be limited to knowledge imparted at a certain time and place but instead is a gateway to further learning. This requires "learning initially not a skill but a general idea, which can then be used as a basis of recognizing subsequent problems as special cases of the idea originally mastered."[9] The learner can then construct new knowledge from old, using intuition as well as the recognition of patterns. Preparing citizens of the twenty-first century requires a method such as this to keep pace with the new information. We cannot teach students what they need to know but rather how they need to be able to learn. Transformative education is moving from what Paulo Freire described as "banking education" to the praxis of the action/reflection model. Education that is liberating takes place in acts and moments of cognition, not in the mere transferring of information.[10]

The third change is an emphasis on teaching as part of a team. Letty's ministry in East Harlem, for example, would not have been the same had she not employed the technique of team teaching. So that the Hispanic custodian could lead Bible studies in Spanish, Letty took his place as the janitor while he met with the Spanish-speaking parishioners. The Sunday sermon was the culmination of the week's dialogic analysis of the texts for the week, with responses about the texts coming to her from all segments of the congregation. As I embarked on my own educational ministry, I tried using her techniques. I reinstituted a summer Bible school, which had nearly as many staff as students. Women in their eighties helped in the kitchen where students prepared matzoth and cookies. High school students helped the children construct a golden calf out of chicken wire and stuff it with yellow tissues. (Unfortunately, when we left it unattended on the town green outside the church, a roaming dog paid it a visit, to the consternation of the students!) Sitting in fellowship hall one day at snack time, a youngster who was on my lap looked up at me and asked, "What do you do here?" Apparently, my delegation of authority and team effort had made my position as the person in charge invisible.

In contemporary teacher-education programs, team teaching is *de rigueur*. Most middle schools employ the team-teaching method, assigning four or five teachers to a team. Teachers are taught not only to participate in team situations but to involve their students in team activities as well. As often happens when idea moves from theory to practice, it becomes formulaic, and this is true of classroom models of "good" group work. The teacher is advised to assign roles to each member of the group—timekeeper, scribe, leader, and so forth. Even with all the roles, children seem to like participating in group work as much as or more than working independently.

Most people familiar with Letty's work know that *production team*—the term she used in the 1960s—became *partnership* soon thereafter and has remained a hallmark of her work since, with two of her books carrying the word in their titles: *The Future of Partnership* and *Growth in Partnership*. (She really wanted to call the second *Growth in Education*, as that is its focus, but her publisher said no one would buy a book with *education* in the title.) Not only was the term used in developing her theology of partnership based on the Greek *koinonia*, but it was one she practiced in her life as an academic as well. Moving from the variety of teams she had developed in East Harlem into the rarified air of Yale University Divinity School, as she did in 1974, might have diminished the partnership proclivity of one less dedicated to that style of work and relationship. For Letty, only the geography had changed.

Although her women colleagues numbered two faculty, one administrative dean, and a registrar, Letty organized the WAFS—the Women Administrators, Faculty, and Staff—to work together on issues of concern for all women at Yale. The 1970s saw a steep increase in the number of women seminarians across the country, which unfortunately was not followed by a comparably steep or even modest increase in the number of women faculty at any institutions. Letty began working with her Yale colleague Margaret Farley and others to strategize about opportunities in theological education for feminists. One outgrowth of their thinking was the Women's Theological Center (WTC), established in Boston in 1982 by women from many schools, with the aim of providing a one-year seminary experience for women eager to study feminist theology and ethics. The vision was for the WTC not only to provide an opportunity for study in a feminist environment but to work to create an antiracist community as well. The struggles toward this end were long and hard, and the work continues as the WTC now has as a major focus work in and among the African American communities of Boston. Letty and Margaret remained on the board for many years and continue to offer their support.

Eventually, the representation of feminists on theological faculties in the United States began to increase, and as this happened, the appeal of the WTC "study/action" year lessened for U.S. participants, though it increased for students from outside the United States. When the legalities of government regulations became too complex for the WTC board, Letty began strategizing to find a place for women, particularly those from the third world, to study feminist theology. In 1987 she helped recruit women for a summer-term course she was teaching in the Doctor of Ministry Program at San Francisco Theological Seminary (SFTS). While there, she began talking with Walter Davis, the director of the program, who had been one of her interns when he was a student at Union Theological Seminary. Letty offered to help organize and recruit students for a new Doctor of Ministry degree, which would be called an International Feminist Doctorate of Ministry. Although the members of that 1987 class consider themselves the foremothers of the tradition, the first class with the new title began in the summer of 1993 in Tokyo, where women from Japan, Korea, and the Philippines gathered. Since then, more than fifty women, 80 percent from the third world, have participated in the program.

The funding for the SFTS International Feminist Doctor of Ministry Program is another example of both the power of partnership and Letty's articulated hope that God is working with others for the mending of creation; and for all that mending, lots of stitchers are needed. Specifically, a coalition of women in Geneva, Switzerland, who staff women's desks for various church and ecumenical organizations has created a fund that provides support for women from the South to participate in the program. The women in the program are themselves ever vigilant, as well, for sources that will enable them and others to participate. The program itself meets for six weeks in San Anselmo, California, but courses take place around the world, from Geneva to Nairobi and from San José to Seoul. Women who have been in earlier programs are invited to join when the new group meets on the continent where the previous students now work, and a newsletter keeps everyone in touch.

The need to create a program such as the International Feminist Doctor of Ministry Program was clear not only from the experience of the WTC and the witness of the women in the 1987 SFTS group but also from conversations with the many women around the world Letty had met through the World Council of Churches and other opportunities. First, very few women in the third world are teaching in seminaries or universities. Second, the feminists in any given country who would like to study with other feminists are often few and far between. Third, many women cannot afford a traditional Ph.D. program because of time, money, or life situation. A doctorate in ministry offers a theological degree that blends current work with study, culminating in a project designed to concretize the women's study and enable them to seek possible new vocational avenues. One South African student in the program was asked to lead a Methodist seminary in her home, and another is now the president of the Presbyterian seminary in her country.

The line between a feminist approach to education, whether secular or religious, and feminist liberation theology is a fine one. In fact, the innovative educational endeavors described above might just as well be gathered under the heading of "Liberation" as "Education." Yet there is something particular about liberation that is perhaps the goal of transformational education, and this is where we shall now move.

LIBERATION

In turning to the *Dictionary of Feminist Theologies*[11] to read the article on liberation, I smiled to see that it was written by Joyce Ann Mercer, a former student of Letty's at Yale Divinity School. In some ways, liberation is a grand letting go. We teach others as well as we know how, and then comes the release. We hope that they are able to meet life and translate the events in their lives into meaningful happenings so that they may then work together with others to bring about God's *oikos*. For so it was with God's design. We were given first community, then the word as text and the word made flesh, and our task is to make meaning and our life's work from our interpretation and understanding of the word.

Although Letty will primarily be known as a liberation theologian and one of the foremothers of feminist theology, her work as a Christian educator was really that of a liberation theologian before the term was in common use. Like Paulo Freire, she had taken as her work the process of enabling the oppressed to analyze their world in relation to God's design, encouraging them to work together with others for their own and their neighbor's freedom. This working together for good has always been at the heart of her theology, both in her days in East Harlem and now when the struggles against the powers and principalities are waged in different arenas. She began her first book with the words:

> My theology is based on the conviction that the resurrection and victory of Christ is the starting and ending point of Christian life and nurture (I Cor. 15:51–58). Certainly this does not mean that I am unaware of the insurmountable problems of the world in which we live, or of the fact that it is only by faith that we can declare that the world has been redeemed in Jesus Christ. Yet with Paul, I am convinced that "in everything God works for good with those who love him," not because sin and death do not abound, but because by the power of God "the grace of that one man Jesus Christ abounded for many" (Rom. 8:28; 5:15–17).[12]

Like Freire, I too am working in a secular context as I seek to educate future educators. One course I teach, "The Social Foundations of American Education," provides the setting for organized reflection on what these social foundations are, who determined them, and what they mean for these future teachers and their students. This is one of the final courses education students take, after most of them have spent at least one semester in a full-time in-

ternship as a substitute teacher in a public school. The students are well aware
of the problems confronting educators in the schools today. We talk about the
stresses they will face as they combat racism, sexism, homophobia, and, one of
the worst ills of teachers, burnout. Together we strategize about how they will
keep on keeping on. They are committed to making a difference in their students' lives and seeking to end the inequalities they see around them. We speak
of justice and of the necessity to be sure that all are included. The one thing
we do not speak of is God. For the class discussion, the passion for justice rests
in each one's individual spirituality. The imperative to work toward mending
the creation has no spoken connection to a Creator who is working with us.
Those who work in secular education may articulate only the ultimate authority of their own conscience; any higher authority is suspect. But my students
know that I am ordained and that I served a church for ten years. They know
that my convictions are rooted in my faith. Though a discussion of that faith
is out of bounds, the faith itself is not irrelevant. The liberation theology of
one who works in secular education must use the language of secular humanism, rather than that of the Christian tradition. This does not mean that God
is not present in that context, going about the eschatological work of mending the creation.

Secular contexts are not the only ones in which there are constraints on language. In the early 1990s, the Peace and Justice Center of the Roman Catholic
Church in Letty's local community decided to start a women's center. Letty
was asked to serve on the board. When the board incorporated, the members
included individuals who were Jewish, Roman Catholic, Protestant, and some
not affiliated with any religious tradition. Issues such as abortion were difficult
to discuss, as they were assumed to be tied to particular religious perspectives.
Letty was asked to lead a discussion about spirituality because some of the
members equated it only with organized religion. Here, as in my "Social Foundations" class, limits were accepted yet transcended. Admirably, no one
wanted to impose a faith stance on anyone else. Yet the discussion of justice
had to go forward.

In the late 1980s, Letty visited South Korea and Japan. When she returned,
she wanted to assist Asian women studying theology in the United States in
forming a support group where they might come together both for encouragement and for the development of an Asian woman's theology. Asian
women studying in the Northeast were invited to Yale for a weekend to discuss the project. The group was enthusiastic and chose a name, Asian Women
Theologians (AWT). The next year, they decided to advertise their annual
meeting to all the seminaries, and the second major gathering was larger than
the first. Once the message was spread more widely, Asian Americans as well
as Asians studying in the United States came, and they objected to the limit-
ing name. Moreover, some were studying for a Master of Divinity degree, not

a doctorate, and therefore wanted to add the word *ministry* to the title. The group then became Asian and Asian American Women in Theology and Ministry (AAAWTM). The group continued meeting at least once a year, still with Letty's support in planning and in fund-raising. Eventually, it became clear to her that the group no longer needed encouragement and interference from a white woman. It was time for Letty to let go, and for Asian women in the United States and Canada to take ownership of their own group. That moment coincided with the appointment of a small number of Asian women to university and seminary faculties. The power of the group is a liberating, creative power.

CONCLUSION

Liberating theology, education, and action take place everywhere—in the world of secular education, in parts of the world where Christian feminists sometimes labor alone, in small towns where women work to increase awareness about women's issues, in churches and schools of all kinds. Out of all of these contexts come clues for ways to live into God's future. These clues provide a fitting conclusion to this retrospective and a challenging call to move into this future.

Letty herself offers three clues, which though first scripted by her in 1967 are as valid now as then. The first is that we need to live with questions rather than answers. "In a changing world, there are only changing answers."[13] Thus my advice to my student teachers is that they are in training to become dancers—people who are attuned to the thoughts and needs of their students and their society, called to dance together into the knowledge of life.

The second clue suggests that we need eyes of faith to enable us to see the world from God's perspective. When we are exasperated because we or someone else has again failed, we need to step back and take God's historical view. A recognized failure has the chance to become a success, or at least an opportunity for learning.

The third clue is that we need to celebrate life, all life, and the world in which we live. What would Letty's classes be without a final shalom meal for celebrating all the learning that had begun? A quarter-century before Alice Walker wrote in *The Color Purple* that we should celebrate the world because God is calling us to do so, Letty wrote that we need to "express the fact that we enjoy the world in which we live simply because it is God's world—a world where [God] makes [God's self] known in the events of history, a world that finds its meaning and purpose in terms of [God's] love for it."[14]

More than a dozen years later Letty continued, "We have no guarantee, simply an expectation of faithfulness and love. We may have different plans and goals to realize, but it is a common hope in the One who is our future that provides a basis for a new focus of relationship in Jesus Christ."[15]

> For surely I know the plans I have for you, says the LORD, plans for your welfare and not for harm, to give you a future with hope. (Jer. 29:11, NRSV)

NOTES

1. Letty M. Russell, *Christian Education in Mission* (Philadelphia: Westminster Press, 1967), p. 85.
2. Letty M. Russell, ed., *The Liberating Word: A Guide to Nonsexist Interpretation of the Bible* (Philadelphia: Westminster Press, 1976).
3. New Revised Standard Version of the Bible (New York: Division of Education and Ministry of the National Council of the Churches of Christ in the U.S.A., 1989).
4. From the "To the Reader" preface written by Dr. Bruce Metzger for each edition of the NRSV.
5. Ibid.
6. Victor Roland Gold, Thomas L. Hoyt Jr., Sharon H. Ringe, Susan Brooks Thistlewaite, Burton H. Throckmorton Jr., Barbara A. Withers, eds., *The New Testament and Psalms: An Inclusive Version* (New York: Oxford University Press, 1995).
7. J. Shannon Clarkson, *Language, Thought, and Social Justice* (New York: National Council of the Churches of Christ in the U.S.A., 1986).
8. Russell, *Christian Education in Mission*, pp. 10–11.
9. Ibid., p. 30.
10. Paulo Freire, *Pedagogy of the Oppressed* (New York: Herder & Herder, 1970), p. 66.
11. Letty M. Russell and J. Shannon Clarkson, eds., *Dictionary of Feminist Theologies* (Louisville, Ky.: Westminster John Knox Press, 1996).
12. Russell, *Christian Education in Mission*, pp. 9–10.
13. Ibid., p. 32.
14. Ibid.
15. Letty M. Russell, *The Future of Partnership* (Philadelphia: Westminster Press, 1979), p. 176.

2

THE THEOLOGICAL VISION
OF LETTY RUSSELL

Rosemary Radford Ruether

Letty Russell has been one of the pioneering feminist activist church leaders, as well as theologians, in the American church for more than forty years. It is indeed a daunting task to pay tribute to her life's work. In this essay I touch on something of the historical context in American Protestant Christianity in which Letty Russell was shaped as a churchwoman and theologian and then speak specifically on what I see as her distinctive theological contribution to feminist liberation theology.

THE HISTORICAL CONTEXT

In the United States, feminist and civil rights movements have historically gone hand in hand. The interrelation between rights for African Americans and rights for women has also sparked movements of theological reflection. This was true in the nineteenth century, and it was again true in the 1960s, when Letty Russell's ministry in East Harlem and her theological reflection on this ministry were being shaped.

In the 1830s the abolitionist movement drew into itself key female leaders, such as Sarah and Angelina Grimké and Lucretia Mott. When conservative male church leaders attacked these women for violating scriptural ordinances that "women keep silence" by speaking publicly on behalf of the slave, the Grimké sisters realized they would have to link abolitionism with the rights of women. Both Blacks and women were being unjustly subjugated by a church teaching which stated that God's mandated "orders of creation" demand both racial and gender hierarchy in church and society.

This insight also drew the Grimké sisters to apply to the issue of the sub-ordination of women the same theological critique that they had used to at-tack slavery. The Grimké sisters took their stand on the belief that God created all humans equally in the image of God. No domination had been given by God to one group of human beings over others, neither Whites over Blacks nor men over women. Such usurpation of power by some groups of humans over others in slavery and sexism does not represent God's creational intention but rather humanity's sinful departure from this intent. The restoration and redemption of creation demands the overthrow of all such constructions of domination of some over others and the restoration of all humans to equality in mutuality with one another.[1]

This first wave of feminism and abolitionism in alliance also sparked the first women's ordination movement. Already in 1848, at the first women's rights gathering in Seneca Falls, New York, led by abolitionist-feminists Lucretia Mott and Elizabeth Cady Stanton, the Declaration of Sentiments culminated in a demand for women's right to preach. The final resolution of the conference reads: "Resolved: that the speedy success of our cause depends on the zealous and untiring efforts of both men and women for the overthrow of the [male] monopoly of the pulpit."[2]

In 1853, the first woman was ordained in the Christian tradition. Although women had been allowed unordained roles of public preaching in earlier eras of Christian history—for example, the twelfth century's Hildegard of Bingen and the eighteenth century's Wesleyan women in England—these roles always came under the rubric of special prophetic gifts given by God to an individual. Only with the ordination of Antoinette Brown to the Congregational ministry in 1853 did a Christian denomination concede that women might share in the ordained ministry as a normal possibility.

The theological basis for this first ordination was argued by Luther Lee, an evangelical preacher who led Antoinette Brown's ordination service. Lee took his text from Galatians 3:28: "in Christ . . . there is neither male nor female" (RSV). He combined it with Acts 2:17–18, where it is said that with the outpouring of the Spirit at Pentecost that founds the church, "your sons and your daughters shall prophesy." Lee argued that the prophetic office is the preaching office. Since the gifts of prophecy were given to women as well as men by the Spirit from the beginning of Christianity, there had never been any excuse for the church to exclude women from ministry. The preaching office was given to women equally by Christ.[3]

In the later nineteenth century, Methodist Protestants, Unitarians, Universalists, and a few other Christian groups conceded ordained ministry to women, but their numbers remained small. The "mainline" Presbyterian, Methodist, and Lutheran churches rejected such a possibility on the grounds of scriptural injunctions. Instead, they invented new lay ministries for women, such as a renewed female deaconate for inner-city work or foreign service.

The movements that raised questions of sexism, racism, and women's full participation in ministry were to be gradually silenced at the end of the nineteenth century, and particularly in the 1920s and 1930s. It would not be until the 1950s and 1960s that a new wave of abolitionism and feminism was to arise, a hundred years after the first wave was sparked in the nineteenth century. Letty Russell's ministry and theology are paradigmatic for this second wave of antiracist and feminist struggle.

Interestingly enough, the turning point for the ordination of women in the American Presbyterian Church and Methodist Episcopal churches took place in 1956, before there was a major development of second-wave feminism. The reasons for the change in the historical policy of the two major denominations are complex. Part of the cause for this change lies in remnants of the earlier movements for the ordination of women that remained in the heritages of these bodies. The Methodist Protestants had ordained women beginning in 1880. They lost this right when they merged into the Methodist Episcopal Church in 1938, but some leaders remained dissatisfied with this loss and sought restoration of the rights of ministry of their women colleagues.

So, too, women deaconesses, returned from foreign service, sought further openings for women. The opening of theological education to women at the turn of the century brought the first women theologians, such as Georgia Harkness and Hulda Niebuhr, into teaching in graduate theological seminaries.[4] Georgia Harkness worked behind the scenes among Methodists to bring about the historic vote in favor of women's ordination in 1956.[5] Also, the Lutheran and Reformed churches in Europe were beginning to ordain women. Liberal Presbyterian leaders in the United States were aware of these developments, and this disposed them to be open to similar changes in their churches.

Perhaps the very lack of a vocal women's movement in American society made this change easier for male church leaders in 1956. No great backlash against movements for women's rights was emanating from conservatives, as would be the case once women again began to speak on their own behalf in the 1960s. Many male church leaders thought it was the "right thing to do" to admit women to ordained ministry but foresaw no great influx of women to ministry occurring as a result of this change.[6]

Indeed, this change attracted remarkably little attention in 1956. Many women in the churches were unaware that ordained ministry had become available to them. It was only when a new feminist movement arose in the late 1960s that the numbers of women seeking theological education and ordained ministry began to grow.

As in the 1830s, the new wave of feminism arose in conjunction with a new abolitionism: in this case, a struggle to abolish the Jim Crow laws that had been put in place in the U.S. South in the aftermath of Reconstruction, and that had created a racial apartheid system that disenfranchised Blacks and deprived them of equal participation in public life and services. This movement to dismantle racist laws and open American society to all citizens regardless of race again drew many new women into the struggle.

The women in the civil rights movement then began to experience sexist discrimination, often in the movement itself from White and Black male leaders. The heightened awareness of human rights inspired such women to begin to articulate their own experiences of discrimination in the movement and in the larger society. A new wave of feminism was born.

With these second waves of abolitionism and feminism came new theological reflections. James Cone began to shape a Black theology to articulate the failure of the churches and seminaries to face racism in their own theological systems and church practices.[7] Women beginning to enter theological education and ministry likewise became aware of the pervasive sexism in church teaching and practice. Their critique of these traditions and practices was the seedbed for a new feminist theology that arose in the 1970s.

LETTY RUSSELL AND FEMINIST LIBERATION THEOLOGY

Letty Russell's entry into training for ministry stands at the starting point of these converging histories of Blacks and women in seminaries and church service in the 1960s and 1970s. In 1954, Harvard Divinity School admitted its first women to its Master of Divinity program but was reluctant to give the only two women in the graduating class the top honors that they had earned, on the grounds that this would put the men in a bad light.[8] One of those two women was Letty Russell.

At that time she was an isolated woman in a system of theological education in which almost all the students and faculty were White males. It is important to remember how recently this was the case as we look at theological education in the 1990s, where women students are now often the majority and women faculty make up about one-third.[9] Blacks, Asians, and Hispanics have also taken their place in theological schools, and there is a growing concern to include the perspectives of Black, Hispanic, and Asian women professors as well. Thus Christian theological education and theology have been decisively reshaped in the last thirty years by the impact of the combined feminist and racial/ethnic liberation movements.

Feminist theology has become a normal part of the offerings of the curriculum at most theological schools, although usually still as an elective, not as a way of rethinking the whole curriculum. Every field of theological studies, from Bible and church history to theology, ethics, pastoral psychology, and worship, now has extensive feminist literature to draw on for its courses. Yet one cannot rejoice that a total change has taken place in how the education in these institutions actually shapes the ministers of today and tomorrow. Most male students and faculty still do not read this literature as a necessary part of their education and scholarship. Women in the Christian churches have come *note this!* a long way since 1960, but the danger of erasure of the memory of this achievement, like that of their foremothers of the nineteenth century, is not over.

Letty Russell is both a pioneer in the development of feminist theology and a continuing prophetic voice in American and international circles for a vision of feminism deeply rooted in a biblically based liberation theology. Russell would describe herself as having spent her whole adult life "trying to figure out how to subvert the church into being the church."[10] In 1954 she was one of the two women admitted to Harvard Divinity School, and in 1958 one of the first women to be ordained by the Presbyterian Church. She spent her formative years in ministry, from 1952 to 1955 and from 1958 to 1968, in the East Harlem Protestant Parish in the poor Black ghetto of New York City, as an integral part of a creative experiment in inclusive ministry across racial and class lines. Her first book, *Christian Education in Mission* (1967), reflects this experience in designing an alternative way of being church in East Harlem.[11]

In the early 1970s, Russell began to reflect theologically on her many experiences of marginalization as a woman in theological education and ministry. This led her to integrate the feminist perspective into the paradigms of Black and liberation theologies that she had absorbed from the Black civil rights movement and from Latin America. Her first explicitly feminist book was *Human Liberation in a Feminist Perspective: A Theology* (1974).[12] Over the next twenty years, Russell moved from East Harlem to become a professor of theology at Yale Divinity School and continues to expand her connections with third-world liberation movements, particularly with third-world feminists in the church.

Russell's books on partnership, on feminist interpretation of the Bible, on authority in feminist theology (*The Household of Freedom*, 1987), and on feminist ecclesiology (*The Church in the Round*, 1993) represent the ongoing growth of her theology.[13] Russell is notable not only as a theologian of continuing practical/prophetic insight but as an enabler of other women, particularly third-world women, to do theology. She has helped sponsor many projects, programs, and initiatives that have given women theologians forums to dialogue together and to develop their theology in their own contexts. This many-sided work of enablement itself is the praxis base and expression of Russell's feminist liberation theology.[14]

Russell's theological methodology can be summed up by her phrase "thinking from the other end." By "other end" she means the perspective of redemption or New Creation.[15] For Russell, much influenced by Jürgen Moltmann's *Theology of Hope,* the norm of Christian theology lies not in the past, either in some ideal moment in the Bible or the early church or in the beginnings of creation, but in the future.[16] This does not mean there are not reference points for Christian theology in paradigmatic memories of the past, in the exodus community of Israel, in Jesus Christ, and in the "original" creation. But all these past moments are to be understood as "memories of the future."

The normative future is the norm of total liberation, the "revolution in which everyone wins."[17] This does not mean that the liberation of everyone into just relations of well-being in communion with God and creation does not involve overcoming the vast evils of racism, sexism, classism, war, poverty, and violence on many fronts, but rather that one does not confuse the overcoming of these evils with the demonization, defeat, and destruction of particular groups of people, namely, White men, capitalists, Christian clergy. One overcomes systems of evil while reclaiming the persons captive in those systems, the oppressed and the oppressors, for a new, liberated humanity on a redeemed earth.

Russell's vision of redemption insists on being all inclusive, without in any way being "Pollyannish" about the many-sided, insidious nature of the evils in which all humans are caught in one way or another. This does not mean conflating White men, White women, Black and third-world men, and Black and third-world women, and the rich and the poor across all these divisions, into a leveling universalism in which "we are all equally oppressed." We are emphatically not all equally oppressed in Russell's view. Sexist, racist, and classist oppression means there are real differences between men and women across these many divides of race, gender, and class. But Russell also makes no simple division of some normative group of the oppressed, who therefore are "without sin," from all the other, "bad guys."

Even those most oppressed by all the many dimensions of violence can nevertheless be caught up in emulation of the dominant class and lateral violence against their neighbors.[18] And affluent White men can sometimes be converted from their privileges of race, class, and gender and enter into real solidarity with the poor. White, middle-class, educated, professional American women—Russell's own context, of which she is always clearly aware—stand *me!* in a position of status ambiguity, sharing some experiences of oppression with other, less-privileged women but also enjoying privileges of class, race, education, and professional status that put them on the side of the oppressors.[19] White middle-class women can become enablers of other women and oppressed men, but only by being critically aware of their own myopia, induced by their own context of privilege. Thus, for Russell, thinking theologically from the "other end" is always complemented by thinking socially from the "bottom," by concrete listening and being taught by women and men of oppressed classes and races.

The vision of total liberation, or the New Creation, is something none of us has experienced. It has never existed in history, either in the early church or in some ideal time at the beginning of creation. Nor have any modern revolutions produced it, although many have worked out of its hopes and some have made some advances for human well-being. Thus the norm of the New Creation by which we must judge the Bible, Christian theology, and social struggles is one that is constantly rising out of an unquenchable hope for a better world, a refusal of humans to settle for oppression as the last word of human life and history. This means that hope takes many different forms in the context of different oppressions. Even among women, what a White middle-class American woman may imagine as liberation, that is, equality with men in a high-status profession, may be very different from the hope of a poor Indian woman, that is, enough food for her family.[20] We also work out of the many "memories of the future" of our particular histories, for instance, the winning of suffrage or ordination for women, a successful organizing of a strike led by union women at a factory, the liberation of a colonized country from colonialism.

For Christians, the paradigmatic memory of the future is Jesus Christ, the one who stood on the side of the oppressed, was crucified for this by the powers that be of religion and state, and yet continues to be alive in our midst, beckoning us into a still unrealized future. Although Russell continues to see Jesus Christ as the normative memory of the future for her (for all Christians, including Christian feminists), she becomes clearer in her later books that this is a contextual norm. Jesus Christ is the normative memory "for me/us," but this does not exclude others' going forward on the basis of other religious memories.[21]

Ultimately, our liberating memories of the future are rooted in God working in history, seeking to make us God's partners in redeeming creation. It is we, all humans, all creation, who are "God's utopia," God's future.[22] Our memories of the many ways in which we have experienced redemption are finally memories of our response to and partnership with God when we acted for transformation and justice, when we celebrated its signs of presence in our midst.

A feminist liberation theology, then, is about reflection on the praxis of acting to overcome injustice in the particular context of how women are oppressed and are struggling for liberation across class and race divisions. It is about questioning and rereading the Bible from the perspective of the liberation of all women and men from this whole nexus of oppression. It is about questioning and rereading theology from this perspective. It is about reshaping the church, its ministry and mission, to become *a* (not *the* or *the only*) genuine sign and means of this praxis of liberation and a place where it is continually remembered and celebrated, equipping the community for continued praxis.

This concern for a theology that enables the praxis of liberation means that

Russell has spent a lot of her work on the issue of partnership. By "partnership" she does not just mean equality between a man and a woman in marriage, although this too is included.[23] Rather, she means a multiplicity of relationships by which we, as White women with Black women, with Black men, with White men, with women and men across many divisions, learn to grow/be converted out of relations of privilege and unprivilege, power and powerlessness, domination and subjugation, into genuine mutuality.

Conversion, for Russell, from domination/subordination to mutuality is always a two-sided process.[24] The subjugated must be empowered into their full potential to be and act; the privileged must learn to listen to the other and give up privilege. The goal is not an exchange of places but a new relation of mutuality. This involves both inner transformation of mind, spirit, and worldviews and a transformation of social structures and systems of power. Russell does not just talk about this process in general but has spent much time trying to do it and then reflect on the processes of this journeying into mutuality in the context of a variety of particular relations: a woman and a man in marriage, two women in a bonded relationship, clergywomen with clergymen, clergy with laity,[25] a woman theologian with her students, a White Christian woman leader in the church in dialogue with third-world Christian women developing their own theologies and leadership in their contexts.

Conversion into partnership, for Russell, is a process that takes place in specific ways in concrete contexts. Conversion from domination/subordination into partnership is what becoming a sign of the New Creation really means in various particular contexts. Her theology is rooted in continual engagement in the praxis circle: seeking to live out this process of conversion, reflecting on her learning from this process in order to return to praxis again, better equipped to do it and to help others do it.

In her forty-five years of thinking out of this engagement in the praxis of liberation, Letty Russell would claim no dramatic victories, many setbacks, but many moment-memories of grace. She (we) cannot give up, not because we know "we can do it if we try" but because we know we are part of God's struggle on our behalf. The assurance for our hope, the ground of our undefeated persistence, lies in our faith that we are joining God in a struggle for the redemption of creation, and God will never give up on us.

NOTES

1. On the theology of the Grimké sisters, see Rosemary R. Ruether, *Women and Redemption: A Theological History* (Minneapolis: Fortress Press, 1998), pp. 160–166. The material in the last two-thirds of this essay is expanded upon in the section on Letty Russell's theology in this book, pp. 211–221.
2. See "Declaration of Sentiments and Resolutions," Seneca Falls, New York, July

19, 1848, in *Feminism: Essential Historical Writings,* ed. M. Schneir (New York: Vintage, 1972), p. 82.

3. Rev. Luther Lee, "Woman's Right to Preach the Gospel: A Sermon Preached at the Ordination of the Rev. Miss Antoinette Brown, at South Butler, Wayne County, New York, September 15, 1853" (Syracuse: n.p., 1853).

4. See Elizabeth Caldwell, *A Mysterious Mantle: The Biography of Hulda Niebuhr* (Cleveland: Pilgrim Press, 1992).

5. Rosemary S. Keller, *Georgia Harkness: For Such a Time as This* (Nashville: Abingdon Press, 1992), pp. 279–280.

6. This analysis was shared with me by Presbyterian women ministers during the celebration of the thirty-year anniversary of the ordination of women in the Presbyterian Church in 1986.

7. See James Cone, *A Black Theology of Liberation* (1970; 20th anniversary ed., Maryknoll, N.Y.: Orbis Books, 1990).

8. Letty Russell, *The Household of Freedom: Authority in Feminist Theology* (Philadelphia: Westminster Press, 1987), p. 12.

9. Rosemary Radford Ruether, "Christianity and Women in the Modern World," in Arvin Sharma, ed., *Today's Women in World Religions* (Albany: SUNY Press, 1994). pp. 276–84.

10. Russell, *Household of Freedom,* p. 88.

11. Letty Russell, *Christian Education in Mission* (Philadelphia:Westminster Press, 1967).

12. Letty Russell, *Human Liberation in a Feminist Perspective: A Theology* (Philadelphia: Westminster Press, 1974). She is also co-editor of *Inheriting Our Mother's Gardens* (Philadelphia: Westminster Press, 1988), and *Dictionary of Feminist Theologies* (Louisville, Ky.: Westminster John Knox Press, 1996).

13. Letty Russell, *The Future of Partnership* (Philadelphia: Westminster Press, 1979); *Growth in Partnership* (Philadelphia: Westminster Press, 1981); *Feminist Interpretation of the Bible,* ed. Letty Russell (Philadelphia: Westminster Press, 1985); *The Household of Freedom: Authority in Feminist Theology* (Philadelphia: Westminster Press, 1987); and *Church in the Round: Feminist Interpretation of the Church* (Louisville, Ky.: Westminster John Knox Press, 1993).

14. The various activities of Letty Russell in enabling other women to do feminist work are only very partially known to me. Among the activities where I have witnessed her work firsthand are: her support from 1983 to the present for the Women's Commission of the Ecumenical Association of Third World Theologians; the sessions of the Society of Biblical Literature on Feminist Interpretation of the Bible, from which flowed publications that she edited, such as *Feminist Interpretation of the Bible;* the organizing and editing, with J. Shannon Clarkson, of the *Dictionary of Feminist Theologies* (1996); the enablement of many third-world women to study theology, including the organizing of the International Feminist Doctor of Ministry Program at San Francisco Theological Seminary for women who are unable to study full time away from their countries; and her many trips to lecture and bring students to study abroad with third-world women. This work of solidarity with third-world women is rooted in thirty-five years of work in key commissions with the World Council of Churches.

15. This motif is found throughout Russell's writings, for example, in *Human Liberation in a Feminist Perspective,* pp. 27–28; *Becoming Human* (Philadelphia: Westminster Press, 1982), pp. 39–41; *Future of Partnership,* pp. 51–53. See also her

"Authority and the Challenge of Feminist Interpretation," in *Feminist Interpretation of the Bible*, pp. 137–146.

16. See Russell's *Human Liberation in a Feminist Perspective*, p. 20. This book also has a preface by Elizabeth Moltmann-Wendel and Jürgen Moltmann, pp. 11–15.
17. Ibid., p. 183; also *Future of Partnership*, pp. 14, 160–163.
18. On horizontal violence between the oppressed, see *Human Liberation in a Feminist Perspective*, pp. 68–69, 118–121.
19. See her remarks on status inconsistency as a White middle-class woman in *Household of Freedom*, pp. 76–77.
20. Russell, *Human Liberation in a Feminist Perspective*, pp. 25–26.
21. For some examples on the role of Christ, see *Human Liberation in a Feminist Perspective*, pp. 65–66, 135–140. On p. 161 of this book, Russell writes, "The church is one of the signs of cosmic salvation and not the exclusive mediator of that salvation." See also *Household of Freedom*, pp. 73–76.
22. Russell, *Human Liberation in Feminist Perspective*, p. 41; *Future of Partnership*, pp. 44–45.
23. Russell, *Future of Partnership*, pp. 49–51.
24. Russell, *Human Liberation in a Feminist Perspective*, pp. 122–125.
25. Russell, *Future of Partnership*, pp. 126–31.

3

JOURNEYING TO THE
HOUSEHOLD OF GOD

*The Eschatological Implications of Method
in the Theology of Letty Mandeville Russell*

M. Shawn Copeland

*The master's tools will never dismantle the master's house. They
will allow us temporarily to beat him at his own game, but they
will never enable us to bring about genuine change.*[1]

Almost from the beginning, women have been outlaws in the house of theology.[2] Their raids posed new questions, critiqued oppression, proposed fresh understandings of God, of the relations between human creatures and God, of the relations between human persons. Moreover, their incursions were motivated by and projected a more holistic vision of human life, of moral and social possibility, than traditional theology accommodated. Because these transgressors recognized not only the nature and extent of their subjugation as women but also the subjugation of theology, their efforts yielded a new intellectual work—feminist theology. In the development of this new theological perspective, feminist scholars set their intellectual, psychological, and social energies against what Audre Lorde has called the "master's house." But how was that house to be brought down, to be dismantled? To be replaced? What tools might and ought to be used? Why are the master's tools so seductive yet so dangerous? So powerful yet so ineffective when turned against the household of oppression? What method do feminist theologians engage to meet these concerns and, more important, to generate a new and better future?

In this essay I discuss the theological method of Letty Russell, who stands in the vanguard of those articulate raiders who seek to liberate women and men, theology and church. I also explore some of the critiques her work has received from other theologians. Russell's genre of theology is too important to be treated with simplistic appreciation.

Why theological method? First, admittedly, it is a particular interest, but a grasp of a theologian's method can uncover her religious and moral commitments as well as her evaluation of epistemological and metaphysical categories. Second, while feminist theologians generally share "common [methodological] basepoints,"[3] and while any differences in their conclusions may be explained on several grounds (e.g., philosophical or religious or confessional), adverting to method furnishes a good way of clarifying those differences. Further, even though there have been cautions against the dangers of "methodolatry,"[4] this issue continues to be "raised in different ways by both Catholic and Protestant feminist theologians, as twentieth-century Christian feminist theology moves into its second generation."[5] Finally, authority is a more than topical issue in theology, especially in feminist theological reflection addressed to the church. Attentiveness to method can uncover the relevant exigencies and contingencies in articulating and living out a vision of human liberation rooted in the eschatological potential of Christian life.

Letty Russell has been doing theology for more than thirty years. The basic content of her theology as well as her method have not changed decisively during this period. Rather, they have been clarified and amplified through the prism of her wide reading, self-criticism, and commitment to solidarity with marginalized persons—women in particular. In the first section, I outline Russell's genre of feminist theology. Russell writes as a feminist committed to the church, even as she wrestles with the intellectual and spiritual tensions that walking with the church poses. The second section examines her theological method and the categories she employs—experience, sisterhood, and authority; social analysis; language critique; and commitment. The third section considers the eschatological openness of Russell's method and theology to the household of God.

RUSSELL'S GENRE OF FEMINIST THEOLOGY

Feminist theology emerged as a critical reading of social and cultural ferment in the United States and Europe during the 1960s. Yet some of its most pressing hermeneutical and methodological questions were anticipated in the late nineteenth century by the work of Elizabeth Cady Stanton.[6] In her introduction to *The Woman's Bible*, Stanton put forward two basic and enduring insights of contemporary feminist theological hermeneutics: (1) neither the Bible nor theology can be presented as intellectually neutral, and (2) the Bible, like theology, is more the product of male (patriarchal and androcentric) inspiration than of divine inspiration.[7] Thus, while feminist theology forms a distinctive discourse within Christian and Jewish academic circles, it is rooted in the history of women's struggle for voice, for room, for justice in society and church.

On Letty Russell's account, feminist theology is a theology of liberation. It is "an attempt to reflect upon the experience of oppression and our actions for the new creation of a more humane society."[8] Feminist theology is inseparably linked to a "commitment to participate in God's liberating actions in mending the creation by working in solidarity with communities of faith and struggle."[9] This commitment not only requires social "discernment and critique" but involves the "willing[ness] to take concrete actions for social change" and presupposes solidarity with the marginalized—even to the point of becoming a "marginal person."[10]

The sharpest way to clarify the genre of Russell's theology is to say that it is a churchly feminist theology of liberation. This theology in feminist perspective is addressed directly to the church, and in the church, primarily to women and men in the pews. But Russell's work is in no sense "popular." It is the immediacy of her effort to conscientize and stimulate dialogue among a worshiping public, that is, among churchgoers, pastors, other clergy, as well as educators and social advocates, that sets Russell's work apart from that of Rosemary Radford Ruether and Elisabeth Schüssler Fiorenza, with whom she shares so many theoretical and practical concerns.

Feminist and other theologies of liberation emerge in human communities that have been structurally exploited, disempowered, and marginalized in history, society, and church. These theologies project the future from the underside of history. Russell searches for a usable past for women by considering its interconnectedness to the future. Taking Immanuel Kant's third question— For what may we hope?—as a kind of lever, Russell constructs a "usable future" from the divine intention that the Christian tradition opens, even though "that *tradition is a problem* in light of historicity."[11]

Feminist theology, like other theologies of liberation, breaks with all oppressive expressions of the Christian tradition, but not with the tradition as such. On Russell's account, feminist theology stands its ground and grapples with what the tradition has taught about liberation and the "eschatological perspective concerning the future of humanity," as this comes from the effort to understand and to live out "God's oikonomia or plan for the world."[12] Russell parses the meaning of tradition quite precisely. She distinguishes among (1) the Tradition, or God's handing over of Jesus Christ into the hands of all generations and nations; (2) the tradition as a witness of scripture and church doctrine, "the deposit of faith"; (3) "tradition," or the traditioning process in human history and society; and (4) "traditions," or the patterns of church life.[13] These distinctions serve Russell in locating a usable past because they sharpen the recognition of tradition as a basic anthropological category related to change in thought and action in history. Russell understands "tradition as a basic anthropological category . . . as the structural element of human existence in which the still living and evolving past calls for commitment in shaping human community in the present and the future."[14]

Still, as feminist theologian Mary McClintock Fulkerson observes, Russell's work can "complicate."[15] Fulkerson holds that for feminist theologies, "no part of the tradition is theoretically exempt from a critical sifting," but Russell has "balance[d] women's benefit against the tradition with her appeal to Christ."[16] If these distinctions complicate, they also counter the frequent dismissal of theologies of liberation as "threat[s] to tradition."[17] Russell comprehends the Tradition in light of its "root meaning of paradosis, . . . [not as] a block of content to be carefully guarded by authorized hierarchies, but a dynamic action of God's love which is to be passed on to others of all sexes and races."[18] Confidence in God's saving action in the world and the coming future of divine judgment brings about new readings and understandings of history by exploited and marginalized communities. Feminist and other liberation theologies refuse to submit themselves or their subjects to invisibility in history or to oppressive misunderstandings of the Tradition. To the contrary, these theologies function as "reminder[s] that the dynamic of God's Tradition transcends and judges all human traditions and action," all of human history.[19]

Russell refuses to relinquish the biblical basis of her churchly feminist theology of liberation. While she acknowledges the male supremacist, androcentric, and sexist elements of the Bible, she strains out those elements through critical exegetical methods and analysis of cultural context. Russell discovers "a critical or liberating tradition embodied in [the Bible's] 'prophetic-messianic' message of continuing self-critique."[20] She weighs this tradition over against the Bible's patriarchal worldviews and androcentric language, thus illuminating the central message of the Bible—human salvation as liberation. Russell finds evidence for this stance not in biblical stories that focus on women or in female imagery for God but in "God's intention for the mending of all creation."[21] Whatever diminishes, denies, or distorts the divine intention for the liberation of creation in all its parts is not authoritative for a feminist theology of liberation. Whatever negates or impedes "the biblical word of promise" to human beings to become what God intends us to become, that is, "partners in the mending of creation," is not authoritative for a churchly feminist theology of liberation.[22] Thus, Russell posits a *critical liberation principle*. This principle translates theologically to the affirmation that whatever diminishes or denies, negates or impedes God's desire for the mending of creation in all its parts must be presumed to be nonredemptive, and it is unauthentically related to the Divine, to the mission and work of an authentic redeemer, and to the mission and work of an authentic community of redemption.[23]

what do i think is Gs' intention?

Although Russell grounds her theology in the Bible's prophetic-messianic tradition and proffers a critical liberation principle, she still must confront Elisabeth Schüssler Fiorenza's charge that her work is aligned with neo-orthodox hermeneutics.[24] Some methodological strategies that Russell employs might overcome this charge. First, to retain the significance of the Bible in Christian life and theology, Russell distinguishes between "script" and scripture; she then distinguishes between two meanings of divine inspiration.

In the first distinction, Russell maintains that "the Bible is 'scripture,' or sacred writing, because it functions as 'script,' or prompting for life. Its authority . . . stems from its story of God's invitation to participation in the restoration of wholeness, peace, and justice in the world."[25] The response of women and men to this invitation is made possible through the "power of the Spirit at work in communities of struggle and faith."[26] Russell considers this distinction analogous to Elisabeth Schüssler Fiorenza's notion of "the Bible as a structuring prototype . . . an open-ended paradigm that sets experiences in motion and invites transformation."[27]

The second distinction follows from the first. Russell maintains that for the Bible to make sense in communities of faith, it is not to be read literally but "through what David Kelsey calls 'imaginative construal' or configuration of criteria that evoke our consent and become normative for the way we would live the life of faith."[28] Particular communities establish the criteria for understanding the Bible as the Word of God by correlating their praxis of faith with the biblical message. However, divine inspiration does not mean the underwriting and authenticating of everything that the Bible contains; to do so is to confuse the Word of God with whatever we read. Instead, the Bible is affirmed as the Word of God when particular communities of faith respond to the Spirit's prompting to struggle for wholeness, justice, and life.

What Russell gains by grounding her reflection in the prophetic-messianic tradition is that cognitive, moral, and social transformation are moved to the center of theology. Theology functions as "a tool for doing something that can become a catalyst for change among those who believe in the Biblical promises for the oppressed."[29] By clarifying the interpretive framework in which the Bible is read and the correlation of that reading with the praxis of faith, Russell integrates hermeneutics with social advocacy. Most important of all, for Russell theology, like the Tradition, has a mission: to show how Christ's love is extended to all people, and "to make that love known as God's will to bring liberation, justice, peace, and reconciliation to all creation."[30] The advance of that mission is the most basic task of theology—of a churchly theology in particular, and especially a churchly feminist theology of liberation.

THEOLOGICAL METHOD AND CATEGORIES

To chart Russell's theological method is to follow a spiral—reflection on experience, an analysis of social reality, the questioning of biblical and church traditions, the pursuit of clues for transformation, and action on behalf of justice. While this method is common to the various theologies of liberation, Russell's appropriation of it comes primarily from two sources. The first source is her critical reflection on her own range of human experience, particularly her life and service as a white female pastor among black and Hispanic/Latino Christians in East Harlem. The second source is her twofold commitment to cultivate the inner resources needed to live toward the divine vision of human community in all its rich diversity and to use her gifts by sharing them. Russell locates and names the dynamic moments in the spiral method by abstracting them from her own lived commitment to God's new creation, to action for justice in solidarity with the marginalized.[31]

The themes and questions pursued in Russell's books follow a spiral pattern as well. *Human Liberation in a Feminist Perspective: A Theology* turned on the metaphor of a journey toward God's household of freedom. That journey began by critically attending to suffering and oppression and called for analysis of the social reality in which such suffering and oppression was characteristic. This work urged Christian solidarity and identified the empowering freedom that comes with relation to God; it concluded with a notion of Christian ministry as social praxis in the service of God's desire for our future. This work was followed by *Growth in Partnership* and *The Future of Partnership*.[32] These companion books dealt with the "practice [of] the liberating presence of God in Christ as partner" in the lives of women and men and advocated their full collaboration in Christian action for healing and creating in history and society.[33] *Household of Freedom: Authority in Feminist Theology* is the published version of Russell's 1986 Annie Kinkead Warfield Lectures at Princeton Theological Seminary. This book emphasized the centrality that Russell accords to freedom in Christian life.[34] Her most recent book, *Church in the Round,* both returns to the themes of *Human Liberation in a Feminist Perspective* and amplifies them. This thematic return is more than simply circular, for new experiences have provoked new questions and new categories in her reevaluation of familiar biblical and social terrain. The aim of Russell's use of the spiral method is tied to a praxis of faith and struggle aimed against the master's house and for the household of God.

Russell's fullest discussion of her theological method is presented in *Church in the Round.* The movement of the spiral begins with "*commitment* to the task of raising up signs of God's new household with those who are struggling or justice and full humanity." The second step invites "*sharing experiences* of commitment and struggle in a concrete context of engagement." The third movement of the spiral "leads to a critical analysis of the context of these experiences" and aims to understand more comprehensively the interconnectedness of historical, political, and economic factors that "affect the community of struggle." The theologian's "commitment to action in solidarity with the marginalized" also involves dialogue and clarification of social analysis with those of differing perspectives. The results of this dialogue provoke "questions about biblical and church tradition." These questions, generated by this spiral of inquiry, can "help us gain new insight into the meaning of the gospel as good news for the oppressed and marginalized. This new understanding of tradition flows from and leads to *action, celebration, and further reflection* in the continuing theological spiral."[35]

For Russell, the purpose of theology is praxis: "action that is concurrent with reflection or analysis and leads to new questions, actions, and reflections."[36] And if commitment to the oppressed and marginalized is the starting point for theologizing, then theology of liberation requires a dialogue in which the "direction of thought flows not only 'downward' from the 'theological experts' but also upward and outward out of the collective experience of action and ministry."[37]

In the remainder of this section, I discuss a few of the key categories that Russell employs in doing theology. These include experience, sisterhood, and authority, which will be taken together and interrelated, since the questions these categories insinuate aggregate as a cluster; social analysis; language critique; and commitment.

Experience, Sisterhood, Authority

The notion of *experience* is a key aspect in all theologies of liberation. A basic insight of feminist liberation theologies and their methods is that gender incriminates perspective. Feminist theologies explicitly name the experience of women as a neglected and crucial source for theological reflection and analysis. By adverting to women's experience, these theologies "contest the male subject as a false universal" and uncover both the contextual character of theology and the situatedness of human knowledge.[38]

Like other feminist theologians, Russell takes women's experience as a proper category and an authoritative source for theological reflection. What differentiates her appeal to experience from those of other white feminist theologians is her early resistance to homogenizing the category of women. Russell's critical analysis of her own social location demonstrates both her resistance to bias and her refusal to support it in any form. Given the role of self-criticism in her reflection, Russell uses social location both analytically and dialogically.

By attending to social location as a category for analysis, Russell is able to determine and to understand the social situatedness of the theologian and the community to whom she is committed. Analysis of social location provides thick description of the experience named by female embodiment, race, class, culture, and sexual orientation. Further, this analysis uncovers the ways in which these experiences are manipulated by heterosexist patriarchy and white supremacist structures in the marginalization of human persons. This category functions dialogically in the spiral method to open Russell's theological praxis to insights and critique from those whose experience of powerlessness and marginalization grants them hermeneutical privilege. Indeed, these so-called nonpersons, Russell asserts, quite possibly may be bearers of an important word from God. This very possibility, perhaps even more than the category of experience per se, opens Russell's theology to the notion of difference.

Since the 1980s, the critiques of Asian and Latin American feminists, *mestiza, mujerista,* and womanist theologians, ethicists, and scholars, have coalesced to displace the notion of *sisterhood.* The new theoretical tool in feminist theologies is the notion of difference. Despite its unifying intention, sisterhood mistook white middle-class women for the universal woman. Functionally, sisterhood erased the actual condition of red, black, brown, yellow, and poor women. The notion of difference destabilizes attempts to analyze or to present women's experience as unitary or uniform. Further, difference problematizes simple binary oppositions, pointing up unsettled and often dynamic relations.[39] Most white feminists have absorbed these critiques and recognize that to overlook or to refuse to engage difference seriously undermines liberation praxis and discourse.

Written in 1974, *Human Liberation in a Feminist Perspective* is a good example of Russell's early theology. While her work always acknowledged differences in the actual conditions of red, black, brown, yellow, and poor women from that of white middle-class women, sisterhood remained a significant theme. Yet even in this early work, Russell's use of sisterhood was never a presumptive category; rather, it served as a strategy in service of the eschatological goal of humanization. Russell conceived of sisterhood as a dynamic process that women achieved by learning to affirm themselves and their sister(s) in their aspirations, "whatever the divergence of race, language, geography, ideology, and tactics."[40] For Russell, sisterhood contested the enforced subordination of women; as a process, it was a task toward mutually supportive community that gave women new identity and hope.

The notion of sisterhood as a dynamic process to be achieved is extended, in *Church in the Round,* as heuristic: "a journey of self-liberation together with others."[41] Here, Russell emphasizes the choice to engage or not in that process and that journey, which has both cognitive and moral dimensions. Each woman or man who desires freedom finds it in learning about who she or he is. For marginalized persons, this self-liberation entails proper self-love and self-acceptance of one's own body and embodiedness, race, sexual orientation, class, and cultural background. In making difference concrete, Russell's work comes closest to accenting the material condition of women and men and naming the damage done to them by the social and cultural forces of hetero-sexist patriarchy and white racist supremacy.

For those who control society or benefit from that control, women and men at the center, self-liberation involves *unlearning* sexism, racism, homophobia, heterosexism, economic and cultural elitism. At the same time, Russell's notion of self-liberation is not to be confused with liberal volunteerism or therapeutic self-help schemes. Self-liberation actuates moral agency for con-version, that is, for authentic change in a woman's or a man's life—a turn in a new direction. As converted moral agents, self-liberated women and men can collaborate in the task of re-creating society with and for those on the margin, of mending God's creation in all its parts.

Russell distinguishes between power and *authority*. She defines "author-ity [as] more than a form of power; it is power that is legitimated by the structures of society. It is exercised in most situations through hierarchy and is control."[42] In feminist theology, women's experience constitutes a source of authority; this controverts the notion of authority as legitimation of op-pressive social structures. Russell specifies and claims women's experience as "not just female (biological) or feminine (cultural) . . . [but] the feminist (po-litical) experience of those advocating a change of society to include both women and men as human beings, created in God's image to participate with God in the fashioning of new creation."[43] This specification situates only relative control of meaning and value in women's critical cognitive, moral, and religious authenticity. This relative control constitutes a new paradigm of authority in which "reality is interpreted in the form of a circle of inter-dependence . . . is explored through inclusion of diversity . . . and is exer-cised in community and not over community."[44] Within this new paradigm, authority does not "guard the Word," interpreting it exclusively through doctrine; instead, authority "tends to incarnate the Word and set forth its in-terpretation through telling stories of faith and struggle."[45] This new para-digm situates normative control of meaning and value in the authority of the Word of God; it is under the aegis of this authority, Russell declares, that as Christians we live.

Social Analysis

Theologies of liberation name and denounce the collusion between personal or individual sin and social sin that results in social evil. These theologies not only promote critical analysis and change of oppressive social structures but call for a person's confession of complicity, repentance, and conversion of life. This is the authentic basis for social transformation.

Social analysis is a conceptual tool utilized by theologies of liberation to obtain a more complete, coherent, and critical understanding of a given social situation. Social analysis asks the question: How and why is a given society ordered as it is? It answers that question by investigating the origins, causes, and interconnections between underlying historical arrangements and the social infrastructure (that is, technology, economics, politics) and by identifying those compromises in the superstructure (common meanings and values) that mediates society. Only when these questions have been answered adequately, their implications for human persons determined, and the social options of Christian communities charted does the task of theological reflection begin.

Russell foregrounds in each of her books stories of suffering and oppression of women and men whom she has encountered directly, personally. She names them, describes their situations, and reports their faith response. The situations, experiences, and responses of parishioners and Yale Divinity School students, members of Philippine communities, the China Dialogue, the NRSV translation committee, along with those of Chong Sun France, Henna Han, Ron Russell-Coons, and Young Sook are recounted in detail. Yet Russell tells us about these women and men without possessing the particularity and substance of their experience or usurping their authority over it.

This anecdotal access to the human side of social analysis discloses more to us about ourselves than about Henna Han or Ron Russell-Coons. At the same time, these situations and experiences do instruct those of us who cling to or stand at the center. The responses of Spirit-filled women and men of faith provoke our reflection on sin and evil in society and our complicity in them. These responses also evoke our decision and commitment to risk partnership, a "relationship of mutuality that requires neither submission nor hegemony on the part of either partner."[46] These narratives instigate a praxis to meet actual needs and heal alienations within our communities. They urge us to change our living and to join women and men on the margin in struggle for God's vision of the future.

If the actual situation in all its complexity serves as the starting point for theological reflection, the criterion for judgment and decision is the liberating Word of God. Like other liberation theologians, Russell tunes her theology to the lived lives of women and men on the margin. To describe their condition, Russell works in broad strokes; her use of social analysis is narrative rather than quantitative. By foregrounding these stories of conversion, faith, and struggle, Russell summons us to attend to the places where we are, to seek glimpses in the here and now of the realization of God's vision of the mending of creation in all its parts.

Language Critique

Russell's search for a "usable language" began more than twenty years ago.[47] In *Human Liberation in Feminist Perspective,* she dismissed the English usage of such words as *man, men,* and *mankind* as universal referents for the human and therefore as including women. Russell called this usage "generic nonsense," since it rendered women and other marginalized peoples invisible in history and society.[48] This invisibility fostered the conclusion that women and other marginalized peoples were not actors or subjects but rather passive objects, acted upon. Here, Russell followed lines put forward by theorists of the social construction of reality. Language expresses ideas; ideas impress human consciousness and thought, which is the generative source of cultural and social structures. In this way, even as it shapes images, roles, and behaviors in society, language is shaped by images, roles, and behaviors in society.

Russell's first response to the problem of "desexing language" was her advocacy for fresh, nonpatriarchal, inclusive linguistic models in worship and biblical interpretation.[49] Practically, this meant relying on biblical exegesis to bring to light "forgotten names of God."[50] Theoretically, it meant accentuating the transcendence and mystery of God and of divine freedom in speech about God. Russell repeated what theologians know but what many simply had overlooked, or perhaps had approved: our language about God derives from limited human experience. Moreover, that language is metaphorical or analogical and can never capture the essence and mystery of God, who is beyond biological (male and female) and cultural (masculine and feminine) determinations. Yet, problematic as the language of the Bible may be, Russell maintained that it serves as an indispensable source in revising our way of speaking and thinking about God. Critical exegesis can uncover images and metaphors for God that have been lost or buried under androcentric language. Furthermore, many of these images and metaphors reflect female and feminine experience. Using these alternatives reinforces our understanding that God transcends absolutely all biological and cultural distinctions of sex. Russell's statement of the problem and solution coincides with those of other feminist theologians and biblical scholars. What distinguishes her position is her insistence that "all people [are to] find for themselves a place in [the] Tradition by perceiving that God offers to them a usable future, a usable history, and a usable language."[51]

Household of Freedom revisited the theme of a usable language by examining the power and authority of women to name and claim their experience. To some extent, naming functions in Russell's theology as a feminist practice. As such, naming returns to women that which has been stolen from them—language. Furthermore, that practice unmasks the role of social and ecclesial "elites" in establishing norms for the appropriation and use of language and symbols, in "control[ling] material resources for education and communication," in assuming "power to describe the social and natural world" and to rank and order human persons according to sex, race, and class. Finally, that practice as an act of authentic power claims and changes reality.[52] But even if the account of language in *Household of Freedom* does not spell out sufficiently either the connection between language, culture, and thought or the relation of power to the functions of meaning or "the complications of conflict and desire," Russell rightly insists "that the power of language is multilayered by the authority invested in the speaker, and that communication is [always] more than language."[53]

Although *Church in the Round* returns to the conditioning relation between language and society, it focuses on women's use of language to decenter patriarchal frameworks in church and society. Borrowing the notion of "talking back" from bell hooks, Russell proposes that women "talk back" to the tradition.[54] This usage interrogates how "contextual theologies are connected to biblical and ecclesial tradition."[55] It also pushes Russell beyond the problem of desexing language to reconsider its hegemonic uses. For talking back is oppositional and disruptive; it is an act of resistance. Feminists talking back in theology and church can shift the margin to the center and introduce other interpretations of what it means to be followers of Christ, partners with him and with one another in contemporary society.

Russell's own language cannot escape scrutiny. To envision this New Creation, she probes several rich metaphors, including those of house and household, housekeeper and householder, good housekeeping, kitchen table, table in the round, church in the round. But as ethicist Christine Firer Hinze comments, Russell's "able mining of metaphors is two edged: she taps their indispensable power to inspire and motivate, yet leaves some theoretical and practical questions unanswered."[56]

Commitment

In Russell's theology, commitment functions as a practice. On this point she and Elisabeth Schüssler Fiorenza agree: "Intellectual neutrality is not possible in a historical world of exploitation and oppression."[57] For theologies of liberation, theologizing is a second step; this is true of Russell's churchly feminist theology of liberation as well. The first step is commitment to or solidarity with those on the margin, expressed in action for justice. To sustain Christian life and theology under the pressure of living *out of time* (that is, not attuned to the *kairos*), inner resources must be developed and nourished. To this end, Russell outlines a "spirituality of connection" in which wholeness of life is nourished.[58] The disciplines of this spirituality affirm the integration of sexuality or embodiment and oppose any "dualistic separation of body and spirit."[59] At the same time, these spiritual disciplines meet the challenge of sitting side by side with "those who cry out for solidarity in the struggle for justice."[60] If the prescriptions for these disciplines are short on personal prayer, they accent partnership, sacrificial service, and communal worship.

Fulkerson, in a review of works by Sallie McFague, Rosemary Radford Ruether, and Letty M. Russell, concludes that all three find "something in the Christian tradition that is usable and expandable." Of the three, however, Russell has remained "the most content with the potential" of that tradition.[61] Russell's theological praxis seeks to mediate an understanding of the tradition in which all forms of exploitation, powerlessness, and marginalization are judged as inimical to the Word of God, but this judgment does not "reduce God's action to [just another set of] politics."[62] Rather, Russell discerns and grapples with what the tradition has handed down concerning the relation between the eschatological reality of God and the cause of the poor and marginalized and their historical struggle for human wholeness, for salvation in liberation.

ESCHATOLOGICAL OPENNESS

In this essay I have sought to clarify Letty Russell's theological praxis—the genre of that theology and a basic outline of its content, method, and some of the key categories. In all this, what is most striking to me in rereading and reflecting on Russell's work is her thoroughgoing preoccupation with the eschatological. Russell's theology invites us to look for God's unexpected reversals, to live in anticipation of the coming of the New Creation, to think and act from a distinctive standpoint—the "other end."[63] In short, Russell challenges the reader, indeed the church, to think *kairotically*.

Yet eschatology is not simply a category among others in Russell's theology. Rather, the eschatological constitutes that basic horizon from which she probes women's experience of coming to sisterhood in difference, encounters and narrates lived stories of faith and struggle, critiques language and ideology and authority, instigates for justice. In other words, what orients Russell's theology is anticipation of God's great reversal in a world of suffering and exile. This orientation explains Russell's regular graced encounters with Spirit-filled persons and communities of courage and hope. It defines her persistent reading of scripture against the grain—even the feminist grain. It explains her "subversive traditioning"[64] and refusal to surrender the Tradition to oppressors. This orientation shapes her joyous celebration of shalom and her celebratory subversiveness. What is at stake in Russell's theology is understanding—cognitively, morally, practically—that we live *already* under the authority of the Word of God. Under that authority, theology is liberated from biased and closed options, so that it might creatively anticipate and seriously participate in the building up of the household of God. To live under that authority is to live a Christian life oriented absolutely in love and service toward God's design for the future.

Those familiar with Russell's work will recall her frequent and appreciative citation of Audre Lorde's injunction regarding the "master's house" and the "master's tools." This same citation serves as the epigraph to this essay. In the eschatological horizon from which Russell's churchly feminist theology emerges, the multilayered metaphor of the "house" functions as a communicative site of dramatic and spiritual tension. In this horizon, eschatological existence involves active partnership with God and with a community in upholding the cause of the poor and marginalized. Using Lorde's cautionary metaphor, Russell paints two portraits, two ends for our choosing—the "master's house" or God's.

The "master's house" is the metaphor for the institutionalization of heterosexist white racist supremacy. This domain of sin and evil is perpetuated by the interlocking structures of sexism, racism, homophobia, and acquisitive capitalism. In this house, intentionally or unintentionally, "reality is seen in the form of a hierarchy or pyramid."[65] This is a place characterized by fear, self-regard, and scramble for position. In this house, authority is exercised from the top down; beliefs, meanings, values, and truth are promoted through domination and competition. Whoever questions this view of reality is undermined or ridiculed. Myths are fabricated to demonstrate the inferiority of those who live outside. Thus, the master's house is off limits to blacks, indigenous peoples, persons afflicted with AIDS, uppity women, Jews, Latinos, Asians, gays and lesbians, the poor and the needy; their critical perspectives are neither sought nor desired. Through aggression and the subjugation of persons, human community is mocked and destroyed.[66] The tools that build and sustain this house include the suppression of new questions and insights; the separation of mind and body, thought and action; domination and control; exclusion and objectification of human persons and nature.

God's household is set against the master's. With the metaphor of the household of God, Russell draws on the ancient biblical image of "God's dwelling with us as One who cares for the world house."[67] The house of God is a place of forgiveness and restoration, of gladness and festivity. In this house, "authority is exercised *in* community and not *over* community and tends to reinforce ideas of cooperation, with contributions from a wide diversity of persons enriching the whole."[68] God's order shatters hierarchy; it is shaped from the bottom up and is ordered around unexpected reversals in which the first rejoice and the last are not grieved. To bring this household to an authentic unity in which difference is valued and respected, the power of the Spirit transgresses all borders of language, race, culture, gender, and sexual orientation. All who are "willing to work for God's covenant purpose of justice [and] shalom" are welcome at the table of the Lord. Tools for life in God's household are partnership, collaboration, interdependence, and mutuality; further, these tools include proper self-love, courage, and a spirituality that nourishes the liberation of our humanity for community and communion with the divine householder.

Yet, given Russell's eschatological commitment, there must be more. In God's household, our freedom is realized through authentic conversion and repentance; spirituality is the foundation of our social praxis. In God's house, we learn to think from the perspective of the end time, to take responsibility for the future, to seek out occasions to promote and to provoke cognitive dissonance and critical thinking, to take on the suffering and marginalization that come with acting for the transformation of society.[69] This is a household in anticipation, built up in a process of mutual subversion. Those at the center and those on the margin acknowledge one another as necessary partners with God in living the *not yet, already* in the present. Thus, for Russell, to take the Word of God as authority is to "appeal to God's future action in creating the world as a household where both humanity and nature can live in a community of responsibility and freedom."[70]

Space prevents me from interrogating the several implications that are embedded in the metaphor of the two households. I choose just one—the challenge to transform the master's house *from within*. With Lorde, Russell recognizes just how compelling the lure of inclusion in that house is. We are dazed by its attraction and cannot grasp it as the strategy of divide and conquer that it is. We must be wary of that house and the tools that have built and sustained it, for Lorde is correct: "They may allow us temporarily to beat him at his own game, but . . . will never enable us to bring about genuine change."[71]

To transform the master's house, rather than merely change the gender or race or sexual orientation of the women allowed to make decisions within it, will take more courage than we alone can muster. Nor can that house ever be our "only source of support."[72] Russell's use of this metaphor implies a twofold trajectory of liberation—one directed toward women, white middle-class women in particular, but also men; the other toward theology and church.

White middle-class women, feminists in particular, because of their "status inconsistency," Russell asserts, can take a role in overcoming the authority of the master's house. With the phrase "status inconsistent" she points out that these women as women are members of a subordinate group, but as *white* women they share in the benefits acquired through relations with the white male dominant group. White middle-class women, indeed all of us, are challenged to defy self-regarding interests and "choose to be status inconsistent."[73] Because the allure of approval from the master is so strong, this is risky business. Moreover, such altruism seems rare, if not impossible. But Russell is confident that "God's action of deliverance makes it possible for persons and groups to be freed from inhuman self-love and to be joined in community with those whom God is delivering from suffering."[74] Grace is in the risk, because the future is in our trust and cooperation with God and in solidarity with one another.

Russell argues adamantly that the paradigm of reality denoted by the master's house is inadequate for Christian theology. "[It] provides a religious rationale for the domination and oppression of the weak by the political, economic, and religious power elites. Such a view is clearly contrary to the prophetic-messianic promise of God's welcome to all the outsiders."[75] In imagining new models for theology and church, Russell advocates no simplistic reversal of the old paradigm of domination, so that now women dictate from the top. To the contrary, she encourages feminists, indeed all theologians and clergy, to take a "revolutionary" stance and "search out alternative way[s] of ordering our reality and our world that [are] less harmful to human beings, to nature, and to all creation."[76]

To imagine and bring about such alternatives calls for new theological and ecclesial practices. Russell's theology offers several, including: (1) seeking, encouraging, and welcoming fresh questions from those on the margin; (2) recovering the "dangerous memories" of those who have placed the authority of God's house above the powers and principalities of this world—foremothers and foresisters in particular; (3) acknowledging that social, ecclesiastical, and academic arrangements are shaped by finite, limited, local human decisions that can be changed in genuine encounter with new questions and needs; (4) recognizing that the liberal logic of token inclusion is but a subtle tool of domination and control; (5) resisting the dualistic split of mind from body, thought from action, and rhetoric from behavior, and nurturing wholeness of living; (6) refusing to emulate the oppressor; and (7) searching out and celebrating hints and clues of God's "coming toward us" in communities of faith and struggle.[77] These practices are tools, Russell asserts, for cleansing and rebuilding theology and church. They turn us toward the future and support us in the effort to realize it, even when what that future brings is opaque. Because of God's liberating promise to bring about a New Creation, these tools enable us "to live with a hope that is strong enough to transform the present."[78]

CONCLUSION

For more than thirty years, Letty Mandeville Russell has been elaborating a churchly feminist theology of liberation. Because the journey of liberation is a long and arduous one, theology has a mission to make known the goal of that journey as well as God's presence in it. Thus, Russell addresses her theology primarily to the church and in the church. Further, she has located her theology within the horizon of proleptic eschatology. Within this horizon, salvation is not conceived in otherworldly or ahistorical terms but rather conjugates humanity and the cosmos in the future tense.[79] Within this horizon, freedom is rooted in the Tradition, that is, the dynamic saving praxis of God's love, and it appeals to the authority of the Word of God. Loyalty to this authority is measured by solidarity with the poor and marginalized, action for justice, and new spiritual and practical disciplines for holistic living. This is what Russell calls full partnership with one another and with God in Christ in the power of the Spirit. And it is just for this, Russell writes, that the created universe is waiting on tiptoe—to see women and men arrive at what they are, God's own household.[80]

NOTES

1. Audre Lorde, "The Master's Tools Will Never Dismantle the Master's House," in *Sister Outsider: Chapters and Speeches by Audre Lorde* (Trumansburg, N.Y.: Crossing Press, 1984), 112.
2. Elizabeth A. Meese makes a similar observation about women as "trespassers [in the] world's literary communities," in *Crossing the Double-Cross: The Practice of Feminist Criticism* (Chapel Hill: University of North Carolina Press, 1986), 5.
3. Rebecca Chopp, "Methodologies," in Letty M. Russell and J. Shannon Clarkson, eds., *Dictionary of Feminist Theologies* (Louisville, Ky.: Westminster John Knox Press, 1996), 181.
4. Mary Daly, *Beyond God the Father: Toward a Philosophy of Women's Liberation* (Boston: Beacon Press, 1973), 11–12.
5. Anne Carr, "The New Vision of Feminist Theology: Method," in Catherine Mowry LaCugna, ed., *Freeing Theology: The Essentials of Theology in Feminist Perspective* (San Francisco: HarperCollins, 1993), 6.
6. Elizabeth Cady Stanton, ed., *The Original Feminist Attack on the Bible: The Woman's Bible*, facsimile ed. (New York: Arno Press, 1974).
7. Elisabeth Schüssler Fiorenza, *In Memory of Her: A Feminist Theological Reconstruction of Christian Origins* (New York: Crossroad, 1983), 7–14; see also Carolyn De Swarte Gifford, "Politicizing the Sacred Texts: Elizabeth Cady Stanton and The Women's Bible," in Elisabeth Schüssler Fiorenza, ed., *Searching the Scriptures*, vol. 1: *A Feminist Introduction* (New York: Crossroad, 1993), 52–63.
8. Letty M. Russell, *Human Liberation in a Feminist Perspective: A Theology* (Philadelphia: Westminster Press, 1974), 20.
9. Letty M. Russell, "Methodology in Liberation/Feminist Theologies: A Theological Spiral of Action/Reflection," unpublished course materials, 1994.
10. Russell, *Human Liberation*, 39.
11. Ibid., 73, 74.
12. Ibid., 57.
13. Ibid., 75; see also Letty M. Russell, *Church in the Round: Feminist Interpretation of the Church* (Louisville, Ky.: Westminster John Knox Press, 1993), 37.
14. Russell, *Human Liberation*, 75.

15. Mary McClintock Fulkerson, *Changing the Subject: Women's Discourses and Feminist Theology* (Minneapolis: Fortress Press, 1994), 38.
16. Ibid.
17. Russell, *Human Liberation*, 78.
18. Ibid., 79; cf. Fiorenza, *In Memory of Her*, 15.
19. Russell, *Human Liberation*, 79.
20. Letty M. Russell, "Authority and the Challenge of Feminist Interpretation," in Letty M. Russell, ed., *Feminist Interpretation of the Bible* (Philadelphia: Westminster Press, 1985), 138.
21. Ibid.
22. Ibid., 139.
23. See Rosemary Radford Ruether, *Sexism and God-Talk: Toward a Feminist Theology* (Boston: Beacon Press, 1983), 18–19, for a discussion of the critical principle of feminist theology.
24. Fiorenza, *In Memory of Her*, 15.
25. Russell, "Authority and the Challenge of Feminist Interpretation," 138.
26. Ibid.
27. Elisabeth Schüssler Fiorenza, "The Will to Choose or to Reject: Continuing Our Critical Work," in Russell, ed., *Feminist Interpretation of the Bible*, 135; cf. Fulkerson, *Changing the Subject*, 38.
28. Russell, "Authority and the Challenge of Feminist Interpretation," 141.
29. Russell, *Human Liberation*, 55.
30. Ibid., 79.
31. Russell, *Church in the Round*, 31; see also her "From Garden to Table," in Katie Geneva Cannon, Ada Maria Isasi-Díaz, Kwok Pui-lan, Letty M. Russell, eds., *Inheriting Our Mothers' Gardens: Feminist Theology in Third World Perspective* (Philadelphia: Westminster Press, 1988), 143–55.
32. Letty M. Russell, *Growth in Partnership* (Philadelphia: Westminster Press, 1981) and *The Future of Partnership* (Philadelphia: Westminster Press, 1984).
33. Russell, *Growth in Partnership*, 141.
34. Letty M. Russell, *Household of Freedom: Authority in Feminist Theology* (Philadelphia: Westminster Press, 1987).
35. Russell, *Church in the Round*, 30–31.
36. Russell, *Human Liberation*, 55–56.
37. Ibid., 55.
38. Fulkerson, *Changing the Subject*, 52.
39. Eve K. Sedgwick, *The Epistemology of the Closet* (Berkeley: University of California Press, 1990), 9–10.
40. Russell, *Human Liberation*, 140; see also her *Becoming Human* (Philadelphia: Westminster Press, 1982).
41. Russell, *Church in the Round*, 183.
42. Russell, *Household of Freedom*, 21.
43. Ibid., 17–18.
44. Ibid., 34–35.
45. Ibid., 50.
46. Mary McClintock Fulkerson, review of *Models of God: Theology for an Ecological, Nuclear Age*, by Sallie McFague; *Women-Church: Theology and Practice*, by Rosemary Ruether; and *Household of Freedom: Authority in Feminist Theology*, by Letty M. Russell, *Signs* 15, 1 (Autumn 1989): 182.

47. Russell, *Human Liberation*, 73.
48. Ibid., 93.
49. Ibid., 93, 95–103.
50. Ibid., 97.
51. Ibid., 103.
52. Russell, *Household of Freedom*, 46.
53. Fulkerson, *Changing the Subject*, 44, 48.
54. See bell hooks, *Talking Back: Thinking Feminist, Thinking Black* (Boston: South End Press, 1989), 10–18.
55. Russell, *Church in the Round*, 21.
56. Christine Firer Hinze, review of *Household of Freedom: Authority in Feminist Theology*, by Letty M. Russell, *Journal of Religion* 69, 4 (December 1989): 573.
57. Elisabeth Schüssler Fiorenza, "Scripture in the Liberation Struggle," in *Bread Not Stone: The Challenge of Feminist Biblical Interpretation* (Boston: Beacon Press, 1984), 45.
58. Russell, *Church in the Round*, 183–208.
59. Ibid., 189.
60. Ibid.
61. Fulkerson, review of *Models of God* et al., 182.
62. Russell, *Growth in Partnership*, 119.
63. Ibid., 94.
64. Elaine Wainwright, "The Gospel of Matthew," in Elisabeth Schüssler Fiorenza, ed., *Searching the Scriptures*, vol. 2: *A Feminist Commentary* (New York: Crossroad, 1994).
65. Russell, *Household of Freedom*, 33.
66. Russell, *Growth in Partnership*, 121.
67. Russell, *Household of Freedom*, 56.
68. Ibid., 34–35.
69. Russell, *Growth in Partnership*, 128–31.
70. Russell, *Household of Freedom*, 20.
71. Audre Lorde, "Master's Tools," 112.
72. Ibid.
73. Russell, *Growth in Partnership*, 121, 124.
74. Ibid., 125.
75. Russell, *Household of Freedom*, 34.
76. Ibid., 64, 35.
77. Russell, *Human Liberation*, 96; Russell, *Household of Freedom*, 60–67.
78. Russell, *Growth in Partnership*, 75.
79. Peter C. Phan, "Woman and the Last Things: A Feminist Eschatology," in Ann O'Hara Graff, ed., *In the Embrace of God: Feminist Approaches to Theological Anthropology* (Maryknoll, N.Y.: Orbis Books, 1995), 222.
80. Russell, *Growth in Partnership*, 160.

PART 2

LIBERATING THE FUTURE:
STORIES AT THE TABLE

4

BIBLE IN THE ROUND

Phyllis Trible

Unlike the apostle Paul, Letty Russell does not claim to "have become all things to all people," not even "for the sake of the gospel" (cf. 1 Cor. 9:22–23). Nevertheless, those who know her may well make this claim about her. No feminist theologian of our time has done more to share the blessings of the gospel with all sorts and conditions of humankind.

The sharing is worldwide. Beginning in the United States, it extends to Guatemala, New Zealand, Korea, India, South Africa, and a host of places in between. As Paul journeyed throughout the world of his time (Acts 13:1–21:14), so Russell encompasses the globe. As he heeded the call, "Come over to Macedonia and help us" (Acts 16:9), so too does she. Specific to situations, the help she gives embraces groups and individuals: prisoners, homeless people, battered women, patients with AIDS, divinity school students, university administrators, clergy, and laity. Bureaucrats to peasants, young to old, color to color, orthodox to heterodox, straight to gay, the foolish to the wise—all these receive the ministry of this professor at Yale Divinity School.

CHURCH IN THE ROUND

In addition to traveling, lecturing, and listening, Russell speaks for the gospel through her writings. Paul wrote letters; she writes books. Prominent among them is *Church in the Round,* a study that inspires this essay.[1] Drawing on thirty-five years of experiences, Russell maintains that if the church is to remain alive, to do more than perpetuate itself as we move into the next century, then it must change. It must reorder, reorient, and rearrange itself through acts of reflection and repentance. The model for change is a common table for hospitality and conversation: a round table that welcomes all who come regardless of status, rank, expertise, or privilege. There is, however, regard for the outcast, for the inclusion of the marginalized.

The images of margin and center loom large in Russell's proposal. To explicate the concept, she uses the biblical story of Hagar and Sarah (Gen. 16:1–15; 21:9–21). First, she acknowledges similarity between the women. Patriarchal oppression marginalizes them both. But then she recognizes difference. Class and national identities drive them apart. Sarah, the Hebrew matriarch, is central to the divine plan; Hagar, the Egyptian slave, is peripheral. In these women, center and margin meet; in them, center and margin clash. Read from contrasting perspectives, their story lifts up terror, survival, entrapment, resistance, and promise.

Appropriating the story, Russell urges those who hold power in the church "to choose the margin as a way of standing in solidarity with those who are oppressed and working for justice."[2] Even as Paul advocated the inclusion of uncircumcised Greeks with circumcised Jews (Gal. 5:6), so Christians are called to include the "other" in the household of God. The goal of such a choice is not to promote marginalization over centralization, for reversal would change nothing. What is needed is the elimination of margin and center through redemptive table talk. This goal both receives and awaits actualization in the Christ, "the One who is at the center of life in the church but dwells on the margin where he lived and died."[3] A transcendent and eschatological perspective thus informs Russell's understanding of church in the round.

Another feature of table talk comes through the image of the spiral in contrast to the circle. To go around the table is not to repeat the conversation and so come out at the same place but rather to change the ways in which we think and talk. The retelling of the Sarah and Hagar story illustrates the spiraling process. As blacks and whites, in their changing contexts, reflect on the biblical narrative, they move from analyses of patriarchal social structures to critiques of racism and classism and even to questionings about divine sanction for child abuse. All such reflections carry the conversation to a level of awareness that engenders redemptive actions. The actions yield new experiences of faith "'til by turning, turning we come round right."

Like the dissolving of margin and center, the movement of the spiral leads to partnership in the Spirit. In writing about this possibility,[4] Russell evokes Paul, first with the admonition "Welcome one another . . . just as Christ has welcomed you, for the glory of God" (Rom. 15:7). After the admonition comes the affirmation "For in the one Spirit we were all baptized into one body—Jews or Greeks, slaves or free—and we were all made to drink of one Spirit" (1 Cor. 12:13).

BIBLE AT THE TABLE

Constructive use of the Bible is a hallmark of Russell's hermeneutics. Unlike feminist commentators who pretend scripture is not there or who condemn it as beyond redemption, she wanders around in it, seeking the lost coin, blessing the five loaves and two fishes, looking for the treasures old and new. Thereby, to some extent, she becomes a marginal thinker within her own discipline of theology. That status extends to the biblical guild, with its suspicion of "outsiders" who dare to interpret the text. But Russell perseveres, and along the way she meets friends. The result is a wondrous act of collaboration, of the removal of boundaries that confine and divide.

Sharing a feminist perspective but coming from different disciplines, Letty Russell and I bring diverse talents to the task of forging a biblical theology for "church in the round." In this essay I envision the two of us at a table with a mixed group of twelve people from ancient Israel. Known only through scripture, they cannot speak directly for themselves. Belonging to a world quite distant in time, place, and culture from our own, their stories nevertheless resound with immediacy. Our task is to listen and report, as initial steps toward reflection and action.

Hosea

The first to speak at the table is a conflicted man named Hosea. This prophet claims that God commanded him to take a wife of whoredom and have children of whoredom (Hosea 1–3). Lashing out at his unfaithful wife, he says that he stripped her naked, denied her nourishment, and kept her captive. When she did escape, he pursued her, spoke tenderly to her, bought her back, and then imposed celibacy on their relationship. All his actions, he insists, were for the sake of love and redemption. Moreover, he maintains that his story carries theological import; it models the relationship between God and Israel.[5]

Hosea's aggressive words disturb us. Often his speech lacks coherence. Yet in the midst of his violence, vindictiveness, and vindication we occasionally hear the clarity of a healing vision. Once, for instance, he approaches a new understanding of God's covenant with Israel that seems to eradicate the inequality of the participants (Hos. 2:16). With eschatological fervor he describes a relationship in which Israel as female spouse will cease to call God "my lord" or "my master" (*ba 'ali*), the paradigm for patriarchal marriage. Instead, Israel will call the deity "my husband" (*ishi*), the language of parity. And Yahweh will answer with the corresponding vocabulary of equality. Israel will be "my wife" (*issa*). To be sure, the vision is not perfect. Yahweh remains in control, locked in male imagery. Nonetheless, Hosea begins to rewrite the covenant, moving from a model of dominance and subordination to domestic mutuality. And this is the man who abuses his wife.

When next Hosea speaks, he has shifted to the metaphor of parent and child. He offers a poem of controlled discipline and unmitigated love (Hos. 11:1–12). The opening stanza depicts Israel as the wayward son running from Yahweh the nurturing parent, the one who has taught, carried, and fed the child. In ancient Israel such activities describe maternal rather than paternal roles. (Whether Hosea intends such a metaphor for God we do not know.) Although the first response of this parent is to punish, the Deity reconsiders. A series of rhetorical questions suggests the impossibility of rejecting the child, and a firm pronouncement to that effect follows. Yahweh will not destroy Ephraim. The motivation for the decision is an extraordinary statement of self-declaration. If earlier Yahweh relinquished his role as master (*ba 'ali*) of Israel to become her husband (*'is*) in mutuality, now this Deity relinquishes male identity altogether: "For I am God [*'el*] and not a husband [*'is;* or 'not a male'], the Holy One in your midst" (Hos. 11:9; my translation).

To church in the round Hosea comes, full of contradictions that terrify and tantalize us. Whatever will we, the gathered community, do? By our own rules, we cannot just denounce or marginalize him. Perhaps we may begin by asking where his wife, Gomer, is. Why is she not at the table? Where is her voice? What is her story?

Hagar and Ruth

Beside Hosea sit two women, Hagar of Egypt and Ruth of Moab. Not unlike the Israelite wife of Hosea, Hagar knows suffering and abuse.[6] (Russell already knows her story well.) She represents many women: the faithful maid exploited, the surrogate mother, the resident alien without legal recourse, the welfare mother, and the black woman used by the male and abused by the female of the ruling class. Yet Hagar brings to the table something other than suffering and rejection. She reports two extraordinary encounters with God in the wilderness of Sinai (Gen. 16:7–14 and 21:17–19). She is the first person in the Bible whom a divine messenger visits, and the only person who dares to name the Deity. She is the first woman to hear an annunciation and the only one to receive a divine promise of descendants. She is the first woman to weep for her dying child and receive divine assurance that he will survive. In time, she finds her son a wife in the land of Egypt and thus secures for herself a future as the founding mother of a great nation. If the biblical tradition rejects Hagar, her presence in it nevertheless brings her to the church in the round. Her story poses upsetting questions for those who claim the center of power.

In contrast to Hagar the Egyptian, Ruth the Moabite brings to the table the experience of acceptance and fulfillment among the people of Israel.[7] Though at first she knows rejection from her mother-in-law, Naomi, soon thereafter the two women bond. Though Ruth knows what it is to struggle for physical survival, she has not lacked for food. Though she knows what it is to struggle for cultural survival, she has not met hostility from those in whose land she lives. By her own initiative, with the support of Naomi, Ruth has received the blessings of husband and child, indeed a child who will become grandfather of the great king David. At the end of the story, however, Ruth seems to lose status. She ceases to speak; the elders of Bethlehem place her in the traditional role of the childbearer, subservient to her husband; and even the women of Bethlehem, who applaud her faithfulness and fertility, subordinate her to Naomi. If Hagar lives on the margins of Israel, Ruth occupies the center. And yet the center paradoxically marginalizes her. The African woman and the Moabite woman have lots to talk about.

Huldah and Jeremiah

The attention of the table shifts now as a third woman approaches. She comes with confidence, for the community respects Huldah the prophet (2 Kings 22:14–20). So powerful is this authority that even the king Josiah and the high priest Hilkiah have deferred to her. Some time ago, while repairs were being made in the temple of Jerusalem, Hilkiah found there a book of the law. He reported the discovery, and subsequently the book was read before Josiah. On hearing it, the king rent his clothes and ordered an inquiry from Yahweh about the validity of the document. Huldah authenticated it, thereby inaugurating a sacred text. The beginning of the canon belonged to this woman. Yet in the biblical account, Huldah spoke not her own words but rather the stereotypical language of the Judean establishment. She chastised the inhabitants of the land for their apostasy and called forth the unquenchable wrath of Yahweh upon them. Then she faded from the story.

Who is Huldah? Is she but a cipher for the politics of the male establishment? Was she discarded once she served the center of power? How do we treat her? Do we appropriate the authority she held to declare canonicity, or do we repudiate all that she authenticated? Do we wish that she had not joined those gathering at the table? Do we fear she will betray us? Not unlike Hosea, Huldah exacerbates the difficulties of table talk in the round.

Her contemporary Jeremiah presents another challenge. Rather than disappearing behind the stereotypical language of establishment theology, this man speaks his own anguish and anger. Pain wracks him. He never wanted to be a prophet. Yahweh forced the role on him (Jer. 1:4–10) and so isolated him in life (Jer. 15:17). Jeremiah resents his lack of wife and children (Jer.

16:1–2), even though, like Hosea, he condemns Judah for being a depraved wife of Yahweh (Jer. 2:1–13). But he also turns on Yahweh, charging that this Deity has raped him and he cannot break loose (Jer. 20:7). With invective heaped on invective he denounces prophets, priests, kings, indeed the entire nation of Judah. He lashes out against the trappings of religion, including the sacrificial system, the ark, and even the temple itself. He knows that danger stalks his life. Already there have been attempts to kill him (Jer. 11:18–19). No one at the table in the round articulates marginalization more vehemently than Jeremiah.

Not surprisingly, in the midst of these assaults, Jeremiah expresses his yearning for comfort and consolation. He remembers his ancestor Rachel weeping for her lost children; he acknowledges that God has shown womb-compassion on them; and he urges virgin Israel to return home, concluding with a cryptic remark that his hearers struggle to understand: "For the LORD has created a new thing on the earth; a woman encompasses a man" (Jer. 31:15–22). Jeremiah also envisions a new day when Yahweh will make a new covenant with the people Israel, a covenant grounded not in obedience to the written law but in the forgiveness and the forgetting of transgressions (Jer. 31:31–34).

The sufferings, insights, and longings of Jeremiah threaten to overwhelm all who come to the table. What manner of man (or woman) dares so to expose himself? His agonies plunge us into the depth of the inner life as they intertwine with the social and political vicissitudes of his time.

Miriam and the Unknown Woman

The isolation that Jeremiah experiences makes him a kindred spirit to the prophet Miriam. Like him, she comes to the table alone, without spouse or children.[8] But she brings the deserved reputation of having worked on behalf of her people. When they crossed the Red Sea, she led them with drums and dances as she sang a song of triumph (Exod. 15:1–21). Yet her face shows the scars of suffering, marks of punishment because she dared to question the sole authority of Moses as spokesman for Yahweh and further to suggest that Yahweh speaks through her as well as through her brother Aaron (Numbers 12). With wounds visible, though healed, the marginalized Miriam seems now to have moved beyond that disturbing encounter. After all, the prophet Micah has openly vindicated her (Micah 6:4), and Jeremiah has obliquely referred to her participation in an eschatological vision of a new exodus (Jer. 31:4). So Miriam appears ready to reclaim the center, to speak a word and sing a song, until she sees another woman approaching the table.

Quite unexpected is the new arrival. No one save Miriam seems to recognize her, so marginal is her presence in the Bible. Is she from Ethiopia or

Midian or Syria?[9] Taking a seat, this woman speaks not a word, but she looks at Miriam, the sister-in-law who long ago spoke against Moses because he had married her (Num. 12:1). The look is a request, perhaps a demand, for an explanation. Silence prevails. The resulting tension instructs all who join the table that closure on the past and celebration for the present are premature.

The Isaiah Family

Not knowing what to do with this situation, the gathered community buys time. It diverts attention to a happy family, Mr. and Ms. Isaiah and their three children. Coming from the upper class, they are prominent people in Jerusalem. Both parents are identified as prophets. They inhabit the centers of power. Ms. Isaiah births prophetic oracles (Isa. 8:3); Mr. Isaiah announces them. He has a reputation for speaking with ease, though with impatience, to the authorities in Judah. He does not mince words in reporting the deficiencies of the government and the desolation he sees on the horizon. But neither is he devoid of hope. In the naming of his children, both facets of the message become clear. Shear-jashub ("a remnant shall return") embodies hope and destruction (Isa. 7:3–9). Maher-shalal-hash-baz ("the spoil speeds; the prey hastens") brings assurance that the enemies of Judah will not prevail (Isa. 8:1–4). And Immanuel ("God is with us") proclaims through his name the presence of God to both comfort and afflict (Isa. 7:14–17; 8:5–8).[10]

What happens when the cuckold Hosea and the reluctant celibate Jeremiah reflect on the happy marriage of Mr. and Ms. Isaiah? What happens when Hagar reflects on the names and treatment of the Isaiah children in the light of her own son Ishmael ("God hears")? What happens when Ruth reflects on her child Obed ("worshiper"), whom she neither named nor raised but who became the ancestor of David? Are the children of the Bible conduits for adult purposes? Rather than modeling solutions, the presence at the table of an intact family increases the questions.

THE CHALLENGE OF AN INVITATION

According to Letty Russell, church in the round is open to all. Having brought to the table some of the people with whom I spend time, I invite my friend Letty to join us—and to bring along the apostle Paul. Though I am unsure where the conversation will go, our common interest suggests that we can engage biblical characters to forge new interpretations of old texts. In a spiraling dialogue, we shall see if the center and the margins dissolve. That prospect is itself a fitting eschatological challenge for Letty as she continues to share the blessings of the gospel with all sorts and conditions of humankind.

NOTES

1. This essay is an expanded version of remarks made at Yale Divinity School on the occasion of the publication of Letty M. Russell's *Church in the Round: Feminist Interpretation of the Church* (Louisville, Ky.: Westminster John Knox Press, 1993).
2. Russell, *Church in the Round,* p. 26.
3. Ibid., p. 27.
4. Ibid., p. 206.
5. For recent discussions of this metaphor of marriage, see Phyllis Bird, " 'To Play the Harlot': An Inquiry into an Old Testament Metaphor," in *Gender and Difference,* ed. Peggy L. Day (Philadelphia: Fortress Press, 1989), pp. 75–94; Tikva Frymer-Kensky, *In the Wake of the Goddesses* (New York: Free Press, 1992), pp. 144–152; Renita Weems, *Battered Love* (Minneapolis: Fortress Press, 1995), esp. pp. 45–52, 92–93; Gale Yee, "The Book of Hosea: Introduction, Commentary, and Reflections," in *The New Interpreter's Bible,* vol. 7 (Nashville: Abingdon Press, 1996), pp. 206–209, 215–233; Yvonne Sherwood, *The Prostitute and the Prophet,* JSOT Supplement Series 212 (Sheffield: Sheffield Academic Press, 1996).
6. Cf. Phyllis Trible, *Texts of Terror: Literary-Feminist Readings of Biblical Narratives* (Philadelphia: Fortress Press, 1984), pp. 9–35.
7. For diverse interpretations of Ruth, cf. Judith A. Kates and Gail Twersky Reimer, eds., *Reading Ruth: Contemporary Women Reclaim a Sacred Story* (New York: Ballantine Books, 1994).
8. In contrast to the biblical depiction, the rabbis insisted that Miriam was married to Caleb and had a son.
9. See Katharine Doob Sakenfeld, *Journeying with God: A Commentary on the Book of Numbers* (Grand Rapids: Wm. B. Eerdmans Publishing Co., 1995), pp. 79–84.
10. Scholars disagree as to whether Immanuel is the child of Isaiah and his wife or of King Ahaz and his wife (cf. Isa 7:10–17).

5

RUTH 4, AN IMAGE OF ESCHATOLOGICAL HOPE

Journeying with a Text

Katharine Doob Sakenfeld

Households of freedom are few and far between, yet they are experienced from time to time as people struggle against forms of bondage and discover glimpses of a new reality for their lives.

—Letty Russell[1]

The goal of this essay is to reflect "outside the box" on the theme of eschatological hope in the Old Testament by turning our attention to the fourth chapter of Ruth, a text not usually presented as an image of hope, much less included in the category of eschatology. Classic "end-time" passages from the Old Testament include texts such as Jeremiah's promise of an era of a new covenant (Jer. 31:31–34) and Ezekiel's vision of a stream issuing forth from the Jerusalem temple to fructify the desert and sweeten the waters of the Dead Sea (Ezek. 47:1–12), as well as the image of the wolf living with the lamb while a child plays unendangered near a snake's den (Isa. 11:6–9). Such passages incorporate pictures of earth and its life so remote from our usual human experience that we almost instinctively regard their content as far distant, even beyond ordinary time, images of a perfected future of the wholeness and harmony of God's creation. At the same time, texts such as these are often identified as eschatological by their literary character (e.g., vision reports, although not all vision reports concern eschatological subject matter) or by characteristic phrases pointing to the future, such as "in days to come."

Classic Old Testament eschatological texts such as those mentioned above focus primarily on the action of God; the promised future is not within human power but belongs to the realm of decisive divine intervention. Only God can write a covenant on human hearts so that no human teaching about the knowledge of God that leads to justice will be necessary (Jeremiah 31).

Only God can undo the predatory behavior of wild animals (Isaiah 11). Only God can send forth a mighty stream from the Jerusalem temple, like the source of those streams that watered primordial Eden (Ezekiel 47; cf. Gen. 2:6, 10). The classic texts provide their hearers with a promise, but they do not in themselves suggest that human beings have any role to play. All is in God's hands.

The importance of such classic eschatological visions of hope must not be underestimated. They provide their hearers, ancient and contemporary, with imagery and vocabulary for imagining God's promised future and thus with categories for assessing, evaluating, judging, and challenging the present world order in which the hearers find themselves. The famous "I Have a Dream" speech of the Reverend Dr. Martin Luther King Jr.[2] offers an illuminating contemporary example. On one level, his vision of a racially integrated and harmonious society remains a future hope that many regard as belonging to the end time, not achievable by human effort. At the same time, however, his words (and his life's work) continue to provide direction and inspiration to those who work individually and corporately to try to bring Dr. King's dream to realization, to live "as if" his dream were a present reality. It is at this point of comparison that the possibilities of considering the story of Ruth can be seen.

Of course, the story of Ruth cannot be classified as a classic eschatological text about an end time. Form-critically it is a narrative, set squarely in a known past-time historical context; it has a geographic locale and a genealogy that relate it to a specific Israelite king. Nor is its content in any usual sense eschatological, since the explicit focus is largely on human rather than divine action. Nonetheless, I suggest that the story, and especially its conclusion in chapter 4, may be regarded as an image of hope, even eschatological hope, in that it presents readers with one of ancient Israel's pictures of ideal human community.

Because it is located in history and focused on human action, this picture of ideal human community in the book of Ruth has a different impact on its readers from that of the classic texts mentioned above. First, the picture is not macrocosmic (the whole earth or universe) but microcosmic (one village or town). Readers are invited to envision an ideal on a scale that can be readily related to their own life circumstances. Second, because the picture remains on an easily recognizable human plane, the picture itself has a "flesh and blood" character to which readers can relate. The future hope embodied in the story is more this-worldly than beyond our earthly imagining. Furthermore, this kind of picture of future hope invites readers to reflect on the relationship between their own actions and God's intention to bring forth the fullness of human community. It is precisely for these reasons that this formally non-eschatological text provides, in my view, an important supplement (and possibly corrective) to images of hope usually considered under the heading "eschatology."

At this point, two obvious objections should be anticipated: (1) that the story has a quite different purpose, and (2) that its picture of human community is far from ideal, even at a village level. The second concern is taken up in some detail in the next section of this essay. Regarding the first concern, scholarly proposals about the purpose of the story, in the sense of the agenda behind its original circulation in ancient Israel, depend to some degree on differing theories about its date of composition. Following the lead of Edward Campbell in his Anchor Bible commentary,[3] a number of recent scholars (notably Kirsten Nielsen)[4] have argued for a date early in the monarchical period. Given this dating, several scholars suggest that the purpose of the text was to defend David's royal line against political opponents who were trying to capitalize on the alleged taint of David's Moabite ancestry. Recent analysis by Frederic Bush, however, shows that an earlier scholarly consensus dating the composition of the story (at least the form we have) to the early Persian (postexilic) era remains viable on linguistic grounds.[5] I follow this tradition of earlier scholarship in dating the story to the general era of Ezra and Nehemiah and in viewing its picture of ideal community as a challenge to the vision of religious and ethnic exclusivism represented in their leadership.

The choice of probable historical context does not finally settle the question of focus or meaning. At a purely literary level, the question of purpose, in the sense of the problem to be rectified within the framework of the story, still remains. In contrast to Nielsen and others, I interpret the concluding Davidic genealogy, even if original to the story, as only supportive reinforcement of the main purpose of the story. My guiding perspective is that the story is intended theologically to offer its readers an appropriate vision of the wholeness of human community. In the course of accomplishing that primary goal, the narrator embodies in the experience of Naomi a contrast between death and life and also offers examples of what it means to "choose life" (cf. Deut. 30:11–20) so that God's desire for the fullness of human community is realized.

READING RUTH 4

We are constantly restless to get an ever-new glimpse of the liberating Word of God.

—Letty Russell[6]

The interpretation of the ending of Ruth as an Old Testament expression of future hope has some continuities with past and current literature, yet it intends to press a step beyond a well-told story with a significant moral component. This section of the essay moves toward my current view of chapter 4 by tracing key moments and dialogue partners in my own journey with this challenging text.

My first work on the story, represented in my dissertation research,[7] focused primarily on the faithful actions of Ruth and Boaz by which human resolution to a human problem was effected. While it will become apparent by the end of this essay that I still hold to the basic insights suggested in my initial publications, those same insights take on a quite different flavor and import in my current perspective. I note especially that my earlier works gave no attention to the kinds of questions feminists would soon be asking of this text. In that early phase, Ruth was just one among many characters whom the Hebrew Bible portrayed as demonstrating *ḥesed,* loyalty or faithfulness that involves both attitude and action.

Phyllis Trible's treatment, "A Human Comedy,"[8] introduced me (and a whole generation of women and men) to the possibilities of an explicitly feminist rhetorical approach to the story. The supposedly familiar story took on new dimensions for me as the place of women in Israel's culture was made a primary lens for a close reading of the text. A story about human loyalty became now a story of *women's* loyalty. In Trible's reading, it is "the brave and bold decisions of women [that] embody and bring to pass the blessings of God";[9] the role of Boaz is here much subordinated to the activity of Ruth and Naomi in the presentation as a whole. Trible titles her reading of chapter 4 "All's Well That Ends Well."[10] This heading, coupled with the title of the essay as a whole, highlights Trible's emphasis on the human aspect of the action: "women working out their own salvation with fear and trembling, for it is God who works in them."[11] Despite her recognition of women and men together at the end of the story, Trible makes clear that in her interpretation it is the women who wrest this humanizing possibility out of the male, patriarchal setting in which they find themselves. I continue to resonate strongly with most aspects of Trible's reading. Yet, to anticipate, I want to hold her focus on women's action in greater tension with the contributions of the Deity to the positive resolution of the story, and also to give even greater theological weight to its concluding vision of wholeness.

A major challenge to Trible's interpretation, and even more explicitly and directly to my own early publication, was mounted by Danna Nolan Fewell and David Gunn.[12] The category of inquiry often called "hermeneutic of suspicion" was applied with unrelenting rigor to a text that heretofore had been presumed to be easily claimed on behalf of women's (and by extension, human) liberation. In particular, suspicion was directed at interpreters such as myself who presumed and lauded Ruth's supposed altruism. Fewell and Gunn pointed to the many gaps in the text, places where information is lacking, and argued for filling such gaps with primarily self-interested motives for the characters, thus undercutting most possibilities for display of altruism and at the same time significantly altering (if not diminishing) the potential theological significance of the story. In their analysis, each of the principal characters gets what he or she wants out of the situation. It is a relatively happy story with a relatively happy ending, to the extent that there happens to be a confluence of each one's personal desire with the personal desires of others. Yet Fewell and Gunn are also highly (and appropriately) suspicious of this supposedly happy ending, for its " 'economic security' masks . . . female economic dependence,"[13] and none of the characters truly escapes the patriarchal system of their culture. Nonetheless, Fewell and Gunn recognize that *ḥesed* is practiced, and God is present in the "mixed motives . . . , complicated relationships . . . , struggle for survival, anywhere there is redemption, however compromised."[14]

Fewell and Gunn provide cogent scholarly information, ranging from text-critical detail to syntactical ambiguities to canonical intertextual readings to rabbinic lore, in support of the unexpected points in their retelling of the story. They properly emphasize the important role of the stance of the interpreter in any reading, and their choices among options developed for filling of gaps are made in the light of the overarching interpretive stance they have chosen: one in which the characters are complex and cannot be subsumed under the single viewpoint of the omniscient narrator, one in which women's contemporary concern for freedom from patriarchy challenges and subverts any reading that unthinkingly praises women's altruism in service of values (such as the importance of preserving the male family line) presumed to be culturally masculine. Thus, I regarded their individual readings as plausible both on the basis of technical scholarly evidence and on the basis of the announced hermeneutical perspective.

A plausible reading is not necessarily a compelling reading, however. I found myself facing two plausible feminist readings, the new reading by Fewell and Gunn on the one hand and the reading by Trible that resonated much more closely with my own initial work on the other. The two readings appeared incompatible at a fundamental level, yet each rang true for me in its own way. The continuing struggle to find my way through this apparent hermeneutical impasse has marked my journey since that time, not only regarding this text but, in principle, regarding scripture generally. How can I lift up even the texts that scripture itself presents positively, since all without exception are in some way products of a patriarchal culture?[15] The questions raised for the story of Ruth in particular are these: What are the continuing possibilities and the dangers of highlighting women's altruism in view of cross-culturally well-documented tendencies for women to value serving others above caring for themselves? Does it make a difference if a woman's primary loyalty is to another woman? Most important, regardless of how the ending is achieved, can chapter 4 be read at all as a happy ending (let alone as a vision of future hope) if the resolution of the story reinscribes a societal structure in which women's economic security is essentially linked to marriage, preferably to a rich man?

One additional challenge from a North American scholar entered the mix of my hermeneutical reflection at about this time. In the introductory section of her *Discovering Eve*,[16] Carol Meyers challenges the alleged sloppiness of the use of the term and conception of *patriarchy* prevalent in much of feminist biblical analysis, including my own. Following the work of M. K. Whyte[17] and M. Z. Rosaldo,[18] Meyers argues helpfully that there is no consistent pattern from one culture to another in the areas in which men exercise greater power or control than women, even though men are generally accorded greater authority. She warns against drawing conclusions about presumed oppressive characteristics of biblical cultures by making easy analogies from the cultures of contemporary readers. Meyers's acknowledgment that the received Hebrew Bible texts do assume male dominance and female subservience[19] raised for me from a different perspective the same question raised by Fewell and Gunn's insistence on the tainted character of the idyllic ending of Ruth. If all the text embodies values I do not share, how am I to accord authority to the text itself at all? At the same time, Meyers's insistent criticism of generalizations across cultures offered an unintended methodological clue. Might there be some fruitful hermeneutical possibility in working with the best images of future hope that biblical tradition has to offer by prescinding from piecemeal criticisms of their components that lead potentially to rejection of every vision of hope we are offered? Can the fact that these images "worked" within their culture be put to good hermeneutical use?

My journey with Ruth continued as I arranged (with help from Letty Russell) a series of conversations about this story with Christian women in Asia. These occasions were spread over several years and a half dozen countries and included women at every level of education beyond basic literacy, women at every level of church leadership, women with and without formal theological education. There were women who regarded themselves as feminist, women who viewed feminism as dangerous, and women who were not familiar with the concept of feminism. The contributions of these hundreds of women to my ongoing search have been invaluable.[20]

The readings of Ruth in these conversations fell broadly into the two types already identified from North Atlantic scholarly readings: those generally appreciative and those deeply suspicious of this story. Significantly, however, the specific details of the story that elicited these reactions often differed from those highlighted by the publications described above. Although many of these reactions were illustrated by immediate situations in the women's various home countries, they were not (as far as I could discern) so much nation-specific as context-specific in terms of varying cultural values or economic status. Thus, the following account of some key reflections is grouped thematically rather than by country of origin.

A cultural tradition of mother-in-law–daughter-in-law relationships very different from that of most North American families shaped many of the conversations.[21] Thus, many women centered their attention on the devotion of Ruth to Naomi, assuming the younger woman's altruistic concern for her mother-in-law. But reactions to this devotion varied. In Burma, for instance, a group of older, married women uniformly praised Ruth as an ideal daughter-in-law, whereas a group of young, unmarried, preprofessional women expressed high anxiety that the story of Ruth would be held before them, by their future mothers-in-law and by the church, as a standard these young women felt it was impossible for them to achieve. They sensed that the traditional family values of their culture matched closely those they perceived in the text. In the face of concern for relating to their future in-laws, the group set aside the potential example of Ruth as a woman who chose an unconventional route for her life as being of little importance. Likewise, in Korea and Japan, the character of the relationship between the two women, especially the care of the younger woman for the older, was a central component in most appropriations of the story. It became apparent that in many instances the church—at least, many of its male pastors—had used this story to urge upon women their traditional role within much of East Asian culture, a role of servant to mother-in-law that was supposed to preclude professional work outside the home. For many younger Christian women, Ruth was an oppressive text.

By contrast, the theme of women bound by economic structures, so significant for Fewell and Gunn, did not arise frequently. Occasionally I raised the topic, and reactions ranged from mystification to dismissal as completely unimportant to enthusiastic discussion of this new angle for viewing the story. As the visitor, I could only begin to guess about the differences in response and could not discern any pattern. In one instance in the Philippines, however, a woman pastor initiated the theme of economic security with an example that continues to haunt all my reflections on this text, and on hermeneutical method generally. A young girl in a remote village had been approached by a "recruiter" and had agreed to go to a wealthy foreign country to work as a "dancer." In response to her woman pastor's concern about this decision, the young girl cited the example of Ruth, who left her home country for a foreign land, made contacts, made herself up attractively, and ended up with a rich husband who supported not only Ruth but Naomi as well. She said that God would take care of her, just as God had taken care of Ruth.

Further details of this sobering report were not available. Whether or not the girl knew she would almost surely become a prostituted child rather than a dancer, exactly what version of the story of Ruth she would have told in more detail, the actual level of desperation of her family's presumed poverty, whether the child was centrally concerned about her family's welfare or just wanted to escape her immediate environment at any cost[22] were not known. Nor was the source of the comparison to Ruth identified—perhaps a relative or the recruiter?—though it seemed unlikely to me that the child thought of it herself. Despite such unanswered questions, the story illustrates starkly the range of warrants for decision and action that believers may find in unlikely places.

Differences in perspective persisted when discussion was focused specifically on chapter 4. In assessing the final chapter of Ruth, Trible draws attention to the male-centered legal proceedings at the gate and the male-focused blessing addressed to Boaz, although she finds a hopeful counterpoint in the women-centered closing scene. Fewell and Gunn emphasize that the "all's well" tone of chapter 4 can be sustained by the hearer only if the importance of a male heir and the customary economic arrangements of financial support through a wealthy husband are accepted as a satisfactory social structure. Aware of these difficulties for Western feminist readers, I found myself entering the conversations with Asian women with curiosity about their views of inheritance structures (those presumed by the Ruth narrative being notoriously unclear to modern interpreters) and still appreciative of the human resolution of Naomi's loss, in which the women of Bethlehem say, "A son has been born to Naomi" (4:17).

It came therefore as a surprise, even a shock, to me when a Taiwanese woman insisted that she wanted to cut the entire book of Ruth out of her Bible precisely because she so hated this verse. Further exploration with women's groups in Taiwan and Japan revealed many women's sense that this expression reinscribed a cultural tradition that the younger generation, especially, sought to resist. Responsibility for child rearing belonged traditionally primarily to the paternal grandmother; the children's mother had little or no role in their upbringing but rather was more of a household servant to their grandmother, her mother-in-law. Inheritance patterns were of little interest, while worries about the role of daughter-in-law extended far beyond questions of working outside the home. What many Westerners might regard as the joyful climax of the book was a "text of terror" for these women. Asian readers thus added a "third strike" against any reading of chapter 4 as a text of future hope.

RETHINKING HERMENEUTICS, RECLAIMING RUTH

A "memory of the future" . . .

—Letty Russell[23]

Given the state of interpretation just described, why try to "rescue" the story of Ruth? What is to be gained by arguing for a text such as chapter 4 as a vision of future hope? And how can that even be done without sweeping all the objections to it under the proverbial rug?

A first step in reclaiming Ruth 4 as such a vision is my rejection of the premise that adopting the vision means adopting the literal village picture offered by the text. This step is perhaps obvious to many readers,[24] yet this hermeneutical move has larger implications. If we know that we are unable or do not expect or intend to replicate actual village life of that ancient place and time, then we must think, by extension, of what else in the story we are not expecting to replicate. Such features may include the specific details of the legal system of decision making, as well as the legal system itself, with its particular categories of inheritance and redemption. Once this much is accepted, then it is not so big a step to suppose that the economic structures implied by or embedded in that legal system are also not necessarily to be replicated. Use of the text to reinforce traditional relationships and patterns of family structures of contemporary cultures or use of the text to reinforce traditional patterns of economic dependence in marriage is an effort to replicate parts of the picture provided by the text without giving proper attention to the goal of the text as a whole.

The second step, then, is to ask after that goal. If we agree that the narrator intends to provide readers with a happy ending, what are the underlying components of that ending, the concluding vision, that would have been recognized by ancient hearers who accepted this particular expression of the vision as adequate? In the case of Ruth 4, we may identify a number of such components: a community that is characterized by reciprocal movement from margin to center and from center to margin, by racial/ethnic inclusiveness, and by adequate physical sustenance for all; a community of upright individuals together creating and affirming justice and mercy; a community in which weeping turns to joy and tears are wiped away; a community in which children are valued and old people are well cared for; a community in which a daughter is greatly valued. It is these features, rather than their specific expression in ancient Israelite culture or the specific means of achieving these ends within the story, that make up the eschatological vision of future hope in this text.

Feminists have long emphasized that biblical language about God is metaphorical. God is not really "male." This fundamental starting point for appropriating God-language has consequences for our interpretation of eschatological texts featuring the righteous (male) ruler or the just (male) judge. Some of those classic eschatological texts describe future hope in imagery of political structures that are inadequate or even offensive to liberationist or feminist readings, yet they are often reconstructed by stating their underlying themes in fresh imagery. In the same way, the vision of hope in Ruth 4 may be thought of as an extended metaphor for God's New Creation that we must find ways to re-express in language appropriate to God's continuing work in our midst.

As I suggested at the outset of this essay, Ruth 4 differs from classic eschatological visions in presenting a vision of hope that is microcosmic and in which human participation plays a critical role. In conclusion, it is important to revisit each of these distinctions. First, the village scale of the vision, while microcosmic and thus more readily imaginable, is not of lesser significance because of its scale. All those fundamental features described above—sustenance, inclusiveness, justice, care for the least ones, valuing of daughters, joy, and the like—can and should be writ large, on a global scale in any Christian vision for the future. The very particularity of the microcosmic image may lead feminist critics more easily to see various culturally specific inadequacies of the vision. Yet the success of our critical hindsight should warn us against placing too much stock in our own restatements of the concrete social structures that we suppose might adequately describe God's vision for the future. It is appropriate to question practices of other cultures past or present as failing to embody even their own best vision; but we are rightly challenged not to absolutize our own ways of concretizing the biblical vision.

Second, like any other story set in history, the story of Ruth could not exist without human participants. Indeed, the book is sometimes spoken of as a "guide for living," in the sense that the actions of the characters, most notably Ruth and Boaz but also Naomi and even the other men and women of the village, provide positive models for our own faithful living. But conceiving of chapter 4 as an eschatological vision modifies that perspective. It is their living out of the *vision* that is as important as their specific behavior. The goal in appropriating the text is no longer emulation of their good actions or even of their best character traits but rather following them in living "as if" the dreamed-of future were now. The focus no longer encompasses just God working through them but also now their participation in God's work. While the book of Ruth does not get to its vision of hope by some cataclysmic divine action, the Deity does have a decisive role, without which the vision would not be achieved. Once the opening verses establish the disastrous situation of famine, flight, and death, the remainder of the story is framed by two direct interventions of God toward the restoration of wholeness and community. The restoration is initiated by God's provision of food in formerly famine-struck Bethlehem (1:6) and is climaxed by God's provision of conception for Ruth (4:13). Mortals are not able to accomplish all that is needed for the vision to become reality; indeed, these two divine acts may represent those aspects of the natural order over which ancient peoples experienced least control.

Elsewhere in Ruth, God is called on to do what human beings believe themselves unable to do (e.g., Naomi's prayer, 1:8) or is portrayed as at work behind the scenes (again Naomi's words, 2:20). How did it "happen" (2:3) that Ruth went to Boaz's field, rather than elsewhere? Surely the storyteller has in mind the providence of God, not sheer random luck. Naomi's prayer commending Ruth to God's hands is fulfilled by the end of the story through the actions of the human characters, but it would not have happened apart from Ruth's arrival at the field of Boaz. The point is that human action and divine action together lead to the coming of the shalom community in Bethlehem that serves as a paradigm for future hope. The very structure of the narrative teaches us that we are not required to choose between God's action and our own. Human beings are living out their "partnership with god and with others . . . , [hoping] in god who is the giver of good."[25]

One must recognize, to be sure, that the story of Ruth does not present great powers of sin and evil as obstacles to be overcome (although the power of death and the evil of ethnic prejudice are certainly conspicuous in the story). For that reason, this text cannot stand alone but must be understood alongside texts such as Jeremiah 31 and a panoply of others that insist explicitly on God's determination to forgive, create clean hearts, begin again, do a new thing. Yet the place of Ruth in the structure of the Protestant canon may offer at least a tentative link to the theme of divine intervention against sin and evil. The story of Ruth takes place in the days of the judges, an era known from the preceding book of Judges as one filled not just with Israelite warfare against external enemies but with the most horrific kind of internecine slaughter and destruction imaginable, destruction in which women are especially victimized (Judges 19–21). Over against this communal implosion stands the seed of a different way, a "household of freedom"[26] watched over by God and initiated through an unexpected human source—a woman, a poor widow, an outsider from a despised group. Surely the story of Ruth does offer us a "memory of the future" of God's promised redemption of all creation.

NOTES

1. Letty Russell, *Household of Freedom: Authority in Feminist Theology* (Philadelphia: Westminster Press, 1987), 26. In Russell's work, "household of freedom" is a metaphor for "glimpses of God's household," understood as "God's new creation" (26).
2. Martin Luther King Jr., "I Have a Dream" (speech delivered August 28, 1963, in Washington, D.C.), reprinted in *A Testament of Hope: The Essential Writings of Martin Luther King, Jr.*, ed. James Melvin Washington (San Francisco: Harper & Row, 1986), 217–20.
3. Edward F. Campbell Jr., *Ruth: A New Translation with Introduction and Commentary* (Garden City, N.Y.: Doubleday & Co., 1975).
4. Kirsten Nielsen, *Ruth: A Commentary* (Louisville, Ky.: Westminster John Knox Press, 1997).
5. Frederic W. Bush, *Ruth, Esther* (Dallas: Word, 1996), 18–30. The argument is based on the presence of grammatical and syntactical constructions characteristic of Late Biblical Hebrew (LBH). Although many features of Standard Biblical Hebrew (SBH) are also present, the later forms appear too numerous to be accidental exceptions to SBH usage.

6. Letty Russell, "Introduction: The Liberating Word," in *The Liberating Word,* ed. Letty Russell (Philadelphia: Westminster Press, 1979), 22.
7. Katharine Doob Sakenfeld, *The Meaning of Ḥesed in the Hebrew Bible: A New Inquiry.* Ph.D. dissertation, Harvard University, 1970; later published under same title (Missoula, Mont.: Scholars Press, 1978), 42–43, 104–7; cf. Katharine Doob Sakenfeld, *Faithfulness in Action* (Philadelphia: Fortress Press, 1985), 32–33.
8. Phyllis Trible, *God and the Rhetoric of Sexuality* (Philadelphia: Fortress Press, 1978), 166–99.
9. Ibid., 195.
10. Ibid., 188.
11. Ibid., 196.
12. Danna Nolan Fewell and David Gunn, *Compromising Redemption: Relating Characters in the Book of Ruth* (Louisville, Ky.: Westminster/John Knox Press, 1990), esp. 12.
13. Ibid.
14. Ibid., 104–5.
15. I use the term *patriarchy* here not just to refer to male–female relationships but to include also the complexity of interacting hierarchies of race, class, religion, ethnicity, and so forth. See Elisabeth Schüssler Fiorenza, *But She Said: Feminist Practices of Biblical Interpretation* (Boston: Beacon Press, 1992), 115. Because the term *patriarchy* is used in such different ways, Fiorenza suggests using the less familiar term *kyriarchy* to indicate this complex of variable patterns of domination.
16. Carol Meyers, *Discovering Eve: Ancient Israelite Women in Context* (New York: Oxford University Press, 1988), esp. 24–26.
17. Martin King Whyte, *The Status of Women in Pre-Industrial Societies* (Princeton, N.J.: Princeton University Press, 1978).
18. Michelle Zimbalist Rosaldo, "Women, Culture, and Society: A Theoretical Overview," in *Women, Culture, and Society,* ed. Michelle Zimbalist Rosaldo and Louise Lamphere (Stanford, Calif.: Stanford University Press, 1974), 17–42.
19. Meyers argues that the perspective in the texts is a later development. She proposes, based on anthropological theory and archaeological data, that premonarchical Israel was characterized by gender equality, and that the cultural practice of female subservience in Israel emerged at the earliest in the monarchical period and possibly as late as post-exilic times.
20. It should be noted that Meyers's challenge to typical feminist modes of criticizing biblical cultures has resonances in the debate about whether persons from a contemporary culture may appropriately criticize practices or values of another contemporary culture, or whether such criticism should come only from within a given culture. While some of my Asian contacts were quite free in criticizing U.S. culture and inviting me to assist them in using Western concepts or values to criticize their own traditions, others expected that neither side should make suggestions to the other. The validity of Meyers's underlying concern was manifested, for instance, in a conversation with Korean women about women's names. Both Korean and U.S. women are moving toward new patterns of family naming to symbolize their new perceptions of married relationships. Many U.S. women are trying to express that they do not "belong" to their husbands by not taking their husbands' names upon marriage. Korean women, in contrast, have never been allowed to take their husbands' names. Some now seek to do so, to express that they in fact genuinely belong to their husbands' families and are not in some subordinate or secondary relationship to them.

21. For a fuller description of this cultural tradition, see Julie L. C. Chu, "Returning Home: The Inspiration of Role Dedifferentiation in the Book of Ruth for Taiwanese Women," in *Reading the Bible as Women from Africa, Asia, and Latin America*, ed. Phyllis A. Bird, Sharon Ringe, and Katharine Doob Sakenfeld (*Semeia* 78; Atlanta: Scholars Press, 1998), 47–53.
22. Compare the approach of Fewell and Gunn, who treat Ruth's expression of loyalty to Naomi in 1:16–17 as a smoke screen that did not reveal her compelling personal reasons for leaving Moab.
23. This phrase appears in several of Letty Russell's works, including *The Future of Partnership* (Philadelphia: Westminster Press, 1979), 157; "Authority and the Challenge of Feminist Interpretation," in *Feminist Interpretation of the Bible*, ed. Letty Russell (Philadelphia: Westminster Press, 1985), 139; and *Household of Freedom*, 27.
24. Although this move may seem self-evident, one must keep in mind the long tradition of communities that have sought to replicate some or all of the supposed features of first-century Christian communities as reflected in the New Testament, whether in terms of musical instruments for worship, hairstyles, use of jewelry, or regulations about ordination. The challenge always is to discern which categories are essential and which are adiaphora.
25. Russell, *Future of Partnership*, 176.
26. See Russell, *Household of Freedom*.

6

DREAMING FROM EXILE

A Rereading of Ezekiel 47:1–12

Elsa Tamez

Today there is a lot of talk about the jubilee, but we all know that it is not just around the next corner. It is far from being a reality, and to make matters worse, it would seem to be moving farther and farther away. What is swarming around us is rather evidence of an anti-jubilee: debts, exclusions, imprisonments, people without land or home, and people dying premature deaths. In spite of all this, however, we affirm the jubilee because that is our task as Christians who believe in the resurrection, who believe in abundant life as a gift from God, and who have hope even in times of messianic drought.

Letty Russell, one of the foremost and most inspiring women theologians for many Christian women throughout the world, has always been concerned not just for the disadvantages women experience but also for people who are poor and excluded because of their race and socioeconomic situation. Much of the power of her writings comes from the fact that she keeps alive the hope for a change for the better, for all people. For this reason her theology inevitably bears an eschatological stamp. This reflection is dedicated to her on the occasion of her birthday.[1]

Is it possible to speak of dreams in a situation that is systematically anti-utopian? How can those dreams be made credible when one cannot count on clear, meaningful signs that verify in some way their feasibility? Today the jubilee is frequently mentioned as a beautiful dream that visualizes justice in relations between human beings and between humankind and the rest of the cosmos, but how can we speak of it without emptying it of its power and trivializing it? I believe that one of the credible ways to do so is to speak from exile, and at the midpoint of the journey, staking one's hope on its future arrival. We encounter elements of this attitude in the oracles of the prophet Ezekiel that announce the restoration. I base this brief meditation on the prophetic vision found in Ezekiel 47:1–12. I am guided by questions related to who speaks of the jubilee, from what context, when, how, and what is said.

WHO SPEAKS OF THE JUBILEE, AND FROM WHAT CONTEXT?

A deportee in Babylon, Ezekiel, from the sixth century B.C.E. The son of the priest Buzi, who assumed he was following the tradition of his father by preparing himself to serve God in the Temple. But things did not work out as he had hoped. The political and economic situation within Palestine was chaotic in the face first of Assyrian and then of Babylonian power. And when Babylonia conquered his homeland of Judah, Ezekiel, together with the king and others, was taken into exile in 598–597. It was the first of four deportations.

With neither Temple nor sacrifices, this man prepared to be a priest is called to prophesy from captivity, where he spends his entire life. From that location, he follows the events occurring between the Babylonian Empire and his insignificant country. In exile he receives three additional waves of deportees. To make matters worse, he hears from his location within the Babylonian Empire itself about the dreadful tragedy of the siege, conquest, and destruction of Jerusalem and its Temple in 589. Fire, violations, brutal deaths—the total demolition of the place of his origin—are images that build up in his heart. Yet even thus, powerless and in the very country that demolished his own, he has the power to see beyond that reality of desolation. He has the faith and the valor to envision a utopia of reconstruction.

When one speaks of the jubilee, it is essential to have before one the concrete situation that one is experiencing: debts, poverty, unemployment, violence, discrimination, exclusion, conflicts, sorrow, dehumanizing consumerism, the lethargy of the churches. For the jubilee is the good news that supposedly puts an end to that reality of suffering and dehumanization. It is, obviously, much more than a "reconciliation" between poor and rich, debtors and creditors, the unemployed and employers, violators and those they have violated. If we speak of the jubilee in a generic sense, the injustice is hidden, and the jubilee loses its power and ceases to be jubilee.

WHEN DO WE SPEAK OF THE JUBILEE?

That depends on the historical moments in which one is immersed. Ezekiel was living in exile and watching from afar his land being laid waste. It would be hard to make his message credible if he were to say that things would soon change for the better. Furthermore, it was not easy to mobilize the exiles. The first little group with whom Ezekiel himself went into exile was composed mostly of members of the nobility. They had little difficulty in accommodating themselves to the new situation. In fact, because of their social position they were not treated very badly by the leaders of Babylon. But the other exiles of the subsequent deportations, who had few resources, also managed to accommodate themselves to their new situation. The majority found the novelties of such a powerful empire more appealing than the tiny, impoverished country of Judah that now was destroyed. Moreover, the question that dominated their thoughts was what they should fight for when their relative power was so thoroughly out of balance. Jon Douglas Levenson notes, "The exiles have passed the point of no-return. [None] of them could report back what the port toward which they were sailing on such a tumultuous sea is like."[2]

The prophet Ezekiel, however, does not allow himself to be crushed by that "tumultuous sea." He knows what the port is like. He dreams from exile and speaks of renewal at the midpoint of the jubilee, in the twenty-fifth year of their exile. He says, "In the twenty-fifth year of our exile, at the beginning of the year, on the tenth day of the month, in the fourteenth year after the city was struck down, on that very day, the hand of the LORD was upon me, and he brought me there" (Ezek 40:1).

Visions are always full of symbolism. Twenty-five years signifies the midpoint of the jubilee, when there was no way to turn back. If we consider the number fourteen symbolically as the double of seven, it would be the culminating moment in the period of a conquered city. That is to say, for Ezekiel or his school the moment has arrived to speak of the reconstruction of the conquered city and its Temple.

In the present reality of the global market economy, many people and even communities throughout the world live as immigrants or exiles in other countries. And from those alien places where they dwell, they observe the deterioration of their own people. Many are homesick to return, but for the sake of survival they close off the ways back home. What is even worse, the governing powers of the countries in which these exiles live also close doors to them. It is as if they are sailing without a course on the tumultuous sea, hoping for the light of a port that will grant them refuge.

In addition, many persons and communities in the poor countries live as exiles on their own continent. With the accelerated movement toward privatization, we have been thrown off our own lands, beaches, rivers, forests, and seas. We have even been alienated from our very selves, as we take on the values of the dominant cultures. When we accommodate to those values and are charmed by the novelties of the market and by technological advances, we do not have eyes to see the misfortunes they cause. We also fail to strive and to remain vigilant to change things. From exile, both within and outside our own land, it is difficult for us to have visions, to dream dreams.

Furthermore, those of us who think differently are like exiled prophets. We have been exiled by the same technocratic and mercantilist current, exiled by the current of the ideology of a lack of faith and hope in more humanizing alternatives, exiled because solidarity becomes each time more tedious. No one wants to hear denunciations of exploitations and injustices, which are the messages of the prophets of the Hebrew Bible. In the book of Ezekiel, for example, only denunciations and judgments are spoken of in the first forty chapters.

Today, no one wants to hear us speak about the poor or from the perspective of the poor. We have the feeling that it sounds anachronistic to speak of injustices. But if that is so, then the reality we see is also anachronistic, because we have many more poor people than in past decades. There are more women and children than can be accommodated by the safe houses for abused women. The numbers of people assassinated—in Colombia, for example— keep growing. In 1998, Monseñor Juan Girardi was assassinated for denouncing the systematic violation of rights in Guatemala. I ask myself, Can it be that assassinations also are anachronistic?

We, the exiled prophets, have two challenges. One is to discern from our "exile" a new reality, in spite of the present realities that systematically deny it. We need the eyes of eagles to distinguish the port toward which we must sail. The second challenge is to convince our people that things will change. Ezekiel does it because he has the necessary confidence in God and believes he is a prophet sent by God. However, in order that our faith not be weakened, it is important to recognize that we are at the midpoint of the journey, and from now on the paths toward the jubilee will be opening up.

WHAT IS THE JUBILEE ABOUT?

Very simply to affirm a life of dignity for all people in a context where justice, liberty, happiness, mutual solidarity, and graciousness prevail. Leviticus 25 describes the jubilee with laws of justice. Jesus of Nazareth takes up the jubilee in his ministry according to Luke 4. Other prophets do it with metaphors.

The visionary prophet relates his or her dream in poetry. Utopia is generally constructed in symbolic language. The poetic form penetrates hearts and consciences better than the literal or rational, because the former is less linear and more embracing or inclusive. Ezekiel envisions the jubilee as a river. The vision is fascinating for the readers. It begins in 47:1: "Then he brought me back to the entrance of the temple; there, water was flowing from below the threshold of the temple toward the east."

Ezekiel is guided by someone who makes him see how the water that flows from the house of God keeps on growing. It begins as simply some water that is flowing out the door. That water becomes a little stream. The guide makes him walk a thousand cubits through the stream that now is ankle deep. Then he makes him walk several thousand more cubits through water that now reaches his shoulders. Then the guide measures thousands more cubits, but now Ezekiel cannot pass through the river, because it covers him. Only by swimming can he continue further. And the guide says to him, "Mortal, have you seen this?" (47:6). Then they go out of the river onto the bank and return toward the city. The prophet observes the river with fascination, and the guide tells him of its prodigious powers.

The symbol of water permeates the account, occurring fourteen times in twelve verses. Most important is the symbol of the river, on a par with the symbols of the wilderness and of the Dead Sea—the latter an accursed place in Palestine where fish cannot live because of the huge quantities of salt. The river flows toward the Dead Sea, that place where there is no life. The waters from beneath the door of the house of God flow toward the eastern region, the one most desertlike. They descend to Arabia and enter the Dead Sea. In that moment the waters are transformed into fresh, living waters. The river heading toward the sea has a miraculous power. The vision evokes the rivers of paradise, the Euphrates and the Tigris. The guide explains, "Wherever the river goes, every living creature that swarms will live, and there will be very many fish, once these waters reach there. It will become fresh; and everything will live where the river goes" (47:9).

This is the vision that Ezekiel dreams from exile. It is his interpretation of the jubilee, which has credibility because he offers it at the midpoint of the journey, as a way to make clear the distance still to be traveled to arrive at the jubilee. In other words, we have to keep on sailing, opening paths, oriented toward the light that reveals the port toward which we are headed.

From exile, Ezekiel sees the radical transformation of a region in ruins, without life, and without signs of restoration. Curiously, the one who had prepared himself to be a priest sees his ministry unfold principally apart from the Temple, and he performs that ministry consciously. From the house of God flows water, scarcely a spring. It is the presence of God, who does not remain in the Temple. The river, as it flows through cities and fields toward the Dead Sea, becomes uncontainable as a project for the restoration of life, healing and revitalizing bodies, societies, and the entire natural habitat.

Those who did not have work now have it, without fear of losing it. The guide says, "People will stand fishing beside the sea from En-gedi to En-eglaim; it will be a place for the spreading of nets; its fish will be of a great many kinds, like the fish of the Great Sea," that is, the Mediterranean (47:10). This part alludes to life that is social and active. En-gedi and En-eglaim are situated opposite each other on the shores of the Dead Sea. In 47:11 the guide explains that the swamps and marshes will be "left for salt." Salt was important, not only to give flavor but also for industry.

In this dream one can observe a harmonious relationship between the natural order and humankind. No one will die of hunger or of illness, for the natural order will not cease to protect human beings throughout the whole year. It will produce even outside the normal season, because beneath it flows the water, symbol of the tender care of God for God's creation. And no one will dare to attack the natural order, because it is a friend who provides protection. The vision ends thus: "On the banks, on both sides of the river, there will grow all kinds of trees for food. Their leaves will not wither nor their fruit fail, but they will bear fresh fruit every month, because the water for them flows from the sanctuary. Their fruit will be for food, and their leaves for healing" (47:12).

Before writing about the river, Ezekiel has the vision of what the Temple will be like; in fact, he dedicates seven rather boring chapters to the precise measurements of the plans for its construction. In the vision of the river the holy place of the sanctuary, where the impure are not permitted to enter, is surpassed by the life-giving presence of God outside God's house, even though the flow of water leaving the Temple is modest, barely a tiny spring.[3]

HOW DOES THE JUBILEE BECOME REALITY?

This is the hardest question when one is speaking of utopias in times when hopes are vulnerable. The jubilee of Leviticus 25 presents it by means of legislation. In fact, this is the most practical means, and it points toward feasibility. However, because it is a law it can be avoided, manipulated, or imposed to such a degree that it produces the opposite of the intended result, because there is inevitably a sentence condemning whoever does not fulfill the law. The meaning is then inverted: whoever does not free the slave is taken prisoner, and whoever does not cancel debts can be condemned to death. Therefore, what must be emphasized in Leviticus 25 is the idea of a coming moment of liberation and the elimination of injustices. Perhaps it is for that reason that the prophets feel they must speak of a law written on the heart. In that way, one will love one's neighbor not because the law says to but through pure grace. At issue is a law permeated by grace.

In Ezekiel there is a deliberate, tense combination of grace and law in the attempt to resolve the problem.[4] The overflowing river, which is pure grace and without limit, occurs in the midst of lists of exact measurements, both before and after. In the previous chapters (40—46) the prophet presents the plans and measurements of the future Temple. After the description of the river that surpasses all measurements we again find exact measurements, but now as part of the legislation of an agrarian reform—that is to say, the egalitarian distribution of the lands among the tribes. These laws, perhaps "contaminated" by the river of God, surpass the Mosaic laws, for in Ezekiel 47:13–48:35 the immigrants not only will be respected as the law stipulated but will also have a right to the land, just like everyone else.

By this I want to say that the dream will always be a dream, and thus it should be: an open horizon that invites us to be human beings with dignity, in order that we might reflect with increasing precision our creation in the image and likeness of God. For that is our identity as human beings, as seen from a theological point of view. But the dream is not sufficient if there are no projects, actions, and concrete laws directed toward it. Both are necessary, and they are in tension. And in that place, to the extent that one feels oneself to be near to that horizon, even in the little things, the jubilee is in process of realization, the grace of God is being felt, and the water of the river is pleasantly refreshing us.

(Translated by Sharon H. Ringe)

NOTES

1. The central ideas of this meditation were presented as a sermon on the occasion of the seventy-fifth anniversary of the Latin American Biblical University in San José, Costa Rica, in June 1998.
2. Jon Douglas Levenson, *Theology of the Program of Restoration of Ezekiel 40—48* (Missoula, Mont.: Scholars Press, 1976), p. 18. *Translator's note:* Tamez understands the second sentence of the quotation to begin with "none" or "no one," but the English original reads "now one," which appears from the sense of the passage to be a typographical error.
3. The Spanish in this case is *un ojo de agua*, literally, "an eye of water."
4. Levenson, *Theology of the Program of Restorations*, pp. 37–39.

7

RACE, SEX, AND INSANITY

*Transformative Eschatology in Hurston's Account
of the Ruby McCollum Trial*

Katie G. Cannon

At 11:34 A.M. on Sunday, August 3, 1952, four shots were fired in Live Oak, Suwanee County, Florida. As a result of these shots, Doctor Clifford LeRoy Adams Jr. became the most prominent White man ever slain by a Black woman in a Southern community. It is not his story that I am concerned with in this essay, however, but the story of the woman who fired the shots, Ruby Jackson McCollum. We have McCollum's story because of the work of Zora Neale Hurston in reporting her trial for the *Pittsburgh Courier*.[1]

Hurston's account of the McCollum trial constitutes a paradigmatic narrative of the injustice in one of this century's most famous murder cases. It is paradigmatic because it places in dramatic relief not only the story itself but the "new possibilities for human existence taking form in the midst of"[2] the existing social order. As such, it offers us a view of womanist transformative eschatology, a form of eschatology that is closely connected with ethics. There are other versions of eschatology that are relevant to ethics—for example, Rudolph Bultmann's "existentialized eschatology," C. H. Dodd's "realized eschatology," and Martin Dibelius's "eschatological stimulus."[3] Womanist eschatology, however, particularly as we may identify it in writings by Hurston, incorporates not only a this-worldly perspective on eschatology but an exposure of the entanglement of race, sex, and class. That is, eschatology from a womanist perspective means that those of us who live in situations of oppression no longer yearn for "pie in the sky, in the sweet bye and bye, when we die," but rather "we find a little heaven right here on earth." This kind of transformative eschatology demands that we seize human possibilities in the here and now and not in the hereafter, morning by morning and day by day. An old African American truism states this succinctly: "Do something, because the time we know now, we shall soon know no more." For Zora Neale Hurston, "doing something" meant exposing the evil forces of racism, sexism, and classism, something she does in her descriptive and interpretive account of Ruby Jackson McCollum's life and trial. This very telling is aimed at moving the Black community and others toward possibilities that would not otherwise be.

Zora Neale Hurston (1891–1960) was not only one of the great American novelists; she was also an essayist, a short-story writer, and anthropologist. Her name "has come to evoke originality and ebullience, sassy behavior and colorful taletelling, intelligence and wit."[4] Though she was never able to gain permission to interview McCollum, Hurston knew that McCollum's "struggle to be saved from the electric chair" needed to be exposed to the eyes of others. In Hurston's distinct voice and powerful prose are embodied the strategies of her efforts against this negative landmark in interracial sexual relations—efforts that were centrally focused on the mobilization of Black resistance. The aim of this essay, then, is to learn from some of her motivating convictions and strategies of Black resistance to racial and sexual injustice, and thereby to gain insight into processes toward individual courage and collective responsibility in the commonwealth of God.

In Hurston's work on the Ruby Jackson McCollum story, we explore first her efforts to demythologize racialized social legitimacy. This involves seeing the McCollum trial in the context of historical and contemporary racially discriminating attitudes and political practices. It involves also understanding the role of journalistic publications at the time and the particular significance of Hurston's use of the media insofar as she had access to it. The second task of this essay is to examine Hurston's opposition to sexual inequalities, especially as these intersect with racial inequalities. This inevitably entails her analysis of the role of class in relation to both race and sex. Finally, all these concerns are brought to bear by Hurston on the question of their specific impact on the psychological perspectives of both Blacks and Whites. The third section of this essay, therefore, explores through Hurston's eyes the ways in which what might be called "mind control" worked in the trial, and in the wider context of the society that produced the trial.

DEMYTHOLOGIZING RACIALIZED SOCIAL LEGITIMACY

The first significant aspect of Hurston's mobilization of Black resistance was not only her reporting of this publicized case for the *Pittsburgh Courier* but the extensive and extremely interesting biography of Ruby Jackson McCollum that Hurston wrote for the *Courier* after the trial ended. Zora Neale Hurston relied on her ethnographical gaze, on the lens of her discipline as an anthropologist in the rural South,[5] not only to report Ruby McCollum's "tragic

drama of life and death" but to demythologize whole bodies of racialized social legitimacy. Hurston created a narrative strategy that combined the personal tragedy of a particular Black woman, Ruby McCollum, with an African
American incarnational recognition of heaven and hell in the dailiness of life.
Hurston's sensitive inquiry gathers up Black voices, past and present, and establishes her own rootedness in the communal understanding of the present
dimensions of the eschaton. By debunking the logic of White supremacy,
Hurston used her authoritative voice to contextualize for her readers the moral
anguish of the Ruby McCollum case.

Hurston's twenty stories about Ruby McCollum were published in the
Courier between October 11, 1952, and May 3, 1953, which places this particular overall narrative within a historical period in which there were numerous changes in African American life. The early 1950s saw considerable
segregation in public and private facilities. In the years between World War II
(1939–1945) and the Korean War (1950–1953), Marian Anderson sang at the
Lincoln Memorial for seventy-five thousand people after her concert at Constitution Hall was prevented by the Daughters of the American Revolution;
A. Philip Randolph of the Brotherhood of Sleeping Car Porters organized
and later called off a march on Washington to protest segregation in the military and employment discrimination; President F. D. Roosevelt issued an executive order forbidding racial and religious discrimination in government
training programs and defense industries. And yet, within the same time period, White mob violence, bloody race riots, and hate strikes broke out in
Northern and Southern cities alike. Substantial amounts of Black-owned
property were destroyed.

Looming large in the historical background of the 1950s are the vestiges of
slavery—lynching, raping, castrating, beating, cross burning, tarring and
feathering, masked night rides, verbal threats, hate rallies, public humiliations,
and random discharging of shotguns in windows by extralegal White vigilante
groups. It is important to note that at least five thousand Black people have
been lynched in the United States. During a fifty-year stretch, lynchings occurred approximately every two and a half days. As a matter of fact, the
Tuskegee Institute reported that 1952 was the first year, in seventy-one years
of tabulation, that no lynchings took place in the United States.[6]

With the historical framework in place, we can turn to the medium of
Hurston's message, that is, her newspaper coverage of the story. While critics
have generated a proliferation of conference papers, journal articles, and
books discussing the significance of Hurston's canon,[7] insufficient attention
has been paid to Hurston's commentary on the Ruby McCollum trial. In its
broadest scope, this particular work warrants serious reflection if for no other
reason than that it provides rich material for an analysis of Black women's
moral agency, an agency that is "profoundly influenced by a legacy of racism,

sexism and classism that is neither linear nor logical."[8] Moreover, this twenty-entry correspondence by Hurston is an important locus for formulating a rigorous critique of any justice-making moral agency in our current social order.

My long-standing desire to address transformative eschatology by focusing on Hurston's *Pittsburgh Courier* account of the Ruby McCollum story against the background of the whole of Hurston's narrative grid received impetus from the publication of Cheryl Wall's excellent two-volume set of Hurston's best writings. These volumes in the Library of America collection contain Hurston's four novels, two books of folklore, an autobiography, numerous short stories, and selected articles. These texts offer a view of the wider scope of Hurston's influence during the twentieth century. In addition, Wall's chronology of Hurston's life sheds fresh light on many aspects of Hurston's career.[9]

In a sensitive reading of Zora Neale Hurston's life, Cheryl Wall points out that the *Pittsburgh Courier* employed Hurston to cover the trial of Ruby Mc-Collum during a period in her life when Hurston was plagued by health problems, including a tropical virus contracted from drinking impure water in Honduras, gall bladder infection, irritated colon, and the effects of obesity. Hurston was having increasing difficulty selling her work. She even declined an invitation to speak at a Taft-versus-Eisenhower forum in Boston in March because she had no winter coat. Despite failing physical health and dire financial circumstances, Hurston continued to search the survival retentions in African American culture for the materials of a justice-making society that would properly preserve and show the significance of the life of this particular woman, Ruby Jackson McCollum.

It is important to keep in mind that the *Pittsburgh Courier*, formally incorporated on May 10, 1910, was a nationally distributed weekly newspaper; its pages addressed the cultural milieu and the sociopolitical issues of fundamental import to the Black community.[10] When we turn to the Black news media in general, we find that Robert L. Vann's *Pittsburgh Courier* (1910), Chris Perry's *Philadelphia Tribune* (1884), John H. Murphy's *Baltimore Afro-American* (1892), William Monroe Trotter's *Boston Guardian* (1901), Robert Abbott's *Chicago Defender* (1905), T. Thomas Fortune's *New York Age* (1907), James Anderson's *Amsterdam News* (1909), P. Bernard Young's *Norfolk Journal and Guide* (1910), and Bill Johnson's *Charlotte Post* (1918) were all part of an influential network of opposition to White supremacy. These newspapers played a vital role in reinforcing and reproducing on a mass scale ethical norms, values, and taboos important to Black resistance.[11] The Black press was an effective, persuasive voice and a powerful force in building self-esteem, racial pride, and community solidarity. Not only did these crusaders for social change serve as vanguards of the National Association for the Advancement of Colored People (NAACP) and independent centers of the civil rights movement, but they advocated for tangible essentials of daily living. In times of crisis, Black newspapers dispensed biting and consistently interesting commentaries regarding relevant contestable issues.

The *Pittsburgh Courier* never suggested that anyone guilty of murder should escape punishment entirely, but it forcefully argued for equity and impartiality in the "evidence" presented and weighed. In this regard, Hurston's reporting fit in well with the long-standing editorial attitude at the *Pittsburgh Courier*. As one of America's most illustrious women novelists, Hurston used her poignant language to bring to the *Courier* readers an interpretive, moving, and descriptive analysis of the hearings and trial of Mrs. Ruby McCollum. Hurston's familiarity with the social identity of her audience situated her at the center of this network of relations between texts and readers, between the hearts and souls of the principals in this case.

The newspaper's editorial column made clear its confidence in Hurston's ability to infuse her reports of McCollum's first-degree murder trial with expressive values derived from African American culture:

> A native of Florida . . . Mrs. Hurston is a recognized authority on the manners and mores of the people about whom she is writing. She knows the people who live on the banks of the Suwanee River. She knows places like Live Oak, Fla. With a searching pen . . . she will report the proceedings . . . the undertones . . . the overtones . . . the implications.[12]

Of the numerous White newspapers in major urban areas, most did not regularly carry Black news. One or two had a Jim Crow column, labeled and identified as "Colored or Negro News." When news coverage about Blacks did find its way into White newspapers, the media-assessment formula consisted mainly of lurid, exaggerated, and gruesome details of African American life that were not only inaccurate and distorted but dangerously inflammatory:

> What little news there was about blacks in Pittsburgh white dailies was invariably bad. Vann, editor of the black newspaper, the *Pittsburgh Courier*, particularly blamed the white newspaper, the *Pittsburgh Press*, for inciting racial unrest through biased writing which stereotyped blacks as criminals and undesirables.[13]

Such hegemonic representation by the White press of demonized or sensationalized aspects of Black life perpetuated the stereotype of Black people as worthless, dangerous, and a liability to civilization, thereby increasing fear and loathing in White society and further polarizing the races. Black newspapers, in contrast, wrote of all facets of the lives of African Americans and their needs for housing, health, education, sports, social news, job opportunities, political awareness, creative poetry. In writing of crime, they offered radical critiques of the misrepresentations printed in the White press.

Why, then, did White newspapers refuse to cover this hot, juicy story about a Black woman killing her White male alleged lover? Why did Hurston aggressively have to convince the White reporter William Bradford Huie (1910–1986), "a journalist and one of the South's best-known White anti-segregationists,"[14] to use his White as well as his male privileges to tear down the wall of silence created by the dominant press concerning the Ruby Mc-Collum case? Hurston knew that Huie, an eighth-generation Southerner, a Phi Beta Kappa graduate of the University of Alabama, could bring credibility and public exposure to the McCollum atrocity. And it was to this end that Hurston insisted that Huie debunk the mainline press as an accomplice in the ideological work of racism during the Ruby McCollum trial.

RESISTING CAPITULATION TO DEMANDS OF SEXUALIZED STATUS QUO

The second element in Hurston's mobilization of Black resistance is found in her opposition to multilayered insidious and subliminal assumptions that reinforce inequalities between women and men. Hurston described at length how, in 1952, Ruby McCollum indeed shot Adams during a quarrel, but Hurston then disclosed that Adams had fathered one of McCollum's children and that McCollum was pregnant by him again at the time of the shooting. More significant, Hurston also provided an analysis of the pervasive presumptions by White men at that time regarding the so-called inherent inferiority of Black women, and their equally strong presumptions regarding their own superiority as White men.

Indeed, here may lie the fundamental reason that Zora Neale Hurston, the most widely acclaimed Black woman author from 1925 to 1960, proactively defended McCollum to the African American community. If we lay side by side racist myths about Black sexuality and the ideology of chattel slavery, we begin to see the contours of Hurston's agenda. Moreover, her strategy becomes even clearer when we note her concerns for a social context wherein all Blacks suffered continuing deprivation and oppression, and wherein the White male subject at the center of power controlled the "Black female body." Hurston thought the whole of this situation was perpetuated not only by racism and sexism but by the classism endemic to a capitalist political economy.

More specifically, Hurston believed that the daily structures and practices of Southern rural culture routinely visited public and private violence on the bodies of African American women. Thus it was that the definitive expressions of racist sexism were lodged in commonplace cultural stereotypes imposed on the Black woman. She was considered incurably promiscuous, sensual, an exotic wench, on the one hand, and a cold, castrating matriarch, on the other; or she was universalized as a fat, jolly, wise, enduring mammy. All of this meant it was acceptable for White men not to understand the word *no* in certain situations. Hence, Hurston's reports pressed the questions: Must Black women kill in order for our "NO" to be understood? What ethical consequences follow when Black women acknowledge the complex baggage of racist fears and sexist fantasies under which they have been forced to live? How shall Black women finally respond to the terrible social situation in which "Black women are not only the second sex, but Black women are also the last race, the most oppressed, the most marginalized, the most deviant, the quintessential site of difference?"[15] Is it realistic to assume that African American women can claim our own bodies peacefully?

Few African Americans of a certain generation can forget that an indelible mark on race relations was imprinted by White men who, wielding an inordinate amount of power, entered the Black community with the assumption that any Black female was available for their possession. Nor can they forget that survival demanded that no Black man, woman, or child say or do anything against such assumptions. A long-standing question therefore acquired urgency as a result of Hurston's coverage of the McCollum trial: In what way does the Black/White duality of race add to the determination of unequal power relations already implicit in the gendered dichotomy between a five-foot one-inch, thirty-seven-year-old African American mother of four and a forty-four-year-old White doctor who is fat, pot-bellied, six-foot two inches, 270 pounds? What kind of power does the woman have, especially when the man is "the biggest, wealthiest and most powerful man in the county," who has just been elected by his local constituency to the Florida State Senate by a landslide? Hurston's juxtaposition of deeply embedded racial suspicions and sexual expectations raised at least implicitly the following questions: When is a liaison between a Black woman and a White man consensual? Whose pleasure is served in elaborate cultural codes that regulate interracial relationships? Does sexual intimacy negate bigotry and economic exploitation? In a real sense, the nature of Hurston's transformative ethics cannot be fully understood without investigating the moral counsel and radicalized wisdom refracted in her overall critique of the particular social mythology and the bizarre circumstances that are integral to the sexual politics of White supremacy.

Details of Hurston's narrative are important. Shortly after the shooting, Mrs. McCollum was hustled out of town under heavy police guard while a hastily formed mob attempted to grab her. Her husband, Sam McCollum, a numbers gambler, tobacco farmer, and successful director of the Central Life Insurance Company in Tampa, fled town with three of the children: daughters Kay McCollum, eleven years old; Sonja McCollum, seven years old; and

Loretta Jackson Adams McCollum, fifteen months old. Nineteen-year-old
Sam McCollum Jr. was attending college on the West Coast at the University
of California in Los Angeles. The strain of the tragedy was too great for
Sam McCollum Sr. When he arrived at the home of Ruby's mother in another
part of the state, he suffered a fatal heart attack. He died on Monday, August
4, the day after the shooting.

To probe the connections between the murder of Dr. Adams on Sunday
and the sudden death of Ruby McCollum's husband, Sam, on Monday, the
narrative allows us to ask: Was Sam McCollum forced to bend under socioeconomic pressure and, in turn, pay Dr. Adams "protection" money for his alleged numbers racket? Were the eighteen one hundred dollar bills that Ruby
McCollum had in her pocketbook when she went to the doctor's office on that
fateful Sunday morning "payoff" money? Did Dr. Adams have Sam's future
in the palm of his hands, with a grip so tight that Sam could not squawk about
anything that the doctor did, "no matter what it was, including being intimate
with Mrs. McCollum?"[16] Is it true that Sam McCollum came home earlier
than expected one day and found Dr. Adams in bed in his house? What might
all this mean?

Questions about class locations complicate this narrative. What happens in
the intertwined politics of race, gender, and class when Black people are of
higher social strata than White folks? A class-conscious axiom gives us this
view:

> Southern whites don't care how close blacks get, as long as we don't get too
> high; northern whites don't care how high blacks get, as long as we don't get
> too close.[17]

Here, for example, we have, on the one hand, Ruby McCollum, the wife of
the city's wealthiest "Negro" businessman, with the McCollum estate worth
more than $200,000; on the other hand, the doctor's farm, owned by the
Adams Company, had to take out a second mortgage from the First National
Bank in Live Oak after the doctor's death, borrowing $20,000 to meet imme-
diate current expenses. Not surprising, Florrie Lee Adams, the widow of
the murdered Dr. Adams (the doctor who was supposed to be the wealthiest
man in the county), ended up suing the McCollum estate for thousands of
dollars in order, according to Hurston, to put the McCollums in their designated class place. In sum, do the socioeconomic divisions exacerbate the sexual
exploitation?

Even though the trial judge denied all members of the press access to the
defendant, saying that "the case is not going to be tried in the newspapers,"
Hurston understood that the judge had no power over the avalanche of
skewed images and slanted speculations of the people in and around Live Oak.
What made Ruby McCollum kill C. Leroy Adams? Almost all the questions,

as well as the answers, immediately implicate sexist stereotypes. Was Ruby McCollum "'the woman scorned' with the 'Hell Hath No Fury'"[18] implications? Was she a hypochondriac, feigning physical sickness and emotional depression for purposes of her own? Is there a romantic angle wherein Ruby, a jilted lover who gave birth to the doctor's daughter and was once again two months pregnant, was now being cast aside by the doctor and was caught up in sudden romantic rage? Hurston pondered whether or not the prosecutors would attempt to prove the rumors going around that Ruby and her husband had not lived together "as man and wife" since the birth of the last child. Or was Ruby McCollum entrapped in "intimacy based on fear?"[19]

Finally, then, why did Mrs. McCollum kill Dr. Adams? One rumor says that Ruby McCollum was "real jealous-hearted over Sam McCollum, her husband, even though 'they never went nowhere like a couple.'"[20] Another speculation put Ruby McCollum down as a very jealous woman under her own roof. She was possessive, and what was hers—or what she considered hers—she must *rule*! Could that be what took place in the office of Dr. Adams on that Sunday morning of August 3? Without thinking about how this particular relationship began, what it meant, or who benefited, a charming, worldly ladies' man told Hurston: "There is nothing so dead as dead love. And no woman can be so thoroughly hated as she who tries to cling, when you have let her know that you no longer want her." "The smart women of the world," he continued, "are those who let you go immediately and without cries of reproach. That kind has a fine chance to win you back by their indifference." "No," he concluded, "men have no pity for a woman they have ceased to love. They can be more cruel to her than to anything on earth. That is why you read so often of men murdering wives and sweethearts. She has committed the unforgivable crime . . . trying to hold him after he is tired of her."[21]

Nevertheless, Ruby McCollum gives us a different story, which Hurston allows us to hear. Mrs. McCollum testified that Dr. Adams had "solicited" their illicit relationship after he delivered her second daughter and that she had submitted "for fear of him."[22] On the fateful Sunday morning, Mrs. McCollum had gone to Dr. Adams's office for medical treatment. The doctor suggested intimacy, but she told her attorneys that she refused because of an ailing arm. Dr. Adams then became enraged, she said, and produced a pistol. She testified that she grabbed the gun and in the struggle it went off. She admitted that she was in a daze after the shooting and could not recall exactly what happened.

There is another cultural commentary to be made on passivity in this network of patriarchal forces. It has to do with the complicity of White women. Hurston challenged her readership to freeze-frame the following problematic representation of the unspoken social relations between Black women and White women:

Down stairs, in the courtroom where the white people sat, the room was nearly full. Four white matrons sat together on the front row. They all leaned forward hungrily to catch every word and every move. The white woman on the center aisle had brought her son, about two years old. The third white woman in the row had brought her knitting, and one was reminded of the females of the reign of terror of the French revolution, who brought their knitting and worked away as they cheered the sharp, heavy blade of the guillotine as the bloody heads fell into the basket.[23]

Given the racial climate and class-determined appropriate gender behavior of the 1950s, did White women have any justice-making agency in these types of situations? How limited were White women's possibilities for cross-race female solidarity? Missing here in Hurston's striking depiction are White women who publicly tried to mitigate androcentric, White supremist patriarchy.

DEALING WITH THE INCOHERENCE OF UNPREDICTABILITIES

The third and final strategy in Hurston's mobilization of Black resistance was exposing the notoriously unfair trial itself. In Hurston's newspaper reports we encounter the pernicious subtleties that suggest the countless, unforeseeable, everyday experiences of White supremacy, androcentric patriarchy, and class elitism that fold into the so-called miasma of Black insanity. Hurston's investigation disturbingly documents White-supremacy cruelties that influence Black people's mental state. The unsuspecting boomerang, the daily defamation, and the sucker punch that pounds the solar plexus of Black folks oftentimes have crippling effects; these may be manifested in incoherent actions that to the members of the dominant stratum appear as craziness, deranged dementia, sheer madness.

Through suggestive imagery, Hurston cryptically illustrates how the Black spectators, all seated in the designated upstairs "Negro" gallery, heard unmistakably racist overtones in the assessment of this Black woman's mental competence. Hurston describes how all the Black people "leaned forward and looked in the same direction like cows in a pasture" when the judge asked whether or not Ruby McCollum was sane. Does she know right from wrong? Judge Hal Adams, the presiding judge (of no blood relation to the slain doctor but an honorary pallbearer at Dr. Adams's funeral), was ready to hear *any* witness concerning Ruby McCollum's mental state, "not specialists in mental diseases."[24]

For all his self-proclaimed position of high moral ground, Judge Adams announced that he did not want tedious, lengthy, technical testimony, nor did he want to do anything to cut anybody off from offering testimony. "I want reasonable progress. Non-expert testimony is wanted today." With clarity and directness that one associates with prophetic utterances, Hurston goes out of her way to critique with perfect candor the judge's single criterion for mental competence—does Ruby McCollum know right from wrong? He never asked whether it is ever right for a Black woman to kill a White man; whether it always wrong, no matter the circumstances.

The "mind control" exercised by implicit appeals to stereotypes was reinforced throughout the trial—for example, by the fact that the court refused to admit testimony that might have spotlighted the intimate relations between McCollum and Adams. Indeed, in almost every instance the court refused to admit this kind of testimony, sustaining the state's objections that Ruby Jackson McCollum's past six-year association with C. Leroy Adams was "irrelevant and immaterial to the present issue." The judge ruled out testimony regarding Adams's association with McCollum "other than as a private physician and doctor" upon the state's objection to that line of questioning.

McCollum's defense team complained that the court refused to admit testimony concerning the birth certificate of Mrs. McCollum's fifteen-month-old baby, which she said was fathered by the White physician. Dr. Adams had entered himself on the birth certificate as the father of the baby. Nor would the court allow the baby, Loretta Jackson Adams McCollum—then present in the courtroom—to be viewed by the jury. The judge would not permit any description of the biracial child. In addition, the jury was not allowed to hear testimony of any maltreatment of McCollum or any altercations between McCollum and Adams—his hitting, slapping, or shaking her at various times, "tearing into Ruby like a lion and then injecting her with shots of medicine."

Furthermore, while Ruby McCollum was in the Women's Department at the State Prison Farm in Raiford, Florida, she was forced to write a letter to her attorney denying sexual relations with Dr. Adams, stating that he was not the father of her child and that she had never had sexual relations with any man other than her husband. When asked, "Did anyone do anything to you to force you to write that letter?" McCollum responded, "I was afraid. A Nurse gave me 2ccs of some drug and it put me to sneezing and feeling very ill. I wrote it because I was afraid."[25] The defense attorney then asked, "Before you wrote that letter, were there officers continually asking you about your pregnancy?" McCollum responded, "I don't know whether he was an officer or not, but a man came in and held my arm while the nurse gave me the shots." "What were you afraid of?" the defense asked. McCollum answered, "Being in such a place, then too, what would they do to me. I was told that I would get a bigger dose next time if I didn't get rid . . . " The prosecution then made an objection, which was sustained. The matter the defendant had begun to speak of dealt with the forced termination of Ruby McCollum's pregnancy while at the State Prison Farm in Raiford.

The defense attorneys attempted unsuccessfully to get a change of venue, so that the trial could be held outside the county and not in the Suwanee County courthouse, which was located directly across the street from the doctor's office where the crime was committed. McCollum's attorneys also argued, in the closing moments of the case, that the state had failed to prove first-degree murder against their client. The state had not proved premeditation and had excluded all evidence that might be helpful to the defendant. The defense asked for a second-degree murder verdict. However, on Saturday afternoon, December 27, 1952, even after Ruby McCollum in a thin, low voice "bared her soul in a vain attempt to save her life,"[26] she was convicted. Her jury was an all-White, all-male jury of twelve, with two alternates; six of the jurors or their family members had been patients of Dr. C. Leroy Adams. In a case that began four and a half months earlier, Ruby Jackson McCollum was found guilty of slaying C. Leroy Adams and sentenced to "death in the electric chair." The reason given for the shooting was an argument or controversy about a bill from Dr. Adams for professional services, even though the contended bill was not introduced as evidence.

"This trial, full of irregularities, made a mockery of the vaunted impartiality of the court,"[27] reported Hurston. McCollum was convicted of first-degree murder, and Hurston reported, "A recommendation of first-degree murder with no mercy makes the death penalty mandatory under Florida law." Later, the Florida Supreme Court overturned the conviction, due to suppressed and excluded evidence; Ruby Jackson McCollum was at that time declared mentally incompetent and committed to the Criminally Insane section of Florida State Hospital in Chattahoochee, Florida.[28] She was released from the mental hospital in 1976, after a twenty-year fight to free her.[29]

CONCLUSION

This study has looked into Zora Neale Hurston's writings in the *Pittsburgh Courier* in order to show one woman's strategic use of another woman's textual persona to fight for basic freedoms in the mid–twentieth century. Looked at in itself, Hurston's coverage of the bench rulings and court protocol of the Ruby McCollum trial critiques the social realities of presupposed normative claims regarding biological inferiority, cultural liability, and a predestined divine order in which some can never be equal to others. Throughout the narrative, Hurston deals with the change of fortune of a Black woman in distress. Kimberle Williams Crenshaw sums up this type of unjust disadvantage:

The gaps between the color-line ideology and the dynamics of racial power are nowhere more acute than in the area of criminal justice, interracial sex, and especially, the intersection of the two.[30]

What is peculiar to this story is that Hurston, who was living in dire existential circumstances, seized the initiative in a timely and clever newspaper writing campaign to revolt against injustice. What she wanted was immediate change and a movement for greater justice in the future. There was no need for Hurston to state her strategy or her hope in theological language. One can speak of "last things," "the rapture," "imminent parousia," and "living as if every day is judgment day" without referring to something beyond this world. This is what Hurston did. She took for granted that the Black community had power already, and in turn, she attempted to mobilize her readers to resist the oppressive character of the established social order. It is Hurston's unrelenting strategy of exposing evil in this whole complex of events that makes this narrative essential to transformative eschatology. Unless evil is named, it cannot be destroyed.

I maintain that the 1952 McCollum case in Live Oak, Florida, is a careful insider representation of the lethal force of racist terror and sexist assault suffered by many African Americans who experienced fierce acts of violence by members of the dominant population. It tells further of Black people's decisive vigilance and definitive hope. In this context, the meaning of transformative eschatology is not a theology for storing up acts of good behavior to cash in on the other side of death, nor is it a theology of purely passive hope. Doers of justice must act directly and speak with immediacy, because "the time we know now, we shall soon know it no more."

NOTES

1. Zora Neale Hurston, in *Pittsburgh Courier*, October 11, 1952, 1, 4.
2. Thomas W. Ogletree, *The Use of the Bible in Christian Ethics*, cited by E. Clinton Gardner, "Eschatological Ethics," in *The Westminster Dictionary of Christian Ethics*, ed. James F. Childress and John Macquarrie (Philadelphia: Westminster Press, 1986), p. 204.
3. For a succinct summary of these theories, see Gardner, "Eschatological Ethics," pp. 201–205.
4. Christine Levecq, " 'You Heard Her, You Ain't Blind': Subversive Shifts in Zora Neale Hurston's *Their Eyes Were Watching God*," *Tulsa Studies in Women's Literature* 13 (Spring 1994): 87. See also Karla Holloway, *The Character of the Word* (Westport, Conn.: Greenwood Press, 1987); Henry Louis Gates and K. A. Appiah, eds., *Zora Neale Hurston: Critical Perspectives Past and Present* (Madison: University of Wisconsin Press, 1993).
5. Lynn Domina, " 'Protection in My Mouf': Self, Voice, and Community in Zora Neale Hurston's *Dust Tracks on a Road* and *Mules and Men*," *African American Re-*

view 31 (Summer 1997): 197. See also Mary Helen Washington, *Invented Lives* (New York: Doubleday, 1987); Robert E. Hemenway, *Zora Neale Hurston: A Literary Biography* (Chicago: University of Chicago Press, 1977); John Lowe, *Jump at the Sun: Zora Neale Hurston's Cosmic Comedy* (Urbana: University of Illinois Press, 1997); Katie G. Cannon, *Black Womanist Ethics* (Atlanta: Scholars Press, 1988).

6. Gripping details of lynchings are reported in Lerone Bennett Jr., *Before the Mayflower: A History of Black America* (1962; 6th rev. ed., Chicago: Johnson Publishing Co., 1993); W. Fitzhugh Brundage, ed., *Under the Sentence of Death: Lynching in the South* (Chapel Hill: University of North Carolina Press, 1997); Ralph Ginzburg, *One Hundred Years of Lynchings* (1969; reprint, Baltimore: Black Classic Press, 1988); Robert L. Zangrando, *The NAACP Crusade against Lynching, 1909–1950* (Philadelphia: Temple University Press, 1980); and Derrick Bell, *Gospel Choir: Psalms of Survival in an Alien Land Called Home* (New York: Basic Books, 1996).

7. Darwin Turner, *In a Minor Chord* (Carbondale: Southern Illinois University Press, 1971); Robert Bone, *Down Home* (New York: G. P. Putman's Sons, 1975); Barbara Christian, *Black Women Novelists* (Westport, Conn.: Greenwood Press, 1980); Lillie P. Howard, *Zora Neale Hurston* (Boston: Twayne, 1980); and Deborah G. Plant, *Every Tub Must Sit on Its Own Bottom: The Philosophy and Politics of Zora Neale Hurston* (Urbana: University of Illinois Press, 1995).

8. Adrien Katherine Wing, ed., *Critical Race Feminism: A Reader* (New York: New York University Press, 1997); Renita Weems, *Battered Love* (Minneapolis: Fortress Press, 1995); Glenda E. Gilmore, *Gender and Jim Crow* (Chapel Hill: University of North Carolina Press, 1996); Delores S. Williams, *Sisters in the Wilderness* (Maryknoll, N.Y.: Orbis Books, 1993); Katie G. Cannon, *Katie's Canon: Womanism and the Soul of the Black Community* (New York: Continuum, 1995); Angela Y. Davis, *Blues Legacies and Black Feminism* (New York: Pantheon, 1997).

9. Cheryl Wall, ed., *Zora Neale Hurston—Folklore, Memoirs, and Other Writings:* Mules and Men, Tell My Horse, Dust Tracks on a Road, *Selected Articles* (New York: Library of America, 1995); Cheryl Wall, ed., *Zora Neale Hurston—Novels and Stories:* Jonah's Gourd Vine, Their Eyes Were Watching God, Moses Man of the Mountain, Seraph on the Sewanee, *Selected Stories* (New York: Library of America, 1995).

10. See Andrew Buni, *Robert L. Vann of the* Pittsburgh Courier: *Politics and Black Journalism* (Pittsburgh: University of Pittsburgh Press, 1974); Roland Edgar Wolseley, *The Black Press, U.S.A.,* 2d ed. (Ames: Iowa State University Press, 1990); Henry G. La Brie, *A Survey of Black Newspapers* (Kennebunkport, Maine: Mercer House Press, 1979).

11. Buni reports that "though hundreds of Black newspapers were started in the United States between 1880 and 1914, most of them were short-lived, one-man projects" (*Robert L. Vann of the* Pittsburgh Courier, p. 44). See also Enoch P. Waters, *American Diary: A Personal History of the Black Press* (Chicago: Path Press, 1987); Frankie Hutton, *The Early Black Press in America* (Westport, Conn.: Greenwood Press, 1993).

12. *Pittsburgh Courier,* October 11, 1952, 1.

13. Buni, *Robert L. Vann of the Pittsburgh Courier,* p. 75. Carolyn Martindale, *The White Press and Black America* (Westport, Conn.: Greenwood Press, 1986).

14. See Wall, ed., *Zora Neale Hurston—Folktales, Memoirs, and Other Writings,* p. 978; William Bradford Huie, *Ruby McCollum: Woman in the Suwannee Jail* (New

York: E. P. Dutton & Co., 1956); William Bradford Huie, *Wolf Whistle and Other Stories* (New York: Signet, 1959); Stephen J. Whitfield, *A Death in the Delta: The Story of Emmett Till* (New York: Free Press, 1988).

15. See Ann DuCille, *Skin Trade* (Cambridge, Mass.: Harvard University Press, 1996), p. 82; Calvin C. Hernton, *Sex and Racism in America* (New York: Grove Press, 1966); Beth Day, *Sexual Life between Blacks and Whites: The Roots of Racism* (Cleveland and New York: World Publishing Co., 1972); and James Reston Jr., *The Innocence of Joann Little: A Southern Mystery* (New York: Times Books, 1977).
16. *Pittsburgh Courier,* January 3, 1953, 4.
17. Adapted from a statement by Thomas Blanton, "The Deacon," *Radcliffe Quarterly* 83 (Fall/Winter 1997): 20.
18. Zora Neale Hurston, in *Pittsburgh Courier,* October 18, 1952, 4.
19. Hurston, in *Pittsburgh Courier,* December 27, 1952, 1.
20. For the details of this discussion, see the *Pittsburgh Courier,* October 18, 1952, 4.
21. Ibid.
22. Hurston, in *Pittsburgh Courier,* January 3, 1953, 1, 4.
23. Hurston, in *Pittsburgh Courier,* October 11, 1952, 4.
24. Hurston, in *Pittsburgh Courier,* October 18, 1952, 1, 4.
25. For the full account of this, see Hurston, in *Pittsburgh Courier,* January 10, 1953, 1, 4.
26. Hurston, in *Pittsburgh Courier,* December 27, 1952, 1.
27. Hurston, in *Pittsburgh Courier,* February 7, 1953, 1.
28. Hemenway, *Zora Neale Hurston,* p. 342.
29. Ibid., p. 352.
30. Kimberle Williams Crenshaw, "Color-Blind Dreams and Racial Nightmares: Reconfiguring Racism in the Post–Civil Rights Era," in Toni Morrison and Claudia Brodsky Lacour, eds., *Birth of a Nation'hood* (Lacour, N.Y.: Pantheon, 1997), p. 99.

8

THEY SOUGHT A CITY

Martin's Dream or Malcolm's Nightmare

James H. Cone

The city has been both a dream and a nightmare, an eschatological symbol of both hope and despair for poor people, especially for the black poor and working class in the United States. This double meaning—dream and nightmare—is symbolized in the black struggle for identity in America. In his classic text *The Souls of Black Folk,* W.E.B. Du Bois called it a "double consciousness," "two warring ideals in one dark body, whose dogged strength alone keeps it from being torn asunder."[1]

Born in slavery and nurtured in the world of Jim Crow, the struggle for black identity exploded in the streets of America's cities throughout much of the twentieth century—Chicago in 1919, Harlem in 1935, Detroit in 1943, Montgomery, Alabama, in 1955–1956, and in almost every metropolis during the 1960s. Relatively quiet during the 1970s, blacks returned to the streets during the 1980s in Miami and then let loose their most violent explosion in Los Angeles in 1992. African Americans were demanding that they be treated as human beings by the government—equal before the law—free of police brutality and racism in the legal system. "No justice, no peace," they shouted in the streets of Los Angeles. The acquittal of four white policemen for beating black motorist Rodney King, which sparked the 1992 rebellion, was reminiscent of the infamous Dred Scott Decision—135 years earlier! In the 1857 verdict, the Supreme Court declared that "negroes . . . had no rights which the white man was bound to respect."

Before the Great Migration to the North in the twentieth century, the struggle for black respect was mostly Southern and rural, with nearly 90 percent of the African American population residing in these areas. The work was hard, the hours were long, the pay was low, and whites were real mean. The rural South provided blacks little economic opportunity to earn a decent living and scarcely any political rights to protect themselves against white brutality. White churches and educational institutions used the Bible and science openly to teach white supremacy and black inferiority. The South was a nightmare of terror and violence, with black men, women, and children being lynched, shot, and beaten for any real or imagined infraction against the etiquette of the white way of life. Historian Rayford Logan called the end of the nineteenth century and beginning of the twentieth the "Nadir" of the black struggle for equality, and John Hope Franklin dubbed it the "Long Dark Night."

The church and the honky-tonk were the only places poor blacks could go to get some relief from the psychological and physical violence of racism and to experience another definition of their humanity. The black church preached hope in despairing circumstances, with words such as "I'm so glad that trouble don't last always." In sermons, songs, and prayers, blacks rejected the white distortions of their humanity and affirmed their identity as children of God with apocalyptic imagination:

> *O, nobody knows who I am,*
> *Till the judgment morning.*

The honky-tonk was a secular expression of the spirituality of black survival and resistance. It was the place where the blues and the dance reigned supreme, as black bodies moved uninhibitedly to the passion and rhythm of life. The blues inspired African Americans to face head-on the harsh realities of life with, as James Baldwin put it, "ironic tenacity,"[2] stubbornly refusing to allow black humanity to be exclusively defined by its sorrows; or as Ralph Ellison wrote, the blues "express both the agony of life and the possibility of conquering it through sheer toughness of spirit."[3] The spiritual energy expressed in the blues and the erotic dance the musical form elicited testified to "the souls of black folk"—their dogged determination to overcome the extreme limits placed on black existence.

> *Ain't it hard to stumble,*
> *When you got no place to fall?*
> *In this whole wide world,*
> *I ain't got no place at all.*

During slavery, the North was often called "Canaan," "heaven," and "the Promised Land"—religious expressions of the black longing for "anyplace but here."[4] The black condition in the South was so bad that many African Americans dreamed of returning to Africa, which was advocated by the African Methodist Episcopal (AME) bishop Henry McNeal Turner of Georgia. "Hell is an improvement upon the United States where the Negro is concerned,"⁵ proclaimed Bishop Turner. After the Civil War, many blacks jumped at the first chance to leave the farm and rural communities of the South and migrate to the industrial cities of the North. But the opportunity did not come for most poor blacks until World War I halted the immigration of Euro-pean workers to the United States and the boll weevil destroyed cotton crops in the South. In response to the promise of jobs and social and political freedom, blacks flocked to Northern cities in droves—going to Chicago, St. Louis, De-troit, New York, Philadelphia, and Los Angeles, searching and hoping for a bet-ter and more fulfilling life, saying, "Hallelujah, I'm on my way to the promised land!" Between 1910 and 1970, nearly seven million blacks left the rural South, about five million of them after 1940. Jacob Lawrence's series of paintings *The Migration of the Negro* (1941) tells the story in powerful images of movement and risk. The city was a dream—like going to a place that was the opposite of everything that blacks hated about the South. Langston Hughes expressed this mood in his poem "One-Way Ticket," when he described the freedom of pick-ing up his life and putting it down in big cities like Detroit, Chicago, and Buf-falo, or "Any place that is North and East/And not Dixie."⁶

The longing to be free in the North was still a potent myth during my youth in rural Arkansas in the 1940s and 1950s. People talked about Chicago, St. Louis, New York, and Los Angeles as if they were totally free of racial dis-crimination. Relatives who made the journey to Northern cities often returned and painted a rosy picture of their lives in the North. Their dressy clothes and fancy new cars seemed to confirm what they said. "Negroes," they bragged, "are free and equal up North. We can go anywhere we please and are not re-quired to go to the back of the bus and are not called 'boy' and 'girl.'" I could not wait to go up North and experience this freedom and equality for myself, which I did to attend graduate school at Garrett Theological Seminary and Northwestern University in Evanston, just north of Chicago.

I soon discovered, however, as many blacks did before me, that the Great Migration to the Northern cities was also a great disappointment. What I saw on Chicago's South Side looked more like a nightmare than a dream. Barred from renting and buying in white neighborhoods with restrictive covenants, blacks in the North were cordoned off into ghettos, where they were charged exorbitant prices for slum tenements, most of which were not fit for human habitation. The chairman of a city housing reform in New York opined in 1927 that "the State would not allow cows to live in some of these apartments used by colored people."⁷ Blacks were given low-paying jobs that whites didn't want and were used as strike breakers against unions that excluded them. In the lean years, such as during the Great Depression, blacks were usually "the first fired and the last hired." As Langston Hughes put it: "The depression brought everybody down a peg or two. And the Negroes had but few pegs to fall."⁸ The white police in the North were just as zealous in keeping blacks in their place as the white law in the South. "I moved to Detroit because I thought life might be better," Elijah Muhammad of the Nation of Islam recalled years later, "but even there . . . I saw my people shot down right on the street without any justice whatsoever."[9]

While the North was different from the South, blacks were not sure that the quality of their lives was much better. As James Baldwin put it, "the North promised more," but "what it promised it did not give, and what it gave, at length and grudgingly with one hand, it took back with the other."[10] Superficially, whites seemed to treat blacks somewhat better. There was no legal segregation, no obscene signs designated where blacks were to eat, drink water, or use the toilet. They could vote, and a few were elected to political office. These differences were important. But still, the North was hardly the promised land of freedom that blacks had hoped to find there. On the contrary, the dream/nightmare contradiction was felt just as deeply in the urban North as in the rural South. The North was cold and indifferent. Langston Hughes expressed this feeling in his poem "Po' Boy Blues" (1932) when he described the sunshine in the South as "gold," but "Since I cam North de / Whole damn world's turned cold."[11]

Today, at the close of the millennium, not much has changed for the black poor in America's cities in the North or the South, except for the worse. There is an enduring and tragic existence for black people in the city—defined by chronic unemployment, economic chaos, inadequate educational facilities, colonial-style police policies, and indifferent political machines. The struggle for meaning and survival takes a terrible toll on the physical and spiritual well-being of black people. The simple wish for a livable wage, humane living conditions, decent schools, and to be both African and American, without being treated like dirt by the dominant white society, still escapes the black poor, most of whom reside in urban centers. In this essay, written in honor of Letty Russell's long-standing commitment to imaging eschatology in urban contexts, I look at the struggle for black identity in the city, paying special attention to the symbolic eschatological significance of the dream/nightmare images as reflected in the lives of two great religious leaders—Martin Luther King Jr. and Malcolm X.

MARTIN'S AND MALCOLM'S
EARLY LIFE IN THE CITY

The double meaning of the city (dream/nightmare) for blacks is reflected in the lives and ministries of Martin King and Malcolm X. Both were born in the city—Martin in Atlanta, Georgia (15 January 1929), and Malcolm in Omaha, Nebraska (19 May 1925). They grew up in the city, Martin in his birthplace and Malcolm in several places—Lansing, Michigan; Boston; and

New York. They conducted their ministries in the city—Martin mostly in the urban South, fighting *de jure* segregation, and Malcolm primarily in the urban North, exposing *de facto* segregation. They gave their most famous speeches in the city: Martin's famed "I Have a Dream" oration was delivered at the Lincoln Memorial in Washington, D.C. (28 August 1963), and his controversial "Beyond Vietnam" speech at Riverside Church in New York City (4 April 1967). Malcolm delivered his well-known "Message to the Grass Roots" speech at King Solomon Baptist Church in Detroit (10 November 1963) and his hard-hitting "The Ballot or the Bullet" talk at Cory Methodist Church in Cleveland (3 April 1964).

Martin's and Malcolm's philosophies of freedom, though vastly different, were developed in and influenced by the city. With the city's access to the national media and to large numbers of blacks and whites, Martin and Malcolm created civil rights and black nationalist organizations that aroused the moral conscience of Americans to take a stand for justice. Both men were assassinated in the city—Malcolm in Harlem (21 February 1965) by a team of black assassins who symbolized the community he loved, and Martin in Memphis (4 April 1968) by a lone white assassin who symbolized the community he sought to transform.

The city is a source of hope and despair, joy and sorrow, life and death. These warring possibilities create ambivalent feelings about the city, causing blacks and other poor people to move constantly in and out of it to different parts of the country as they search for a safe place to work, play, worship, and assert their dignity.

Martin Luther King Jr. and Malcolm X exhibited this ambivalence that many blacks experience. Both were infused with the double aspects of the dream and the nightmare. Sons of rural Georgia Baptist preachers, Martin and Malcolm were nurtured in the black religious tradition, which was created out of an amalgamation of African spirituality and white evangelical Protestant Christianity of the rural South. These two religious roots influenced the black Christian and Muslim religions in which Martin and Malcolm became ministers.

Martin's father, Martin Luther King Sr., left rural Stockbridge, Georgia, for the city of Atlanta and later became the prominent pastor of the influential Ebenezer Baptist Church. Malcolm's father, Earl Little, left Reynolds, Georgia, and drifted from city to city—Montreal, Canada; Philadelphia; Omaha; Milwaukee; and Lansing, Michigan. His status as a minister did not exceed that of a "jackleg" preacher who never was called to a permanent church. Martin's father was a well-known civic leader, an active participant in the NAACP—the largest civil rights organization, and the most feared by whites of that time. It defined the idea of integration as the goal of the black struggle for racial justice in America. Like King Sr., Little was deeply involved in the black struggle for justice. But unlike King Sr., he was no integrationist. Earl Little was rather a devoted disciple of Marcus Garvey, the black nationalist leader who left Jamaica for New York and organized more African Americans than anyone in U.S. history. Little was elected president of the Omaha branch of Garvey's Universal Negro Improvement Association. The different journeys of King Sr. and Little profoundly influenced the lives and messages of their sons, Martin and Malcolm.

Martin Luther King Jr.'s dream was partly derived from the middle-class success of his parents and the Christian teachings they used to account for it. Through hard work, clean living, and an active faith in Jesus Christ, the Kings believed that blacks could overcome the legacy of slavery and the disadvantages of segregation and become the proud people God created them to be. The self-help philosophy of Booker T. Washington, the protest philosophy of the NAACP, and the eschatological faith of the Christian religion were combined to motivate blacks to fight against economic oppression, social degradation, and political exploitation.

"Daddy King" (as King Sr. was affectionately called) preached and embodied the philosophy of the American dream: "If you work hard and play by the rules you should be given a chance to go as far as your God-given ability will take you."[12] Against great odds, he pulled himself up by his bootstraps and demonstrated that deep faith and hard work could overcome the most dire circumstances. Even during the depression years of the 1930s, when 60 percent of blacks in Atlanta were on public welfare, the King family had plenty of food to eat, a nice place to stay, and, as King said, they never had to ride long in a car for which money was still owed.

But no matter how successful blacks became, they could do only so much to shield their children from racial discrimination. No blacks could escape it— whether in the city or the country, up North or down South. Young Martin was only six when he first became aware that his color set him apart for ridicule by the dominant white society. The father of a white playmate told him that his son could no longer play with him because he was "colored." That was Martin's painful introduction to America's racial nightmare. Though his parents assured him that he was as good as anybody, the experience was one he never forgot. Other racial incidents happened that reinforced the rule of white supremacy in the city of Atlanta. Martin overheard a white policeman call his father a boy and was with him when a shoe-store clerk told his father that he could only be served in the "colored section." Martin was also forced to ride at the back of the bus and behind the curtain on a train. Racial discrimination affected him so deeply as a child that he initially "was determined to hate every white person."[13]

It was the black community in the city of Atlanta which gave Martin hope that the world could be changed and that things need not stay the way they were. He saw many signs of hope—the eschatological faith of Ebenezer and other black churches, the enlightened faith of Morehouse College and other educational institutions in the Atlanta University Center, the economic faith of black businesses, and the political faith of the NAACP and other protest organizations. Blacks in Atlanta represented one of the most progressive black communities in America, especially in the South. They inspired Martin to believe in himself, in black people, and in America's possibilities.

While Martin was a student at Morehouse, President Benjamin E. Mays and religion professor George D. Kelsey showed him that the ministry could be a vocation that contributes to the freedom and dignity of black people. The church was the soul of the city of Atlanta in the African American community. Blacks of all ages and classes flocked to their favorite churches to have their spirits uplifted and to experience another dimension of their humanity.

Malcolm X's early life was much more stressful than Martin's because his parents were not able to protect him from the pain of poverty and the violence of white supremacy. A white hate group burned down the family home when he was only four. He called it the "nightmare night of 1929, my earliest vivid memory":

> I remember being suddenly snatched awake into a frightening confusion of pistol shots and shouting and smoke and flames. My father had shouted and shot at the two white men who had set the fire and were running away. Our home was burning down around us. We were lunging and bumping and turning all over each other trying to escape. My mother, with the baby in her arms, just made it into the yard before the house crashed in, showering sparks. I remember we were outside in our underwear, crying and yelling our heads off. The white police and firemen came and stood around watching as the house burned down to the ground.[14]

Significantly, Malcolm called the first chapter of his autobiography "Nightmare." As his nightmare was created by the violence of white America, his dream was inspired by his childhood memories of Africa and race pride he experienced with his father at the Garveyite meetings. "Up, you mighty race, you can accomplish what you will," Earl Little thundered, repeating a popular slogan of Marcus Garvey: "Africa for the Africans. Ethiopians Awake." Unlike his reaction to his father's sermons about Jesus, which left Malcolm "confused and amazed," he listened attentively to his father's proclamations about "the hour of Africa's coming redemption."

Malcolm's African dream, however, died with the death of his father, who many blacks said was murdered by the same white hate group that burned down the Littles' house. Malcolm was only six when his father died. The Little family became destitute. Unable to support eight children, Malcolm's mother had a complete nervous breakdown and was put in a state mental hospital in Kalamazoo. Malcolm became a delinquent and was sent to a reform school in Mason, Michigan, where a few nice white people helped him turn his life around. The only black in his class, Malcolm became an outstanding student, popular among his white classmates, and was elected the president of his seventh-grade class.

Malcolm was living the American dream of token integration. Everything went well for him until his English teacher discouraged him from becoming a lawyer and suggested carpentry as a more "realistic goal for a nigger." At that moment, Malcolm's attitude toward whites began to change. He realized that no matter how smart he was, he was still just a nigger in the eyes of white America. Malcolm dropped out of school and went to Boston and later to New York, where he became a con artist, thief, pimp, drug dealer, and numbers runner—living, as he put it, by "my wits," "like a predatory animal."[15]

New York and Boston were both a dream and a nightmare for Malcolm X. As a dream, they were places where blacks had their own communities—such as Roxbury and Harlem—with churches, speakeasies, nightclubs, street talkers, and other prophets. Blacks defined their space in the city. They developed a style of their own, creating new blues, jazz, and gospel music as they remembered the spirituals, secular rhymes, and work songs of their slave grandparents. There were black poets, novelists, short-story writers, and other literary men and women who described the *everydayness* of black life in fresh and powerful ways. This is the world that defined Malcolm X.

In contrast to Martin King, the church did not appeal to Malcolm X. Its message was too otherworldly and thus did not speak persuasively to his life in the fast lane of Harlem and Roxbury. He reveled in the style of the ghetto—smoking reefers, shooting craps, and lindy-hopping to the sounds of the big jazz bands of Count Basie, Duke Ellington, and Lionel Hampton. The world Malcolm loved was also the source of his nightmare. Before he reached his twenty-first birthday, Malcolm was sentenced to eight to ten years in a Massachusetts prison for armed robbery (February 1946). In prison, Elijah Muhammad's Nation of Islam entered his life, re-created his African dream, and defined the cause and the meaning of the American nightmare. The African dream and the American nightmare guided Malcolm's ministry and defined the content of his black nationalist message. As an interpreter of the meaning of the city for its black population, no one's insight was more profound and compelling than Malcolm's.

MINISTRY IN THE CITY

When nineteen-year-old Martin King left Atlanta for Chester, Pennsylvania, to attend Crozer Theological Seminary (1948) to deepen his intellectual understanding of the Christian faith, Malcolm X had been in prison two years,

studying the teachings of Elijah Muhammad's Nation of Islam and vora-
ciously reading books in history, philosophy, sociology, and religion. Crozer
Seminary was Martin's first opportunity to live and study in a predominantly
white community, whose openness to racial justice deeply impressed him.
Prison was Malcolm's first occasion to study critically world history and culture. Martin's social and academic exposure to a larger world made him more
open to the goodwill of liberal whites, whereas Malcolm's exposure to the
prison population and guards, as well as his reading, had the opposite effect,
making him very distrustful of whites. In the Atlanta black community and at
Crozer Seminary, Martin was taught that God created all persons as brothers
and sisters who should treat one another with love and respect. Through Malcolm's study of history and Muhammad's religious teachings, Malcolm came
to believe that genuine community between blacks and whites was impossible
because white supremacy and black inferiority were the defining elements of
white religion, culture, and history.

As Christian and Muslim ministers, both Martin King and Malcolm X
preached love. Martin focused on "love your enemy," and Malcolm accented
"love yourself." Although both spoke to urban audiences, Martin spoke primarily to Southern black Christians and white moderates and Northern white
liberals. He used the language of love, which he equated with nonviolence, to
empower blacks and to arouse the conscience of whites to oppose segregation
and create the beloved community of racial integration. Malcolm spoke
mainly to Northern ghetto blacks, whom he loved, and to white do-gooders
and "Negro Uncle Tom leaders," whom he despised. He used the language of
self-love, which he equated with self-defense, to empower poor blacks to reject the self-hate philosophy of nonviolence and integration and to affirm the
spiritual power of black love and separatism.

In the South, black Christianity was much more spiritually powerful and
oriented toward community building than was its Northern transplantation.
In Northern cities, black Christianity lost much of its power to inspire hope
in ghetto blacks. The same sermons, songs, and prayers that helped blacks hold
their humanity together in rural Mississippi, Alabama, and Georgia could not
duplicate that power in New York's Harlem, Boston's Roxbury, and Chicago's
South and West Sides. Jesus'turn-the-other-cheek philosophy did not ring
true in the inner-city ghetto. A "pie in the sky," "wait 'til I get to heaven" religion seemed grossly out of place for people who needed food and shelter
now. The black urban poor therefore turned to a variety of home-grown sects
and cults, such as Daddy Grace's United House of Prayer for All People, Father Divine's Peace Mission, and Elijah Muhammad's Nation of Islam. These
offered poor blacks a way out of hell *now,* and not in some distant, undefined
future. As Father Divine put it:

I would not give five cents for a God who could not help me here on the earth, for such a God is not a God at hand. He is only an imagination. It is a false delusion—trying to make you think you had just as well go ahead and suffer and be enslaved and be lynched and everything else here, and after a while you are going to Heaven someplace. If God cannot prepare Heaven here for you, you are not going anywhere.[16]

To understand the urban ghetto today, with its proliferation of religious sects and cults, the violence and the drugs, teen pregnancy and the breakdown of family values, we need to focus on the loss of meaning that overwhelms inner-city residents from the time they draw their first breath in this world. Considering what they are up against, the persistent and self-destructive forces of hate, I am amazed that any poor ghetto blacks ever manage to survive America's colonial-style police policies, economic chaos, and indifferent political machines. If one-third of white men in their twenties were involved in the criminal justice system or were killing one another at as astounding a rate as blacks are today, a national state of emergency would be declared. The churches and seminaries would focus their spiritual and intellectual resources on the creation of alternative human possibilities. But poor blacks are expendable. They do not count for much in the white society or their churches. That is why their life experience is hardly present in our political and theological discourse. The poor attract negative attention when politicians talk about what is wrong with America and positive attention when liberal-minded religious people want to feel morally superior to conservative politicians and corporate capitalists. This is the reality that Malcolm understood so well and addressed with profound insight and absolute rage. Speaking to Harlem blacks on August 10, 1963, Malcolm said:

Unemployment and poverty have forced many of our people into this life of crime; but . . . the real criminal is in City Hall downtown. The real criminal is in the State House in Albany. The real criminal is in Washington, D.C. The real criminal is the white man who poses as a liberal—the political hypocrite. And it is these legal crooks, posing as our friends, [who are] forcing us into a life of crime and then using us to spread the white man's evil vices among our own people. Our people are scientifically maneuvered by the white man into a life of poverty. You are not poor accidentally. He maneuvers you into poverty. You are not a drug addict accidentally. You are maneuvered into drug addiction. You are not a prostitute accidentally. You are maneuvered into prostitution by the American white man. There is nothing about your condition in America that is an accident.[17]

Martin understood the complexity and the depth of racial oppression in the urban North only in his later years. His transformation began when he went to Los Angeles to quiet down rioting blacks in August 1965. "Get out of here, Dr. King! We don't want you!" blacks screamed. "Long live Malcolm X!" Four months later, Martin took the civil rights movement to Chicago, moved his family into a slum apartment on the South Side, and discovered the depths of meaninglessness in the lives of city blacks. He could see hopelessness in the eyes of the people, the way they walked, talked, and related to one another. "Been down so long, / Till down don't worry me." Self-hate was so deep and the living quarters so crowded and dirty that one slight insult or any perceived expression of disrespect could get a person killed.

In Chicago, the radical King began to emerge. He called the ghetto a form of internal colonialism wherein the people are relentlessly dominated, segregated, and exploited by the political, economic system in which they are caught. He quit talking about his dream, because, as he said, he saw that dream turned into a nightmare. Martin King declared that there was more racism in Chicago and other Northern cities than in Mississippi and the rest of the South. This militant Martin began to sound like an angry Malcolm X.

Today, although the church may be physically located in the city, it has not been transformed by the reality of the urban plight. Its members live in the suburbs, on the outskirts of the city. The church serves people who are safely removed from city problems—drugs, gang violence, and the homeless. Those churches that try to cope with these complex urban issues rarely have the intellectual and material resources even to make a dent in them. Preachers still preach that God can "make a way out of no way," that God is "a heart fixer and mind regulator," but most do not *really* believe that gospel anymore. Preachers still preach that God loves the poor, but they have not the faintest clue why the poor are cast so low.

No longer interested in the worn-out gospel of Christian preachers, many urban blacks turn to other sources for relief from the daily pain of meaninglessness. In the North, where the forces of white domination are more hidden and thus more dangerous, and where community is more difficult to establish, blacks long for a spiritual message that will create a deep bond among themselves. In the old South the bond was found in the church, where the love of Jesus flowed like a river "from heart to heart and breast to breast." But in the move to the North, Jesus' love lost its power to bind together the broken lives in the city. Jesus was too white, too identified with the cultural and political forces of racial oppression. Blacks needed a bond that was identified with their history and culture, a bond that separated them from white America's racist values and connected them with their glorious African past.

For Malcolm the bond was *blackness*, a solidarity based on a common history and culture and a fierce resistance to white supremacy. He said that blacks must recapture their heritage if they are to free themselves from the bonds of white supremacy. They must engage in a cultural revolution aimed at unbrainwashing an entire people. Through the power of his oratory and the sincerity of his commitment to black liberation, Malcolm transformed docile Negroes into proud blacks. For example, the actress Denise Nicholas recalls that she never knew she was black until she had read Malcolm.

Still today, the legacy of Malcolm X resonates with the experience of blacks in the inner city. Remnants of his meaning abound in popular culture, especially among the rap artists and other articulators of black cultural nationalism. His voice is the one the people listen to, because he, more than Martin, understood the desperate plight of the down and out in the ghetto—the ones, he said, "deepest in the mud." The future of black city dwellers is found in an affirmation of blackness and a rejection of whiteness—embracing difference in community and the world. We must fight sexism, classism, and heterosexism as fiercely as we fight racism. To embrace blackness is to embrace humanity in all its manifestations. Black and womanist theologies are seeking in a variety of ways to incorporate this insight in black religious communities.

Unfortunately, there is a leadership vacuum in the inner city, and questionable voices have filled it with black nationalist rhetoric that sounds like Malcolm but is actually a great contradiction of what Malcolm represented. The man who proclaimed Malcolm a hypocrite, "worthy of death," is now the most influential leader among ghetto residents—Minister Louis Farrakhan of the Nation of Islam. No other black leader could have called the Million Man March and achieved the great success he did. The spirit of togetherness that moved through the throng of one million black people captivated the world. I was there and experienced the power of blackness, a deep and profound spiritual experience. If that spirit could take over the culture of the inner cities, then the future of black people would be in their own hands. But I am not so hopeful about that these days. While Minister Farrakhan's call for the march unleashed a powerful black spirit of unity, his sexist, homophobic, and anti-Semitic declarations undermined black solidarity and thereby undercut the potential role he could play in creating a meaningful future for black city dwellers. Like so many Christian ministers and theologians, he speaks only a partial truth. We need, therefore, critical insight to discern when he is on target and when he is off.

Minister Louis Farrakhan can step into the leadership vacuum because he can speak effectively to black hurt and pain, so pervasive in the urban ghetto. He speaks a truth that blacks know and understand. Mainline black leadership seems bankrupt, unable to develop a creative vision that is capable of capturing the imagination of people whose backs have been pushed up against the wall. It is oriented too much toward the interests of the black middle class.

Churches should be able to speak to the urban poor, but most are too frightened of the black nationalist rhetoric they speak. Churches criticize but offer little. They run from Malcolm X's rage and ignore the militant preaching of Martin King.

Although I am still in the church and serve as one of its theologians, I am not convinced that most churches even care about the poor in the city, except perhaps a few of those churches that are locked in and cannot get out. The churches are blind to problems in the city. Their ministers are like the priest and the Levite in the Lukan Jesus' parable of the Good Samaritan, who, seeing the robbed man on the Jericho road, "passed by on the other side."

Seminaries and divinity schools prepare ministers for middle-class congregations that are able to shield themselves from the homeless and jobless in the city. One of my former biblical colleagues at Union said he did not see why white students needed to study black theology or even be concerned about the problems in Harlem, since they will be ministers in white communities. With professors like that, it is no wonder that white churches run from urban problems. Their members may go to arts events in the city and take advantage of the cultural and educational opportunities that cities offer, but churches are too inwardly focused to recognize that they no longer know the gospel of the one whose name defines their identity.

Like ministers, seminary and university professors of religion also do not know the gospel. We know things *about* Jesus and have amassed a great deal of historical information about his time. We can talk for hours about the "old quest," "new quest," and the "newest quest" of the historical Jesus, holding seminars and deciding which words of Jesus in the Gospels are authentic. But we know not Jesus, the one who came to preach good news to the poor and to set the captives free. Our books often make for interesting reading for our academic peers, and that in itself is not a bad thing. That's a good thing. But we ought to call it what it is—academic discourse about Jesus. It is not discourse that empowers the marginalized in Chicago or New York City, the people whom Jesus' message was intended to liberate.

As churches, ministers, and theologians, we have failed to embrace and be embraced by the harsh realities of the city. How can we dream with people whose nightmares we fail to recognize? Without consideration for "the essential bleakness of black life in America,"[18] we often dismiss the uncomfortable lyrics of rap music, labeling it violent and sexist. And some rap music should be rejected for those reasons. But not all. Who is more likely to provide today's message on the city—preachers and theologians or Grand Master Flash and the Furious Five, whose song "The Message" describes the dehumanization and destructiveness of ghetto existence as a "jungle" where you can hardly keep from "goin' under"?

Is there any hope for America's cities, especially for young black men and women, boys and girls whose lives are emotionally and physically destroyed by the violence, drugs, and meaninglessness that overwhelm them? Where is hope to be found? Is it located in America's political leaders—the white Democrats and the Republicans? Is it found primarily among the African American political leadership—the liberals or conservatives?

Do we have any reason to believe that America's universities and colleges will show us how to save the poor in the city? There are so many intellectuals whose minds are devoted to knowledge production, seeking solutions to complicated and difficult human questions. Scientists know how to clone sheep, create a cyberspace informational highway, and build spaceships that explore the mysteries of the universe. It seems there is no limit to humanity's technological capability. But do we know how to mend the twisted lives in America's treacherous inner cities? Can we create communities in our cities where men and women have meaningful jobs, and where boys and girls can go to school and play without fear of being beaten, raped, and shot?

The Bible says, "Where there is no vision, the people perish" (Prov. 29:18, KJV). Does the church not have a vision for young black lives in the city? Is there no balm in Gilead? Is there no physician who can heal broken lives?

There is tragedy in this land, and most of our theologians are blind. If our theologies do not seek to empower and to bestow meaning on "the wretched of the earth," to use Frantz Fanon's (*The Wretched of the Earth*, trans. Constance Farrington, 1961; reprinted New York: Grove, 1968) words, they are not worth the paper we write them on. I conclude with the words of Stevie Wonder, physically blind but spiritually clear, who reminds us in his song "Living for the City" that if we do not begin to change, the "world will soon be over."

NOTES

1. W.E.B. Du Bois, *The Souls of Black Folk* (1903; reprint, New York: Fawcett, 1961), pp. 16, 17.
2. James Baldwin, *The Fire Next Time* (New York: Dell Publishing Co., 1964), p. 61.
3. Ralph Ellison, *Shadow and Act* (New York: Quality Paperback Book Club, 1994), p. 94.
4. See Arna Bontemps and Jack Conroy, *Anyplace but Here* (New York: Hill & Wang, 1966).
5. Henry McNeal Turner, "The American Flag" (1906), in Edwin S. Redkey, ed., *Respect Black: The Writings and Speeches of Henry McNeal Turner* (New York: Arno Press, 1971), p. 196.
6. Langston Hughes, "One-Way Ticket": (1948), in *The Collected Poems of Langston Hughes*, ed. Arnold Rampersad (New York: Alfred A. Knopf, 1995), p. 361.
7. Cited in Gilbert Osofsky, *Harlem: The Making of a Ghetto*, 2d ed. (New York: Harper & Row, 1971), pp. 135–36.
8. Ibid., p. 187.
9. Cited in Hatim A. Sahib, "The Nation of Islam" (M.A. thesis, Department of Sociology, University of Chicago, 1951), p. 90.

10. James Baldwin, *Go Tell It on the Mountain* (New York: Dell Publishing Co., 1965), p. 163.

11. Langston Hughes, "Po' Boy Blues," *Collected Poems,* ed. Rampersad, p. 83.

12. This is a classic statement of the American dream that is deeply embedded in American history and culture. It was repeated in a speech by President Bill Clinton, cited in George M. Fredrickson, "Land of Opportunity," *New York Review,* 4 April 1996, p. 6.

13. Martin Luther King Jr., "The Autobiography of Religious Development," in *The Papers of Martin Luther King, Jr.,* vol. 1: *Called to Serve* (January 1929–June 1951), ed. Clayborne Carson, Ralph Luker, and Penny Russell (Los Angeles: University of California Press, 1992), p. 362.

14. Malcolm X (with Alex Haley), *The Autobiography of Malcolm X* (1965; reprint, New York: Ballantine Books, 1973), p. 3.

15. Ibid., p. 134.

16. See Robert Weisbrot, *Father Divine and the Struggle for Racial Equality* (Urbana: University of Illinois Press, 1983).

17. Cited in James Cone, *Martin and Malcolm and American: A Dream or a Nightmare* (Maryknoll, N.Y.: Orbis Books, 1991) p. 89.

18. Richard Wright, cited in Ellison, *Shadow and Act,* p. 93.

9

A COMING HOME TO MYSELF

The Childless Woman in the West African Space

Mercy Amba Oduyoye (Amba Ewudziwa)

Reflecting on "liberating eschatology," I am reminded that the seven signs of human well-being as viewed by the Akan of Ghana include the power of pro-creation. Fruitfulness of plant and animal life is the prayer of African religion. Eschatology, concerned with the end, the aim, the goal of life, for many Africans focuses on the fullness and fruitfulness of life here, in this land of the living. The end is to be found in the quality of life possible to us now. Fruit-fulness has traditionally been considered necessary for a good quality of life, for the immortality of humanity and the survival of the clan; ancestors return to be born into this realm of life. Perpetuation of family names and preserva-tion of the memory of those who have borne these names reveal the power of a clan's fruitfulness through procreation. In most African cultures, naming has religious and spiritual significance, and it is tied to the experience of child-bearing.

In the context of this festschrift, in my honoring of Letty Russell, it seems appropriate to reflect once again, as I have with her in the past, on the power of naming. In a book whose theme is liberating eschatology, it seems partic-ularly appropriate to consider African women's experience of naming insofar as it is tied to their fruitfulness. There is a part of this experience that has not received adequate theological reflection, a story of women's experience that has yet to be told. What I do in this essay is reflect on the experience of women who belong to traditions where naming is according to fruitfulness in child-bearing, but who for whatever reason do not join in "increasing and multiply-ing" the human race. This is an area of silence crying out for insight and for words.

But let me begin by apologizing to all who call me Mother, Mama, Ma, es-pecially to the nieces and nephews for whom I have had particular responsi-bility in accompanying them to adulthood. I love you all, and I appreciate and will continue to bask in your love and care for me. Nevertheless, I would like to come home to myself as a woman who has no biological progeny. To all those worldwide who, though not blood relations, have come to call and to refer to me as Auntie, Ma, Mother, I say the same. I love you all. Your friendships and solidarity have nourished my life and strengthened me with a reason to live and to struggle to contribute to what we have in common, the quest for humanization, for justice, and for community. I want to hold you all in my embrace, and to have you hold me in yours. Nonetheless, I want to come home to myself as a woman without biological progeny. I want to be known and called Amba Ewudziwa, as I was named on the eighth day of my sojourn on earth. This is my name forever, my "primal name"; all others are secondary.

Named after my paternal grandfather according to Gomoa tradition, I bear the feminine form of his name. Just before sitting down to write this essay, I visited his grave in the vicinity of the new Methodist church in Asamankese; it is one of two left standing by the roadside after the cemetery was razed to the ground to give way to roads and housing. The bicultural naming of Africans, both Christian and Muslim, is evidenced on his gravestone, which reads as follows:

> *To the glory of God in memory of*
> *Isaiah Yamoah alias Kodwo Ewudzi*
> *The leader of the founders of*
> *Methodist church in Asamankese.*

One of the leaders referred to is his spouse, Martha Aba Awotwiwa Yamoah, now gone to rest and interred in her hometown, Apam. With these two began the Christian patriarchal naming of wives and children on my father's side of the family. Nana Ewudzi was born in 1880 and died in 1944, thus witnessing the height of British colonialism in the former Gold Coast and passing on before the changes that came in the wake of the Second World War. Descending from these two and others of their generation, I lay claim to an ancestry of women and men of tremendous faith, adventurous spirit, and initiative, people who were community builders.

Coming home to myself means lifting up my primary names, Amba Ewudziwa. I do not deny that I am known by most persons and identified in official documents as Mercy, named by my father after the woman who made him a biological father. I do not deny that I am Yamoah, the firstborn and daughter of my father, who in Western Christian fashion and against Akan practice had to name his children after himself, and who in compliance with British and Christian practice had to continue the patriarchal family tree begun by his father. I do not deny that I am Oduyoye, spouse of Adedoyin Modupe, the man who, in 1968, with a lot of hope and admiration, lent me his name in compliance with Western patriarchal matrimonial law; and who, in spite of my inability to make him a father, remains a husband to me. I love and honor and hold both father and husband in high esteem. Nevertheless, I would like to come home to myself as the individual who on that eighth day was named Amba Ewudziwa.

That this naming was critical even for my relationships with my Yoruba in-laws was brought home to me in their concerted effort to make me a biological mother. That was the name demanded by those who wanted to pray for me, that I might become an expectant mother. Their hope was that my soul (*kra/chi/ori*) would respond more readily when called on by this primal name. As it turned out, Amba Ewudziwa had come to the world with an expectant *kra* whose expectations did not include biological children. As I was born to Christians, no oracle had been consulted at my birth on my life plan. Hence the fretting that accompanied the child factor in my life. For me now, however, claiming my primal name is my way to claim my mythical and legendary foresisters—African women with no biological progeny, many of them Nigerian—and to style myself a scion of Efuru, Anowa, Tinubu, an incarnation of Uhamiri, and kin to the biracial Mammy-wata.[1] I would like to claim who I am as a "woman alone" who inspires community; a woman who prays that the men and women she touches and who touch her will grow and prosper as God would have all humans do; a woman whose life helps effect an earth that is prosperous and at peace.

African women's creative literature is replete with what has come to be named the "child factor."[2] That is, central to the narratives of women's lives is the importance of biological reproduction; central to the spirituality that is developed for women is their role in relation to children, family, and community; central to women's identity is their healthy biological functioning. Thus far, only Flora Nwapa has been able to give voice to the view that a woman's worth includes but goes beyond biological procreation.[3] The other side of the coin, fecundity, is examined by Buchie Emecheta in *The Joys of Motherhood*.[4] Both views are aptly captured in the Akan adage "Wo wo a amane wannwo a amane" (Both bearing children and bearing no children are accompanied with troubles [or challenges]).

But now I must tell my own story, not only to reclaim my name but to provide a context for theological reflection on the experience of childlessness among African women. In the Circle of Concerned African Women Theologians,[5] the age gap among members has prevented most from raising the issue with me on a personal level. Resources for theological reflection are in many ways limited. Not much can be drawn from African religion and culture, though Nwapa's writings have presented examples of female water deities and a role of social mothering. African women's literary and historical writings, as I have already suggested, provide an important source for relevant spiritualities. But the voices of theologically trained women who are Christian and

without biological children must still be heard. In Africa, lives and relationships are ruined daily because of the "child factor," especially by childlessness
within a marriage. The burden of the silence on these matters causes me to
come home to myself and to take up my primary names in order to express
what is specifically myself.

THE SILENCE

Childlessness is a taboo subject. Even among women, one has to live with non-
starters in conversations, such as:

"How are the children?"
"I have no children."
"Oh?"

Or:

"How is the family?"[6]
"Everyone is doing well, thank you."
"How old are the children?"
"I have none."
"I am sorry."

Or:

"Do you have children?"
"No."
"Don't say 'no,' say 'not yet.'"

Not yet, not yet, not yet. Until when do I continue to expect to become "expectant," so that I can fulfill the expectation of both church and society that I
shall increase and multiply? These conversations show that there is nothing to
talk about beyond children when one meets a married woman. One mother of
four said to me, "Go and bring children from Ghana. It is necessary for your
integration into this community. You will take them to school and meet other
parents, you will attend functions involving children and feel at home. Otherwise your life here is going to be very lonesome." She was right. Except for
people like her, the silence around childlessness is so loud it is almost deafen-
ing. I plucked up courage to ring this bell after several women dealing with the
issue in their ministry said to me, "You have got to write about this. So far, the
women writers who have faced this are all biological mothers. They cannot tell
your story."

Some of the women who have urged the breaking of this silence are wives and mothers; others are mothers but have never been wives; still others are neither wives nor mothers. All these women have one thing in common: they are the ones whose final word to me was not "Oh?" or "No" or "Not yet." They talked about their own experiences to me. Or they shared the experiences of other women they knew. Some offered help and advice and directed me to doctors and healers. I felt supported, cared for, and loved by all these sisters, and some brothers, too. They also all have another thing in common: they never give up, and they would not say or even give a hint that life could be fulfilling without biological children. My expected agony becomes their agony, for none has a theology that responds to the absence of fruitfulness. Nor have we tried together to plumb the depths of our faith for one. "What happened to the diversity of gifts?" I would ask myself but not speak out.

I originally wrote this part of the essay in response to those who, after a long time, asked hesitantly, "Why don't you share your story? It may help open this taboo subject for discussion rather than allow it to cause the breakup of marriages, schizophrenia, suicidal quests for pregnancy and sterile sublimation." After two decades of life as a childless wife, I felt free to break the silence. But the first attempt was marked "Draft—Not for Publication," and it was shared for comments and discussion only with a few sisters of the Circle. Now, a decade later, I share it through the medium of this festschrift for Letty, my mentor and guide in my journey toward wholeness as an African Christian woman engaged in theological reflection and theological education.

EXPECTATIONS

I was thirty-plus when I finally got around to accepting that getting married might be a good idea, though somewhere down the line I had considered alternative lifestyles. My father was the first to be puzzled. "At your age?" was his response. We had a long conversation about the implications of my decision. I began to doubt the wisdom of my new choice. I remember saying to him, "My one worry is what will happen if I do not have children. Right now no one expects me to have children, but when I am married, it will be different." That gave words to what I knew was the unasked question in the conversation between Papa and me. "You are not pregnant then?" "Oh no! Should I be?" And there was no answer.

Somehow the subject was changed, and I went through the marriage, all three phases—traditional African in Accra, Western matrimony at the government registry in Ibadan, and a Christian church ceremony at Sekondi. Two people could not have been more married. We had done what was expected of us, though rather late. More expectations were to surface during the process of getting married. My prospective mother-in-law (may her loving soul rest in peace) arrived in my parental home during the first of the three phases, saw the grandchildren—offspring of my siblings—tumbling around, and said to me, beaming, "I want you to give us children like these." I smiled back and directed the request to the right place: "There we go, dear God, you have heard."

I was marrying into another culture, one that counts fathers and ignores mothers. My maternal grand-uncle was happy that I was finally getting married. He was well known for the premium he placed on education and was very proud of my achievements in that direction, but an Asante woman must get married and be the vehicle for the reincarnation of her ancestors. He was relieved, until I explained the origins of the other protagonist of the drama that had begun to unfold; then he got worried: "I have heard that when you have children with a Yoruba man, they will be taken away from you. We do not do that. We are Asante, and our children belong to their mother." My husband (Modupe) and I were one in affirming that a child is a gift of God to the whole human community. Given such a gift, parents are simply custodians. Our children would belong to neither of us. We would be jointly responsible for them to God. We would bring them up to feel as at home in Ghana as in Nigeria and hope they would be able and enabled to contribute positively to any other human community in which they might find themselves. Such was the idealism of the Christian and ecumenical commitment that had brought 'Dupe and Amba together. The question, however, remains: "To whom do children belong?"

Then no children came. Two years after we were married the same grand-uncle asked, "What is my *in-law* doing about your situation?" (Modupe is not simply my husband, he is an in-law among my people, as I am among his.) I must admit I was confused until he added, "If nothing is done, it will bring disharmony in future." Others were equally concerned. The immediate circle of parents, aunts, uncles, sisters, and brothers advised, took me to doctors, said special prayers, greeted me with "Next year this time we shall hear cries of children in this home." It was moving and disturbing at the same time. Once I wept out of sheer anger when Swiss immigration authorities said to me, "She is your niece, not your natural daughter. Our law cannot give her the privileges of a daughter, unless you show adoption papers." "Really!" I retorted. "Adopt my sister's daughter? We do not do that in Ghana."

What a strange world the Swiss must live in; but of course, the Swiss are not Asante. I could not blame the Swiss for too long, however. African governments, like most others, have punitive taxation for childless persons, knowing full well that no African escapes financial and moral responsibility for members of the extended family, especially if they themselves are childless. Moreover, unlike the Swiss, Africans have no homes for the elderly or old-age pensions in the traditional economy. One's old age is in the hands of the young people one has enabled to become economically stable adults. This is why I count my niece as "my daughter." There are no aunts in Akan language; there are only younger mothers and older mothers. Of course, Westernization has changed all that, and now people speaking their African language intersperse it with references to uncles and aunts, cousins and second cousins. The nuclear family is taking over, making the factor of childlessness even more critical.

In spite of the cultural expectations among my own people that every woman, whether or not she has "womb-children," must be ready to assume a mothering role to children of other women of the family, there is usually frantic activity on the part of all to ensure that each member of the family, woman or man, joins in actually reproducing the human race. My case was no different. One uncle undertook to send me to a Harley Street doctor. My mother-in-law was tireless in prayer. The whole community was in agony. One traditional doctor, an expert in such cases, said to me, "I cannot believe that a woman of your physique is unable to have children." And he asked a question so embarrassing that I could not answer with my father and mother sitting in on the consultation. Now that I relive that scene, I find that the question is also unprintable, and shall remain so. My answer was a deliberate lie. He knew it was, and so did my parents, but I wanted to hear what he would say to it. He said nothing. He simply gave me the herbs I was to brew and drink. All the bitterness that is expected to go with childlessness must have been ground into those barks and roots and leaves. My palate rejected the brew as my soul eschewed bitterness of any sort. Such are the indignities that women go through to fulfill religiocultural expectations. Remember Tamar and her father-in-law; remember Ruth and her late husband's kinsman Boaz. Both women were doing their duty as dictated by their culture.

A childless marriage was an embarrassment. I myself regretted the decision to get married when I was "past my prime" and with less than a perfect womb, having been operated on for fibroid tumors with a warning that they were likely to return: "If you hope to have children, start soon, for after two years your chances will be slim." The year we married was the fourth after this Addenbrooks specialist's advice. But I was joining with a man of exceptional faith. So I hoped his faith would make me whole; I hoped God would send us children for his sake. Images of all the biblical "faith-births" became my spiritual well. I convinced myself that the codices that attributed the Magnificat to Elizabeth were the more authentic. What shame does one have who is a virgin and childless?

Modupe sustained the Abraham-and-Sarah paradigm, and only once did he articulate what amounted to blaming me for our childlessness. I had come back from my travel to one ecumenical meeting and was talking of the possibility of another when he asked, "Did you plan children into this marriage?" I did not answer. One colleague, a woman, was sure I should stop work or at least stay home on a month's leave during certain periods. I had shared in detail with her what was happening to me. Once I tried for a week, and it almost worked. But that miscarriage was also the most traumatic. Many are the traumas in the quest for a child of one's own.

An experience I cannot leave out is the one in which I was asked to come to clinic at seven in the morning without breakfast, then discovered that I could not see the doctor till three in the afternoon, and only then was told that the machine they were to use had broken down. Another time, it was a matter of no bed in the ward. I finally freed myself from the hospital when the doctor, famous for having helped many women and sympathetic to our situation, told Modupe and me, "You are both healthy. The only problem is Mercy's fibroid. I hesitate to counsel another operation, since she has had one before. She still has a fifty-fifty chance of retaining a pregnancy, though it may mean long weeks in a hospital bed. At any rate, unless you two are expecting a virgin birth, I'd say you are not giving yourselves the best of chances with your traveling schedules."

That was sufficient. I knew I was incapable of that sacrifice. Why go through six months of lying in bed expecting to become a mother? For what sort of a child? Is the devil I know (that is, myself) not better than the angel that may or may not survive the ordeal of a "hostess" who does not walk? When the fifty-fifty chance waned, I offered to leave Modupe so that he could fulfill fatherhood elsewhere. Why should he bear my burden? Why should he pay the price for my lack of faith and unwillingness to make the adjustments to my lifestyle the doctor had outlined? I was determined that the fullness of my life and the contribution I could make to the communities to which I belong not be belittled. The abilities and skills I have are also given me by God, with the responsibility to utilize them. If children cannot come through me, then I should free Modupe and not force my choice on him, for the stigma of childlessness can be just as devastating for African men as for African women. He was not convinced by my arguments. I was relieved that we could continue to share our lives. We had so much else between us and for us. But I still wished he would have children elsewhere. That he, too, does not have children is therefore a deliberate choice of his; for in the normal run of things in Africa, he is considered justified to find another woman. I have lived in my own life one of the central reasons for polygyny in Africa.

THE ULTIMATE FAILURE

The rest of the world was ambivalent toward us. The bruises and the sounds of the stone throwing, intentional and unintentional, are still fresh in my mind. Only my soul remains undaunted and unembittered. "Are you still here? Where are the children we brought you here to produce?" "Let us hear you call some other names in this house. 'Dupe,' 'Dupe,' 'Dupe,' call some other name." I called Jesus. Modupe had become to me both husband and son. The culture was expecting me to call him Baba Ade, or whatever the name of the firstborn would have been. He would have ceased to be Modupe and become known and called "father of Ade," and I would have become Mama Ade, "mother of Ade." Naming persons without indicating status embarrasses some African peoples. In situations where Mrs. Oduyoye was considered too formal and distant I became Mama Daystar, because I lived in Daystar House. Rather than call me Mercy, several Nigerians would call me Iyawo Wa, our wife, a designation reserved for young wives before they have had their firstborn. In West Africa, human beings are not just Modupe or Mercy; they have to be linked to other people, and it is best if that link is to one's child.

This is one of the reasons for the deep-seated antipathy and embarrassment related to childlessness in Africa. "We brought you here to give us children, not to grow corn to feed us; we Yoruba women do not farm" was the response of a Christian woman, an academic to whom I was serving freshly boiled maize, plucked from my backyard garden, grown with my hands on land that my father, on a visit, had cleared for me. The anguish was not only on my Nigerian side of the family. At the naming ceremony of a close Asante relative's fourth child, waxing eloquent as usual in his speeches the relative burst out: "It is only a foolish woman who stays in a childless marriage." There was I in the circle, sharing his joy, and he was voicing his indictment of me, even though what he had given was a general declaration. True, in our culture my people would have seen to the termination of the marriage, for a childless marriage for an Asante woman is like unpaid labor. Keeping vigil at my father's funeral, a cousin in my age group raised a song with a chorus "Aba Egyir, my sister, it is taboo not to give birth to a child [*Annwo ba a wogyir*]."

At funerals in Nigeria, I would join the procession to the cemetery but not sing the song that asked, "Obi mo abi oobi mo?" (Did this person have children or not?). This is largely a rhetorical question, the children making a display of how well the one who had died had nurtured them into prosperous adulthood. Yet it expresses the importance of one's own biological progeny. In Africa, it is at one's death that children count most, for reproducing the human race is seen as a religious duty. One is never really a full and faithful person until one has a child. Among the Asante, burial rituals for childless persons are enacted in a way that is supposed to ensure that they are not reincarnated. Some would not call on childless ancestors in libation or name children after them. It is an inauspicious state, not to be encouraged and not to be celebrated.

FRIENDS OF JOB

In this situation I was viewed as vulnerable. Several solutions were suggested. From the most unexpected quarters—for example, my father—came the question "Does your husband have any children?" "My husband?" I was shocked.

Why such a question? Why should he have children when I do not? He saw the puzzle on my face and added gently, almost in a whisper, "Then both of you should see a doctor," and changed the subject. This was only two years into the marriage! Later, when the real impact of the question dawned on me, I sought occasion to tell him what the problem was. It was after that conversation that we all went to see the herbalist.

African culture has ways of providing for surrogate fatherhood just as modern science has finally recognized the need. Men I have known as colleagues and friends would say to me, joking of course, "If our brother is the problem we stand ready to help." Generally, there is an embarrassed laugh when I say no, thank you, what I need is a sister to lend me her womb. This was well before surrogate motherhood made the headlines in Western countries. These men were not licentious, promiscuous persons, ready to take advantage of desperate women. They, too, were socialized by a culture that requires them to hide "the brother's shame." They were responding to religious and cultural demands that they believed would become problematic for us in the future, especially if both of us died childless. How easily rules against adultery get swept away when people are desperate for children!

Almost all the men we knew whose wives were, like me, unable to be fruitful had children, sometimes with no questions asked, sometimes openly and with the agreement and even the connivance of their spouses. Once I sat in church stunned as the orator at the funeral of a prominent clergyman said the deceased had no children by his wife, and since his passing away, no "hidden children" had appeared. This was, in the eyes of the orator, a mark of greatness for this man, who was a fine human being and a faithful servant of the ecumenical movement. But at his funeral, the "child factor" had to be raised. Modupe, like this clergyman, was not doing what was expected of him. Children are welcome in or out of regular marriages, and a wife who accepts a husband's children gives additional evidence of her commitment to her husband's welfare. As it happened, even my father's counseling for legal adoption was rejected by 'Dupe. "Do you lack children to look after?" 'Dupe asked me. I had no lack of demands on my mothering instincts, and I shared the duties, joys, and sorrows of this form of parenting with 'Dupe. But both of us had hoped for children of our own. I prayed for one girl; maybe he prayed for one boy, I never asked him. There was no occasion to do so.

Friends of Job would in such cases admonish persons for not taking the traditional route. I confess to wishing at one time that 'Dupe would in this case be a traditionalist—that is, that he would seek another mother for his children. I was saved the temptation of seeking a sperm donor because I knew where the problem was; it was with me. Children are central in every aspect of human interaction in Africa, and no one lightly forgoes the "duty" to have them. But is the personal relationship one builds up in marriage worth nothing apart from children? If donated sperm were an option for me, the challenge would have been whether I care what happens to my body when I die, or whether anybody would name a child after me or remember me in libation.[7] But are there not other memorials I can raise for myself? I prayed to God to help me live creatively even in what the world sees as a shameful and pitiable void.

This is my personal story, but I know there are many others, and not only in African cultures, who have stories that the "shame" of childlessness prevents telling. Perhaps some who read this will respond, "Oh, it *is* such a shame!" But worse shame is that Christianity does not seem to have stories from which the childless can draw strength. If there are such stories, we must find them for the sake of the many who suffer in silence.

THE POSITION OF THE CHRISTIAN CHURCH

The Christians of the early church were not preoccupied with biological fruitfulness. The "end times" were imminent; Jesus was expected at any moment. Hence, the key concern was not the number of children to be born to the Christian community but rather the fruits of the Spirit in the faith community and in the life of the individual Christian. The central hope for the Christian community was that when Jesus the Christ returned there would be people of faith on earth to offer welcome. We have no indication of what the early Christians taught, preached, and counseled regarding unchosen childlessness, especially within marriage. Through the centuries, however, the Christian church has not been helpful in this regard. Indeed, it has often made the suffering of the childless more painful.

Alternative lives and lifestyles are all that the Bible offers. Where in the Bible are the children of Miriam, Deborah, and Esther? Where are the offspring of Mary and Martha, John and James, Priscilla and Aquila? There was no shame in childlessness for virgins. But it is a mystery to me why a church that at least for a time upheld celibacy (and thereby relativized the importance of biological progeny) could not develop a theology that would help the enforced childlessness of many who are married. On the contrary, the Jewish and Christian traditions tell and retell stories of the Ruths and the Tamars of this world, who will pursue their men until they fulfill their cultural roles as wives and mothers. These are hailed as "mothers" of Jesus. Notable patriarchal, priestly, and prophetic names refer to the sons of women who passed through the agonies of childlessness to have baby boys—Isaac, Samuel, and John the Baptizer. The response of "not yet" that I received was in accord with this strand of the biblical tradition. But when "not yet" is no longer an appropriate response, silence reigns uncontested.

The church joins in debates about the so-called population crisis, and in these it takes various stances. But nothing is said to enrich the lives of those who have childlessness thrust upon them. Here, truly, there is no balm in Gilead. If the Bible does not finally anchor people's worth solely in their power of procreation, then why is there not a stronger eschatology that would counter the craving to continue particular genetic lines, to reproduce ourselves as concrete evidence of our immortality? What constitutes immortality? The immortal ones whose "photocopies" we see around us are themselves no longer here; only their spirits and what they stood for abide. To be remembered by children is not the only way to desirable immortality. The "immortal" ones who people our archives and history books were not all persons of honor and great love. What kind of immortality are we craving?

On marriage and childbearing the Christian church is often as unswerving as the Hebrew and African religions and cultures. The wedding ceremonies of traditional Africa do not explicitly articulate a "fruitfulness" requirement, but it is a basic assumption within the whole of the marriage transaction. The traditional Christian marriage ceremony, still often read to new couples, makes children a primary reason for getting married. The church continues to include Psalm 128 as part of a wedding ritual: "Your wife will be like a fruitful vine within your house; your children will be like olive shoots around your table. . . . May you see your children's children" (vv. 3, 6). There is no empowering word and no ceremony to strengthen what may, for many reasons, turn out to be a childless marriage. On this, the church is at best simply silent. Later, it may join the world in leaving a man to his own devices and agonies (though in the past it also refused to baptize the children he begot outside the matrimonial home). For the woman it will be worse. The general taunting of the community is reflected in sermons from our pulpits. Whether intentionally or not, the church participates in blaming her and casting stones:

"She must have misused her youth, getting pregnant and aborting."

"She has been promiscuous, earning sterility through disease."

"She has wasted her fertile years on education and a profession."

Nor does the church actively dispute the traditional condolences and indictments: "Poor girl, she is plagued by witches and evil spirits." "She is a witch. She has exchanged fertility for fame, and maternal instincts for the power to become wealthy." There is no aid for the judgments of inferiority and shame, no clarity for the childless couple from an alternative theological view of their forms of fruitfulness, their participation in the glory of God. Only passive resignation is offered in an inadequate eschatological perspective.

I therefore had to work things out for myself, believing that I am no less in the image of God because I have not biologically increased and multiplied. I reflected on the taunts, the condolences, the blaming, and I concluded that these efforts to explain "why" one is childless are futile and false. I knew women who were accused of these things but had children. I knew women of whom these things were not true but they had no children. I found models of faith who had not biologically increased and multiplied but who participated in glorifying God. I prayed for strength to move beyond the theological impasse and to be at home with my *kra Amba*. I believed that what my soul desires is in what I am and in what I live.

AND HANNAH ROSE (1 SAMUEL 1:9)

How did I come to where I am now? the Circle readers of a first draft wanted to know. Well, it was like this: I remember clearly one morning on the island of Crete, during a World Council of Churches consultation, when I woke up singing:

> *King of Glory, King of Peace,*
> *I will love thee. . . . Thou hast heard me.*
> *Thou hast spared me. Thou didst clear me. . . .*
> *Seven whole days, not one in seven*
> *I will sing thee. In my heart, though not in heaven,*
> *I can raise Thee.*[8]

My singing was the continuation of a dream that had haunted me through the agonizing days of my pursuit of pregnancy, in which there was always a child too heavy for me to lift from a rapid stream full of rocks. My interpretation of the dream was that the fibroid that competed with my pregnancies always won and succeeded in getting into my subconscious to become dreams. Whenever I had that dream, I could count on seeing blood in under a week, and so it was on the island of Crete. But after the Cretan manifestation, I never had the dream again. And I never again worried about whether or not I would become pregnant. That morning I got out of bed cleansed, feeling light, singing "King of Glory" again and again. It was a resurrection. It was a transformation out of which I received a new perspective. It did not bring resignation; it brought acceptance of what my church and African community considered my limitations but what my soul recognized as home.

Later, I was to read and reread the third and last stanza of this hymn, which ends:

> *Small it is, in this poor sort*
> *To enrol Thee:*
> *E'en eternity's too short*
> *To extol thee.*

So I said to myself, so be it that I am too small to enroll God. Should that prevent me from exalting God? The answer was a clear *no*. I became expectant:

What is God trying to say to and through me? I have to listen hard. I had risen from my bed as Hannah rose from her prayers. I had heard the voice of God and needed no priestly confirmation. God knows the priests are taught by African culture and by biblical narratives to confirm only the dreams of a child that is to be born. God had to deal with me directly, speak to me as I am. God knew the church had as yet no affirming word for me. God knew how the church joined the African community to declare that children are wealth, so it is better to have them and be poor. Once I was told of a woman whose husband, a minister of the church, told her it was better for her to die struggling to have a child than not to have any. She went along. She had a son. And she died in the birth of the child. Her husband was happy. God has located my happiness elsewhere.

Just as Hannah rose, so that day, on the island of Crete, Amba rose to the realization that children are God's gift to creatures who need to survive by procreation. I had prayed to join in obeying the command to increase and multiply, and God was saying a clear no to my offer. I felt free; I felt open and fertile, a new person for whom God has a purpose. It was like putting my life on the altar for God to consume what is not necessary for my journey. Rather than being consumed by childlessness, I rose, like Hannah, as one who had experienced a secret conversation and a secret pact with God. I was convinced that something would be born of this experience. I was pregnant with expectation of great things to come to me from God. I have not been disappointed.

What do we expect from the hand of God? For me, it is life lived fully as God would have it, life as a doxology to God, who first loved us. The creative command became for me:

> Increase in humanity.
> Multiply the likeness to God for which you have the potential.
> Multiply the fullness of humanity that is found in Christ.
> Fill the earth with the glory of God.
> Increase in creativity.
> Bring into being that which God can look upon and pronounce
> "good," even "very good."

This is what theologians should enable the church to understand and to give to the childless, so that they can actively embrace this state of life, this call with which the traditional culture cannot now cope. The church can thus empower childless couples to sing, "Behold the servant of the Lord." Let them sing Mary's song (or is it Elizabeth's?), and God will deal greatly with them.

Living in obedience has been for me to try to labor with those who work to enhance and enrich humanity, and to suffer with those who suffer as did Jesus

Christ. To participate in the ever-widening stream of resurrection people is to know fruitfulness and to be transformed.

> *As torrents in summer*
> *Half dried in their channels*
> *Suddenly rise though the sky is cloudless,*
> *So hearts that are fainting*
> *Grow full to overflowing*
> *And they that behold it marvel. . . .*[9]

For me, then, childlessness in the West African space has been a challenge—to my womanhood, my humanity, and my faith. To say that I have overcome would be sheer arrogance, for we live by grace, and it is by the grace of God that I am who I am. It is for the church to acknowledge and raise up the diversity of God's gifts and to celebrate all the ways of bringing forth life. My concern is for a theology of procreation that responds to this challenge, a theology and eschatology that will speak to both those who reproduce themselves biologically and those who do not, a theology that embraces forms of fruitfulness, biological and beyond.

The issue I have been addressing may have only marginal relevance for feminists, womanists, and *mujerista* theologians, the theological sisterhood in the Western world; but in a community of women-centered theologians, where one hurts, all should hurt. In the context of liberating eschatology, therefore, I make bold to raise a question so personal and so "old-fashioned" that it may embarrass even my African sisters. The "child factor" in Africa (and perhaps elsewhere) is complex, and its public faces are daunting; but nothing is more oppressive than the ordinary meanings imposed on the absence of children in a marriage. The silence that shrouds the issue compounds its potential for the disempowering of women. Shall we continue to be silent, or shall we help shape a theology that is life-giving in a situation that is otherwise a context of death? The one who sits on the throne says, "See, I am making all things new" (Rev. 21:5). Shall we not seek new life for the childless?

NOTES

1. For the significance of these names and the stories of these women, see Chikwenye Okonjo Ogunyemi, *Africa Wo/Man Palava: The Nigerian Novel by Women* (Chicago: University of Chicago Press, 1996).
2. The term is Ogunyemi's. Major works of African women writers that have influenced my thinking on childlessness include Ogunyemi, *Africa Wo/Man Palava;* Ama Ata Aidoo, *Anowa* (Accra, Ghana: Sedco Publishing Ltd., 1985); Flora Nwapa, *Efuru* (London: William Heinemann, 1966); and Flora Nwapa, *Idu* (London: William Heinemann, 1970).

3. See Nwapa, *Efuru* and *Idu*.
4. See Buchie Emecheta, *The Joys of Motherhood* (New York: George Braziller, 1979).
5. This Circle of Concerned African Women Theologians (hereafter referred to as the Circle) was initiated by Mercy Amba Oduyoye in 1989 to encourage gender-sensitive research and writing by women in the area of African religions and culture.
6. This question in Africa can only be answered in the affirmative, for the family goes beyond spouse and children and certainly is not limited to biological children.
7. This is, for me, the core of the demand that arises out of African religion. So though a Christian, I wept with disbelief when a younger brother named a son after me and another brother named a daughter for me. Both brothers were not following tradition, so I took this as a special recognition of all the mothering I do. Though this is not "the men's story," I was relieved that my husband's nephew named his daughter Modupe.
8. Based on lines from George Herbert (1593–1632), used in "King of Glory, King of Peace," hymn 23 in *The 1933 Methodist Conference Office London Hymnal*, 34th ed.
9. This song has accompanied me all my life, from an unknown source in the long history of African Christianity.

PART 3

LIBERATING THEOLOGY:

The Work of the Table

10

TO FOLLOW THE VISION

The Jesus Movement as Basileia *Movement*

Elisabeth Schüssler Fiorenza

To express my great appreciation for the feminist leadership and to honor the theological work of Letty Russell, I want to approach the topic of eschatology in and through a critical discussion of the politics of meaning at work in historical Jesus research.[1] Such a critical discussion seeks to explore the nexus between reconstructions of Jesus and those theoretical, historical, cultural, and political conceptual frameworks that shape malestream[2] biblical as well as feminist christological discourses.

A politics of meaning contends that, like research in Bible, history, and theology, so also Jesus research[3] is of significance not only for religious communities. Rather, as master narratives of Western cultures the products of this research, as well as the methods, are always implicated in public discourse. They collude with the production and maintenance of systems of knowledge that either foster exploitation and oppression or contribute to a praxis and vision of emancipation and liberation. Hence, a politics of meaning must make visible the contesting political interests and theoretical frameworks that determine the articulations of malestream and feminist Jesus research.

The sociopolitical context in which feminist theology as well as malestream Jesus research take place is constituted by the resurgence of the religious Right around the world, claiming the power to name and to define the true nature of religion.[4] Right-wing, well-financed think tanks are supported by reactionary political and financial institutions that seek to defend patriarchal capitalism.[5] The interconnection between religious antidemocratic arguments and the debate with regard to wo/men's[6] place and role is not accidental or of merely intratheological significance. In the past decade or so, right-wing movements around the globe have insisted on the figuration of emancipated wo/men as signifiers of Western decadence or of modern atheistic secularism, and they have presented masculine power as the expression of divine power.[7]

In this context of struggle, the production and proliferation of Jesus books for popular consumption by malestream biblical and theological studies seem to function as the reverse side of the fundamentalist literalist coin. In and through a literalist, dogmatic reading, fundamentalist christologies seek to "fix" the pluriform expressions of Christian scriptures and traditions and to consolidate the variegated texts and ambiguous metaphors of Jesus Christ into a definite, single discourse of meaning.

In response to such literalist readings, "liberal" scholarship insists on its scientific character, stressing its objectivity and detachment from all theological interests. Jesus books often reassert historical positivism in order to shore up the scholarly authority and universal truth of their research and portrayal of Jesus.[8] Hence the proliferation of "new" Jesus books does not undermine and undo but rather reinforces the literalist desire of religious fundamentalists for an "accurate," reliable biography of Jesus.

The refusal of malestream scholarship to reflect on its own ideological or theological interests and its restoration of historical positivism[9] corresponds to political conservatism. Its emphasis on the *realia* of history[10] serves to promote scientific fundamentalism, since the "newest search" generally does not acknowledge that historians select and interpret archaeological artifacts and textual evidence, and that they then incorporate these materials into a scientific model and narrative framework of meaning.[11]

The present proliferation of historical Jesus books and articles proves that the judgment of Albert Schweitzer is correct after all: scholars and writers inescapably fashion the image of Jesus in their own image and likeness. At best, we can glimpse the historical shadow of Jesus, but how we develop "his picture" will always depend on the lens we use, that is, what kind of reconstructive model we adopt. This holds true also for the earliest portrayals of Jesus in the canonical and extracanonical Christian literature. Any presentation of Jesus—scientific or otherwise—must therefore own that it is a "reconstruction" in order to open up its historical models or patterns to critical inquiry and public scrutiny.

Reconstructive models must be scrutinized not only as to how much they can account for our textual and archaeological information on the Jesus of history and his sociopolitical contexts but also as to how much they are able to inquire into the rhetorical interest and theological functions of the production of historical knowledge about Jesus. Moreover, the ethics of interpretation[12] requires that such reconstructive models be tested as to whether they reinscribe mind-sets of discrimination and exclusion. For not just hegemonic but even feminist Jesus studies have reinscribed both anti-Judaism and white racism.

First: The Jewish theologian Judith Plaskow has again and again pointed to such anti-Jewish inscription in malestream[13] and feminist Jesus research:

I find it especially disturbing, therefore, that the tendency to define Jesus as unique over and against Judaism remains even in feminists who do not make use of the Jesus-was-a-feminist-argument, who are quite aware of Christian anti-Judaism, who are freely critical of Christian sources, and who have gone very far in deconstructing notions of Jesus' divinity. . . . It seems as if the feminist struggle with patriarchal christologies itself . . . leads back into the trap of Christian anti-Judaism. . . . Can Christians value Jesus if he was just a Jew who chose to emphasize certain ideas and values in the Jewish tradition but did not invent or have a monopoly on them?[14]

The obstinate persistence of veiled or explicit anti-Judaism in Christian arguments for the liberatory uniqueness of Jesus raises two sets of epistemological questions: the first is *historical,* the second *theological* or ideological. The first set of questions asks not only *what* we can know historically about first-century Judaism and the relations between Jesus and wo/men but also *how* we know what we know, *who* has produced this knowledge, and *to what ends.* The second set of questions explores what kind of theological interests compel Christian anti-Jewish reconstructions of the historical Jesus.

Second: The African American theologian Jacquelyn Grant[15] has criticized "white" feminist christological discourses as also tainted by racism. She distinguishes between biblical or evangelical feminists, feminist liberation theologians, and rejectionist feminists who repudiate biblical tradition and faith. Grant argues that all three directions in feminist theology adopt a white racist frame of reference, both insofar as they universalize the experience of white wo/men in articulating feminist christology and insofar as they do not take the experience of wo/men of color or poor wo/men into account. Although liberation theologians such as Letty Russell, Carter Heyward, and Rosemary Radford Ruether analyze racism and classism, in Grant's judgment they nevertheless remain caught up in the dualistic gender framework of malestream scholarship. Grant summarizes the position of Russell and Ruether as follows:

The historical Jesus was a man, but men do not have a monopoly upon Christ, and Eve was a woman but women do not have a monopoly on sin. For 'Christ is not necessarily male, nor is the redeemed community only women, but new humanity, female and male'. . . . The maleness of Jesus is superseded by the Christness of Jesus. Both Russell and Ruether argue that the redemptive work of Jesus moves us toward the new humanity which is in Jesus Christ. But whereas Russell still holds to the unique Lordship of Jesus, Ruether raises the possibility that this Christ can be conceived in nontraditional ways,—as in sister.[16]

I am interested here not in assessing whether or not Grant's reading is correct but rather in highlighting its methodological implications for feminist theology. Grant formulates two important criteria for the evaluation of feminist christological arguments. First, she insists that all theoretical frameworks of white feminist christology must be scrutinized as to whether they employ a one-dimensional gender analysis or whether they develop a multisystemic analysis of sexism, racism, and class exploitation. Second, Grant argues that feminist christology must emerge from the experience and situation of the least, because "Jesus located the Christ with the outcast."[17] Therefore, she insists that the experience of black wo/men must become the second norm against which the limitations of feminist theological perspectives must be judged.

Like other two-thirds-world wo/men before her, Grant challenges white European and American feminists to abandon their dualistic gender analysis. Responding to this challenge, I have developed an analytic of kyriarchy conceptualized as an interstructured pyramid of multiplicative oppressions. The neologism *kyriarchy*, which connotes the rule and domination of the lord/master/father/husband, is a more apt analytical tool than *patriarchy*,[18] which in white feminist theory has been understood as the domination of all men over all wo/men equally. Whether one looks at feudal, late capitalist, monarchical, democratic, national, or global systemic forms of kyriarchy, its structures of domination and exploitation always are determined by male elites and affect different wo/men differently.

A critical analysis of systemic kyriarchy allows one to trace not only the historical roots of domination and exploitation but also its ideological mystifications, such as anti-Judaism and white supremacy. The ideological mystification of Western systems of domination is already found in classical philosophy. Greco-Roman philosophy has legitimated elite male domination and the subordination of marginalized wo/men. This ideological argument has found its way into the Christian canon in the form of the so-called neo-Aristotelian household-code texts.[19] Their claim to divine revelation has determined subsequent Christian theology and practice decisively. Although this ideological-religious legitimization of the Western system of domination has continued throughout Christian history, it has never been total; alternative voices and egalitarian visions advocating a domination-free world and church have also been codified in Hebrew and Christian scriptures.

Such a systemic analysis of kyriarchy provides a different hermeneutical lens for feminist Jesus studies. It does not compel one to position feminist Jesus research theoretically within the patriarchal sex-gender system but rather allows one to situate it within wo/men's historical-religious experience of domination and their feminist struggles for liberation. Whether black or white, rich or poor, lesbian or married, Christian wo/men until very recently have been excluded from church leadership and have been silenced and marginalized by law and custom. Although all wo/men have been marginalized and silenced by kyriarchal theology, such marginalization and exploitation have affected wo/men differently depending on their social location within the kyriarchal pyramid.[20]

The full oppressive power of kyriarchy is manifested in the lives and struggles of the poorest and most oppressed wo/men, who live on the bottom of the kyriarchal pyramid. The feminist movement has not succeeded as long as the oppression of wo/men who suffer under multiple, interlocking exploitative structures continues. Although wo/men may experience moments of liberation in the struggles for both survival in and transformation of kyriarchal structures, no wo/man is free and liberated unless all wo/men are full citizens in society and church.

In contrast to Jacqueline Grant, I do not seek, however, to derive the criterion and norm of feminist Christian theology from the option of the historical Jesus for the poor and the outcast. Being poor and outcast does not, as such, manifest G*d's[21] grace and liberation. Rather, I seek to ground this norm in the emancipatory historical struggles for the transformation of kyriarchal relations of domination. Scripture, tradition, theology, and Jesus research are to be critically analyzed and tested as to their ideological-political functions in legitimating or subverting multiplicative kyriarchal structures of domination. They are to be judged on whether and how much they articulate Christian identity and faith in terms of kyriarchal dehumanization or in terms of emancipatory subversion.

Such a struggle-oriented feminist hermeneutical perspective has been articulated already in the last century, although its theoretical implications as yet have not been fully reflected or explicated theoretically. I think here of the often-quoted speech of Sojourner Truth, an African American wo/man and a former slave who could not read or write. Sojourner Truth gave this speech in 1852 at a mostly European American suffrage gathering in Akron, Ohio. It owes its historical transmission to the collaboration between a black and a white wo/man.[22] Since I do not want to reduce Sojourner Truth's very particular experience and its paradigmatic articulation to mere abstraction, I quote it here extensively:

> *That man over there say*
>   *a woman needs to be helped into carriages*
> *and lifted over ditches*
>   *and to have the best places everywhere.*
> *Nobody ever helped me into carriages*
>   *or over mud puddles*
>   *or gives me best place . . .*
> *And ain't I a woman?*
>   *Look at me!*
> *Look at my arm!*
>   *I have plowed and planted*
> *and gathered into barns*
>   *and no man could head me . . .*

And ain't I a woman?
  I could work as much
and eat as much as a man—
     when I could get it—
and bear the lash as well
     and ain't I a woman?
I have born 13 children
     and seen most all sold into slavery
and when I cried out a mother's grief
     none but Jesus heard me . . .
and ain't I a woman?
     That little man in black there say
a woman can't have as much rights as a man
     cause Christ wasn't a woman
Where did your Christ come from?
     From God and a woman!
Man had nothing to do with him!
     If the first woman God ever made
was strong enough to turn the world
     upside down all alone
together women ought to be able to turn it
     right side up again.[23]

My theoretical elaboration of this statement is not so much interested in the answer to "Ain't I a woman?" but in its methodological implications for feminist Jesus studies and christology. This address contains several hermeneutical insights that are important. In distinction from the feminist critique of christology put forward by Elizabeth Cady Stanton, for instance, Sojourner Truth does not apply her critique directly to the doctrinal christological system but to those who have articulated it. She points to the political interests of those who are the theoreticians not only of the myth of "true womanhood" but also of kyriarchal christology. She confronts them with her own concrete experience of slavery. Confronted with the experiences of a slave, the myth of the "eternal feminine" and its concomitant sex-gender theology turns out to proclaim the ideal of the "white lady" that is promulgated by white, elite, educated men. In other words, I do not argue that the question "Ain't I a woman?" serves to elicit white feminist identification with Sojourner Truth, as the productive misreading of Karen Trimble Alliaume claims.[24] Rather, I argue that it unmasks the ideology of elite white femininity.

The myth of true womanhood[25] promotes not only sexist but also cultural, racist, and classist interests. This Western ideological construct of femininity cannot be fully recognized within the framework of gender theory but only within a complex theory of interlocking kyriarchal structures. The experience of the former slave Sojourner Truth underscores that the theoretical construction of gender difference is not primarily anthropological but social. It serves to maintain kyriarchal relations of domination. Consequently, Sojourner Truth sees christology as enmeshed in the societal and ecclesial web of kyriarchal structures. She explicates the interconnection between the ideology of the "white lady" and christology by pointing out that elite clergymen ("That man over there say"; "that little man in black there say") continue to produce such kyriarchal theology in order to maintain the status quo ("woman can't have as much rights as a man / cause Christ wasn't a woman"). Over against such kyriarchal christological claims, Sojourner Truth appeals to her own experience as a hardworking slave and mother whose children were sold into bondage. Her experience of exploitation and domination compels her to formulate the following two arguments, and she does so with reference to the Bible, which she herself could not read because of kyriarchal prohibitions.

On the one hand, Sojourner Truth points out that the incarnation of Christ must be correctly understood as the collaboration of G*d and a wo/man. On the other hand, she stresses that redemption from sinful structures can be experienced only when wo/men come together for turning the world "right side up again." Truth accepts the claim of kyriarchal theology and traditional doctrine that wo/man caused original sin, but she draws a different conclusion from it. Exactly because a wo/man was implicated in and collaborated in the original fall, wo/men cannot continue to understand themselves as innocent victims but must get together to make right the perversion of the world that is wrought by oppression and domination. Taken together, both arguments articulate a theological norm that locates G*d in wo/men's struggles for "mending creation"—to use a focal expression of Letty Russell.[26]

Like white suffragists, Sojourner Truth sees incarnation and redemption as intrinsic elements of doctrinal christology that perpetrate the marginality and oppression of wo/men. However, she understands the christological system as intertwined with the cultural system of essential or natural gender difference. She understands wo/men not simply as oppositional "others" of men or as innocent victims who can disassociate themselves from the responsibility for kyriarchy. Rather, she sees wo/men as deeply implicated in generating and sustaining the kyriarchal perversion of the world.

In short, Sojourner Truth does not advocate a new feminist christological principle or system as normative for Christian experience and identity, nor does she appeal to the historical Jesus. Rather, by pointing to her own concrete experiences of dehumanization, she unmasks kyriarchal christology as a rhetorical construction of male clerics. However, it is not her personal spiritual experience of Jesus but her call for wo/men to get together in order to turn the world "right side up again" that provides the theoretical breakthrough that I have in mind. Neither Sojourner herself nor even Jesus is the locus of liberation and salvation but rather wo/men's movements for change and transformation. In my view, her speech pioneers a theological approach that locates G*d, Christ, and the possibility of salvation in a wo/men's movement concerned with justice and well-being for all.

By invoking this theological argument of Sojourner Truth, I do not want to canonize her or uncritically subscribe to her point of view. Nor do I suggest that feminists who call themselves Christians must express their liberation experience in similar terms. Nor do I want to use Sojourner as a Jesus figure. I also do not celebrate her as an *academic* theologian, as Karen Trimble Alliaume[27] suggests. Rather, I want to lift her up as a *feminist* theologian who, like many wo/men, does theology from her own daily experience of struggle. Hence I do not see her either as a spokeswo/man for the least of the oppressed or as representing them, nor as their or white feminists' surrogate. Rather, I see her as an Africana feminist[28] theologian who calls on every wo/man who is implicated in structures of oppression to get together with other wo/men for righting the wrongs. Since Sojourner's call is not limited to a specific group of wo/men but nevertheless is rooted in her particular experience of oppression, it can claim universal significance.

Rather than reinterpret the historical maleness of Jesus in humanist,[29] trickster,[30] transvestite,[31] or feminine terms, I have argued, feminist theology must join Sojourner Truth in insisting on the wo/men's movement for change as the space where G*d and liberation are to be located. Hence, feminist theology must reject the hegemonic cultural gender framework of the scientific quests for the Jesus of history, as well as the belief that Christian identity must remain contingent on the scientific reconstructions and dogmatic constructions of the divine maleness of Jesus. This is not to say, however, that Christian feminist scholars must eschew all historical reconstruction of their own theological and historical roots.

My work has sought to spell out an alternative reconstructive model to that of gender. This model seeks not only to address the question raised by decades of historical Jesus research but also to make explicit its own hermeneutical perspective and theological framework. Popular and scholarly discussions of the *topos* "Jesus and wo/men"[32] tend to adopt the objectivist, value-detached postures of historical criticism and the androcentric categories of the social sciences in order to justify the kyriarchal cultural or ecclesial status quo that marginalizes or excludes wo/men. Christian feminist assertions about "Jesus and wo/men," in turn, are often seen as apologetic attempts to challenge the dominant positivist historical and theological constructions of Jesus and his movements. Yet such arguments collaborate with hegemonic kyriarchal ones when, on exegetical grounds, they seek to show that Jesus was the exception from the patriarchal rule.

Although such malestream and feminist apologetic arguments today are generally formulated in historical terms, they nevertheless remain caught up in the doctrinal paradigm of interpretation that utilizes the scriptures as a storehouse of proof-texts for furthering kyriarchal Christian identity and an exclusivist historical imagination. Rather than begin with a kyriarchal model of historical reconstruction that assumes wo/men's marginality or absence as historical agents, a critical feminist historical reconstructive model, as I have developed it, begins with the assumption of wo/men's presence and agency, rather than with the kyriarchal preconstructed discourse of their marginality and victimization.[33]

Such a contention shifts the "burden of proof" to malestream biblical scholarship, which assumes that Jewish wo/men were *not* active and present in the development of early Christian life and theology. Only the presumption of wo/men's—slaves and freeborn, rich and poor, black and white—historical and theological agency, I argue, will allow us to read the slippages, ambiguities, gaps, and silences of androcentric (that is, grammatically masculine) texts[34] not simply as properties of language and text but as the inscribed symptoms[35] of historical struggles.

Feminist christological reconstruction must not limit itself to an investigation of texts about wo/men and Jesus or simply focus on gender relations, I have argued. Rather, it must conceptualize early Judaism and early Christianity in such a way that it can make marginalized wo/men visible as central agents who have shaped Jewish and Christian history and religion. This requires a reconsideration of the theological framework that—as Rosemary Radford Ruether has put it—has produced Christian anti-Judaism as the left hand and divine masculinism as the right hand of christology. In short, only an emancipatory feminist model of historical and theological reconstruction can do justice both to our common struggles for transforming religious kyriarchy and to our particular historical struggles and differing religious identity formations.

Such a change of theoretical framework or hermeneutical "lens" makes it possible to understand Jesus and early Christian beginnings as shaped by the agency and leadership of Jewish, Greco-Roman, Asian, African, free and enslaved, rich and poor, elite and marginal wo/men. Those who hold the opposite view, for instance, that slave wo/men were not active shapers of early Christian life, would have to argue their point. If one shifts from a kyriarchal, preconstructed frame of reference to that of a discipleship of equals, one no longer can hold, for instance, that wo/men were not members of the communities that produced the hypothetical Sayings Source Q.[36] If one cannot show definitely that wo/men were not members of this early Christian Jewish group, so my argument goes, one needs to give the benefit of the doubt to the textual traces suggesting that they were. Rather than take the kyriocentric text at face value, one must unravel its politics of meaning.

The objection that this is a circular argument applies to all hermeneutical practices. For instance, social-scientific studies that presuppose the "precon-structed"[37] dualistic opposition of "honor and shame" as given "facts" of Mediterranean cultures will read early Christian texts "about wo/men" within this theoretically preconstructed kyriocentric frame of reference.[38] Their nar-ratives, however, appear to be more "realistic" and "objective" than feminist ones because kyriocentric discourses function as ideologies, that is, they mys-tify the "constructedness" of their account of reality. Therefore, such hege-monic narratives of how the world of early Christianity "really was" are considered to be "commonsense," "objective," "scientific" historical accounts, although they are as much a "construction" as feminist ones are. Undergirding this reconstructive model are four basic assumptions:

First, the assumption of anti-Judaism is contrary to a Christian feminist theology of liberation because such a historical assumption does not recognize that Jesus and his first followers were Jewish wo/men. They were *not Chris-tian* in our sense of the word. Rather, as Jewish Galilean wo/men they gath-ered together for common meals, theological reflection, and healing events. They did so because they had a "dream" and followed a vision of liberation for every wo/man in Israel.

Second, who Jesus was and what he did can be glimpsed *only* in the inter-pretations and memory of the Jesus movement, understood as a first-century Jewish movement. Therefore, the Jesus movement must not be separated methodologically from other messianic movements in first-century Judaism. Moreover, one must keep in mind that just as there was no unified early Chris-tianism, so also no "orthodox" singular Judaism existed yet in the first century C.E.[39] Orthodox Judaism, like orthodox Christianity, emerged only in subse-quent centuries.

Third, this emancipatory movement of Galilean Jewish wo/men must be seen as a part of the variegated *basileia* and *holiness* movements that in the first century sought for the "liberation" of Israel from imperial exploitation. The concrete political referent of these movements was the colonial occupation of Israel by the Romans. Hence, it is no accident that in this political context they invoked the covenant promise of Exodus 19:6. Some of them, such as the Pharisees or Essenes, stressed the notion of "priesthood and holy nation." Others, such as the apocalyptic prophetic movements—among them the Jesus movement—stressed the political notion of the *basileia* (empire/common-weal) of G*d as counterterm to the Roman Empire.

Fourth, the emerging, variegated, predominantly Galilean Jesus movement understood itself as a prophetic movement of divine Sophia-Wisdom.[40] That it named itself after Jesus, the Christ, was probably due to the conviction, which emerged after Jesus' execution, that he was the vindicated or resurrected One. This conviction, I have argued, had its base in the wo/men's tradition of the "empty tomb," which centered on the proclamation that "Jesus is *going ahead* of you to Galilee," the site where the antimonarchical prophetic traditions of the Northern Kingdom were still alive. This tradition manifests the self-understanding of the inner-Jewish, Galilean *basileia* of G*d movement as an ongoing and inclusive movement of prophets and messengers sent to Israel by divine Wisdom. The *basileia* movement is thus a Wisdom-Sophia movement in which Jesus is *primus inter pares*, first among equals.

Such an egalitarian reconstructive model, I submit, is able to place the beginnings of the Galilean prophetic-wisdom *basileia* movement within a broader, universalizing historical frame of reference. This frame allows one to trace the tensions and struggles between emancipatory understandings and movements in antiquity inspired by the democratic logic of equality, on the one hand, and the dominant kyriarchal structures of society and religion, on the other.

Ancient movements of emancipatory struggle against kyriarchal relations of exploitation do not begin with the Jesus movement. Rather, they have a long history in Greek, Roman, Asian, and Jewish cultures.[41] The emancipatory struggles of biblical wo/men must be seen within the wider context of cultural/political/religious struggles. Such a historical model of emancipatory struggle sees the Jesus of history and the movement that has kept alive his memory not over and against Judaism but over and against kyriarchal structures of domination in antiquity.

This reconstructive frame of reference, I submit, is able to conceptualize the emergent Jesus movement and its diverse articulations as participating in popular movements of cultural, political, and religious resistance. To variegate Bultmann's well-known scholarly dictum: Jesus did not just rise into the kerygma as "dangerous memory." Rather, he is "going ahead" in the emancipatory struggles for a world of justice, liberation, and freedom from kyriarchal oppression. He is "going ahead" in wo/men's struggles to "mend the world."

Yet to speak about the Jesus movement as an inner-Jewish renewal movement, as I have done in *In Memory of Her*, still provokes several misunderstandings between Jews and Christians. Jacob Neusner has rightly pointed out that the notion of "renewal" still carries traces of supersessionism, insofar as it suggests that Christianity is a "better" form of Judaism. In other words, the notion of a reform movement still can be made to fit into the hegemonic Christian construct of the *Judeo-Christian* tradition that posits a supersessionist continuity between Judaism and Christianity.[42] Only if one explicitly acknowledges that Judaism and Christianity are two different religions that have their roots in the Hebrew Bible and in the pluriform religious matrix of first-century Israel can one avoid reading "renewal movement" in a supersessionist fashion. As Alan Segal has aptly put it, early Judaism and Christianism are Rebecca's children, twin siblings of the same mother.[43]

Moreover, to speak about the Jesus movement as an inner-Jewish renewal movement of the first century can be, and has been, further misread as implying that the Jesus movement was the *only* reform movement at the time, and that Jewish or Greek wo/men who did not join this movement suffered from a "false consciousness."[44] Furthermore, if read in a preconstructed frame of meaning that maintains the uniqueness of Jesus, the expression "renewal movement" suggests not only Christian particularity and exceptionality but also superiority. For that reason, one cannot stress enough that the Jesus movement must be understood as *one among several prophetic movements* of Jewish wo/men who struggled for the liberation of Israel.

As a result, I have replaced the notion of "renewal movement" with the concept of the Jesus movement as an *emancipatory movement.* The central symbol of this movement, the *basileia* of G*d,[45] expresses a Jewish religious-political vision that spells freedom from domination and is common to all the different movements in first-century Israel. It is difficult to translate the Greek term *basileia* adequately, because it can mean kingdom, kingly realm, domain, or empire, or it can be rendered as monarchy, kingly rule, sovereignty, dominion, or reign. In any case, it has not only monarchical but also masculinist overtones.

According to Gustav Dalmann, the Hebrew equivalent of *malkuth* when applied to G*d always means kingly rule and never has the territorial sense of kingdom. Following him, most exegetes translate *basileia* with "kingly reign" and understand it as G*d's all-overpowering initiative and sovereign ruling. Moreover, most reviews of scholarship on the meaning of the expression "*basileia* of G*d" do not even discuss its political significance in a context where people must have thought of the Roman Empire when they heard the word.

To lift the political meaning of *basileia* into consciousness, I suggest that it is best translated with words such as *empire, domain* or *commonweal.* Such renderings of the word *basileia* underscore linguistically the oppositional character of the empire/commonweal of G*d to that of the Roman Empire. Since such translation is generally not understood in an oppositional sense, however, but rather as ascribing to G*d imperial, monarchical power, I have tended *not* to translate the Greek word *basileia* but to use it as a tensive symbol that evokes a whole range of theological meanings and at the same time seeks to foster a critical awareness of their ambiguity. The translation of the term with "kin-dom" that has been suggested by Ada María Isasi-Díaz also loses the political overtones of *basileia.* Such a symbolic rendering of the term seeks to bring to the fore its political impact and eschatological significance in the first century C.E., at the same time problematizing its kyriarchal politics of meaning.

Exegetes agree that the Roman form of imperial domination signified by the term *basileia* determined the world and experience of all Jewish movements in the first century, including that which named itself after Jesus. Jesus and his first followers, wo/men and men, sought for the emancipation and well-being of Israel as the people of G*d, a kingdom of priests and a holy nation (Exod. 19:6). They announced the *basileia* (commonweal/empire) of G*d as an alternative to that of Rome.

The *basileia* of G*d is a *tensive* religious symbol,[46] not only of ancestral range, proclaiming G*d's power of creation and salvation. This term was also a political symbol that appealed to the oppositional imagination of people victimized by the Roman imperial system. It envisions an alternative world free of hunger, poverty, and domination. This "envisioned" world is already anticipated in the inclusive table community, in the healing and liberating practices, as well as in the domination-free kinship community of the Jesus movement, which found many followers among the poor, the despised, the ill and possessed, the outcasts, prostitutes, and sinners.[47]

The story of the Jesus movement as emancipatory *basileia* of G*d movement is told in different ways in the canonical and extracanonical Gospel accounts. These accounts have undergone a lengthy process of rhetorical transmission and theological edition. The Gospel writers were concerned not with antiquarian historical transcription but with interpretive remembrance and rhetorical persuasion. They did not simply want to write down what Jesus said and did. Rather, they utilized the Jesus traditions that were shaped by Jesus' first followers, wo/men and men, for their own rhetorical interests and molded them in light of the political-theological debates of their own day. What we can learn from the rhetorical process of gospel transmission and redaction is that Jesus as we still can know him must be "re-membered," contextualized, discussed, interpreted, questioned, or rejected within not only an intertheological and interfaith but also political-cultural debate.

However, one must be careful not to construe the Jesus movement as free from conflict and kyriarchal tendencies, lest in so doing one idealizes it as the very "other" and positive counterpart of Judaism understood negatively. From the very beginnings of the Jesus movement, differences, divisions, and conflicts existed, as the variegated, if not contradictory, articulations of the extant Gospels indicate. For instance, the varicolored *basileia* sayings tradition that surfaces in Mark 10:42–45 and 9:33–37 par. is an antikyriarchal rhetorical tradition that contrasts the political structures of domination with those required among the disciples.[48] Structures of domination should not be tolerated in the discipleship of equals, but those of the disciples who would be great and would be first must become slaves and servants[49] of all. While this tradition advocates nonkyriarchal relationships in the discipleship of equals, its grammatical imperative simultaneously documents that such relationships were not lived by everyone. Especially, the would-be "great" and "first" seem to have been tempted to reassert kyriarchal social and religious status positions. The argument of the Syrophoenician wo/man, which has given my book *But She Said* its name, provides another example for such debates, since this story criticizes the ethnic bias of Jesus himself.

One also must not overlook that all four Gospel accounts reflect the controversies with and separation anxieties from hegemonic forms of Judaism. Consequently, they all reinscribe Christian identity as standing in conflict with Judaism. A good example of this kyriocentric process of anti-Jewish and anti-wo/man inscription can be found when one traces the transmission history of the story about the wo/man who anointed Jesus as the Christ. The Gospel of Mark places this story at the beginning of the narrative about Jesus' execution and resurrection.[50] Here, Mark probably takes up a traditional story that knows of a wo/man anointing Jesus' head and thereby naming him as the Christ, the anointed One.[51] A revelatory word of Jesus links her prophetic sign-action with the proclamation of the gospel in the whole world.[52] The community that retells this story after Jesus' execution knows that Jesus is no longer in their midst. They no longer "have" Jesus with them.

Either in the course of the transmission of this story or at the editorial stage, three kyriocentric interpretations of the wo/man's prophetic sign-action are introduced. First, the objection and debate among the male disciples introduces a kyriarchal understanding that sees "the poor" no longer as constitutive members of the community but as "the others," as people who deserve alms. The second interpretation construes the unnamed wo/man's sign-action in feminine kyriocentric terms: she does what wo/men are supposed to do, prepare the bodies of the dead for burial.[53] Finally, the third interpretation reframes the story as an ideo-story or example story that counterposes the action of the wo/man to that of Judas, the betrayer of Jesus.[54]

Insofar as the wo/man disciple remains unnamed, whereas the male disciple who betrays Jesus is named Judas, the text evokes an androcentric response that, contrary to the word of Jesus, does not comprehend the significance of the wo/man's prophetic naming. It also elicits an anti-Jewish response by underscoring that the name of the betrayer is Judas, a response that is intensified in the course of the passion narrative. Thus we still can trace the Gospels' anti-Jewish rhetoric in the reinterpretations of the anointing story, which was potentially a politically dangerous story. This depoliticizing rhetoric not only has engendered anti-Jewish interpretations of Jesus' suffering and execution but also forged Christian political adaptation to Roman imperial structures that opened the door to the co-optation of the gospel in the interest of domination.

Since the process of the kyriarchal reinterpretation of the story in the Gospels has produced the "preconstructed," by now commonsense, kyriocentric frame of meaning that marginalizes wo/men and vilifies Jews, it is necessary to dislodge our readings from such a preconstructed frame of reference and to reconfigure the Christian testament discourses about Jesus. Constructing the Jesus movement as one among many *emancipatory movements* in the first century, as I have argued here and elsewhere, provides such a different historical frame of reference. It allows for a Christian self-understanding that neither is articulated over against Judaism nor remains intertwined with theological masculinism. Such a christological rereading does not need to relinquish the quest for its historical Jewish roots or end in Christian supremacy and exclusivism. It does not tie Christian self-identity to its previous stages of formation and their sociocultural contexts but remains obligated to the messianic *basileia* vision of G*d's alternative world of justice and salvation.

In sum, a feminist Christian identity is to be articulated again and again in the emancipatory struggles for the vision of G*d's *basileia*, which spells well-being and freedom for all in the global village. Similarly, a Jewish feminist identity is to be articulated within the emancipatory struggles for the "restoration of the world," of *tikkun olam*[55] as the social, political, and religious transformation of kyriarchal structures of injustice and domination. The one G*d of Jews, Christians, and Muslims today still calls wo/men of faith to engage in the prophetic-messianic vision of justice, freedom, love, and salvation that has inspired our historical predecessors in their religious-political struggles for a more just world.

NOTES

1. For extensive documentation, see my book *Jesus: Miriam's Child and Sophia's Prophet* (New York: Continuum, 1994).
2. I use this term in a descriptive way to indicate that scripture, tradition, church, and society have been and still are determined and dominated by elite men.
3. To mention just a few references: Marcus J. Borg, *Jesus in Contemporary Scholarship* (Valley Forge, Pa.: Trinity Press International, 1994); idem, "Portraits of Jesus in Contemporary American Scholarship," *Harvard Theological Review* 84, 1 (1991): 1–22; James H. Charlesworth, "Annotated Bibliography," in James H. Charlesworth, ed., *Jesus' Jewishness: Exploring the Place of Jesus within Early Judaism* (New York: Crossroad/The American Interfaith Institute, 1991); John F. O'Grady, "The Present State of Christology," *Chicago Studies* 32, 1 (April 1993): 77–91; Werner G. Kümmel, "Jesusforschung seit 1981," *Theologische Rundschau* N.F. 53 (1988): 229–249 and 54 (1989): 1–53; Dieter Georgi, "The Interest in Life of Jesus Theology as a Paradigm for the Social History of Biblical Criticism" *Harvard Theological Review* 85, 1 (1992): 51–83; Daniel Korsch, "Neue Jesusliteratur," *Bibel und Kirche* 48 (1993): 40–44; Ferdinand Hahn, "Umstrittenes Jesusbild?" *Münchener Theologische Zeitschrift* 44 (1993): 95–107; Jeffrey Carlson and Robert A. Ludwig, eds., *Jesus and Faith: A Conversation on the Work of John Dominic Crossan, Author of the Historical Jesus* (Maryknoll, N.Y.: Orbis Books, 1994); Luke T. Johnson, *The Real Jesus: The Misguided Quest for the Historical Jesus and the Truth of the Traditional Gospels* (San Francisco: Harper & Row, 1966); Robert W. Funk, *Honest to Jesus: Jesus for a New Millennium* (San Francisco: HarperCollins, 1996); see also my article "Jesus and the Politics of Interpretation," *Harvard Theological Review* 90, 4 (1997): 343–58.

4. See the varied contributions in Hans Küng and Jürgen Moltmann, eds., *Fundamentalism as an Ecumenical Challenge* (Concilium; London: SCM Press, 1992).
5. For an excellent critical analysis of the involvement of religion in this global struggle, see especially the work of the late Penny Lernoux, *Cry of the People* (New York: Penguin Books, 1982); idem, *In Banks We Trust* (New York: Penguin Books, 1986); and her last book before her untimely death, *People of God: The Struggle for World Catholicism* (New York: Penguin Books, 1989); Robert B. Reich, *The Work of Nations* (New York: Vintage Books, 1992); Joan Smith, "The Creation of the World We Know: The World-Economy and the Re-Creation of Gendered Identities," in Valentine M. Moghadam, ed., *Identity Politics and Women: Cultural Reassertions and Feminisms in International Perspective* (Boulder, Colo.: Westview Press, 1994), 27–41; see also Diana L. Eck, *Encountering God: A Spiritual Journey from Bozeman to Banaras* (Boston: Beacon Press, 1993), 176, who writes: "A new wave of exclusivism is cresting around the world today. Expressed in social and political life, exclusivism becomes ethnic or religious chauvinism, described in South Asia as communalism. . . . As we have observed, identity-based politics is on the rise because it is found to be a successful way of arousing political energy."
6. For the problematic meaning of the term *woman/women*, see Denise Riley, *"Am I That Name": Feminism and the Category of Women in History* (Minneapolis: University of Minnesota Press, 1988); Judith Butler, *Gender Trouble: Feminism and the Subversion of Identity* (New York: Routledge & Kegan Paul, 1990). My way of writing *wo/men* seeks to underscore not only the ambiguous character of the term *wo/man* or *wo/men* but also to retain the expression *wo/men* as a political category. Since this designation is often read as referring to white women only, my unorthodox writing of the term seeks to draw to the attention of readers that those kyriarchal structures that determine wo/men's lives and status also impact that of men of subordinated race, classes, countries, and religions, albeit in different ways. The expression *wo/men* must therefore be understood as inclusive rather than as an exclusive, universalized gender term.
7. See especially the declaration of the Division for the Advancement of Women on "International Standards of Equality and Religious Freedom: Implications for the Status of Women," in Moghadam, ed., *Identity Politics and Women*, 425–38; Rebecca E. Klatch, "Women of the New Right in the United States: Family, Feminism, and Politics," in Moghadam, ed., *Identity Politics and Women*, 367–88; Most of the contributions in Moghadam's edited book are on women and Islam in different parts of the world. However, see Sucheta Mazumdar, "Moving Away from a Secular Vision? Women, Nation, and the Cultural Construction of Hindu India," in Moghadam, ed., *Identity Politics and Women*, 243–73; and Radha Kumar, "Identity Politics and the Contemporary Indian Feminist Movement," in Moghadam, ed., *Identity Politics and Women*, 274–92.
8. See the critical review by N. T. Wright, "Taking the Text with Her Pleasure: A Post-Post-Modernist Response to J. Dominic Crossan, The Historical Jesus: The Life of a Mediterranean Jewish Peasant" (Edinburgh: T. & T. Clark; San Francisco: HarperCollins, 1991). "With Apologies to A. A. Milne, St. Paul and James Joyce," *Theology* 96, 112 (1993): 303–10, from the perspective of a critical realistic reading. However, it is regrettable that Wright's critical essay resorts to sexist "figuration."
9. See my critique of positivism in biblical studies in "Text and Reality—Reality as Text: The Problem of a Feminist Social and Historical Reconstruction on the Ba-

sis of Texts," *Studia Theologica* 43 (1989): 19–34; and in *But She Said: Feminist Practices of Biblical Interpretation* (Boston: Beacon Press, 1992), 79–101.

10. James H. Charlesworth, ed., *Jews and Christians: Exploring the Past, Present and Future* (New York: Crossroad, 1990).

11. Cf. James H. Charlesworth, "From Barren Mazes to Gentle Rappings: The Emergence of Jesus Research," *Princeton Seminary Bulletin* 7, 3 (1986): 221–30, with annotated bibliography.

12. Elisabeth Schüssler Fiorenza, "The Ethics of Interpretation: Decentering Biblical Scholarship," SBL presidential address," *Journal of Biblical Literature* 107 (1988): 3–17.

13. For instance, Luke T. Johnson, "The New Testament's Anti-Jewish Slander and the Conventions of Ancient Polemic," *Journal of Biblical Literature* 108, 3 (1989): 419–41, cavalierly solves the problem of anti-Judaism in the Christian testament by pointing out that such slanderous behavior was common in the first century. He seems not to have read anything I have written when he characterizes my approach as liberationist censorship, "which is frequently based on the premise that texts should reflect our liberated self-understanding and practice. If they offend our sensibilities, they are dispensable" (421). In a footnote (n. 4) he credits Rosemary Radford Ruether as having defined the "basic liberationist approach" and me for having extensively developed it in *In Memory of Her: A Feminist Theological Reconstruction of Christian Origins* (New York: Crossroad, 1983). He probably would justify such a sloppy but politically expedient scholarly procedure, which still seems to be widespread in biblical studies today!

14. Judith Plaskow, "Feminist Anti-Judaism and the Christian God," *Journal of Feminist Studies in Religion* 7, 2 (1991): 106. For her early critique see Judith Plaskow, "Christian Feminism and Anti-Judaism," *Cross Currents* 33 (1978): 306–9; for her most recent contribution, see her "Anti-Judaism in Feminist Christian Interpretation," in Elisabeth Schüssler Fiorenza, ed., *Searching the Scriptures: A Feminist Introduction*, vol. 1 (New York: Crossroad, 1993), 117–29, esp. 118. See also Susannah Heschel, "Jüdisch-feministische Theologie und Antijudaismus in christlich-feministischer Theologie," in Leonore Siegele Wenschkewitz, ed., *Verdrängte Vergangenheit, die uns bedrängt feministische Theologie in der Verantwortung für die Geschichte* (Munich: Kaiser, 1998), 54–103; and Susannah Heschel, "Anti-Judaism in Christian Feminist Theology," *Tikkun* 5, 3 (1990): 26–28.

15. Jacquelyn Grant, *White Women's Christ and Black Women's Jesus* (Atlanta: Scholars Press, 1989); see also Kelly Brown Douglas, *The Black Christ* (Maryknoll, N.Y.: Orbis Books, 1994); and Delores Williams, *Sisters in the Wilderness: The Challenge of Womanist God-Talk* (Maryknoll, N.Y.: Orbis Books, 1993).

16. Grant, *White Women's Christ*, 144

17. Ibid., 6

18. *Patriarchy* in the "narrow sense" is best understood as "father right and father might." However, this translation overlooks that the father as the head of household was, in antiquity, also lord, master, and husband. Consequently, *patriarchy/patriarchal* connotes a complex system of subordination and domination. Moreover, the patriarchal system of the household also was the paradigm for the order of society and state. For a review of the common feminist understanding of patriarchy, see V. Beechey, "On Patriarchy," *Feminist Review* 3 (1979): 66–82; G. Lerner, *The Creation of Patriarchy* (New York: Oxford University Press, 1986), 231–41; C. Schaumberger, "Patriarchat als feministischer Begriff," in *Wörterbuch der feministischen Theologie* (Gütersloh: Gerd Mohn, 1991), 321–23. For Roman

patriarchal structures, see W. K. Lacey, "Patria Potestas," in Beryl Rawson, ed., *The Family in Ancient Rome: New Perspectives* (Ithaca, N.Y.: Cornell University Press, 1986), 121–44.

19. Cf. Klaus Thraede, "Zum historischen Hintergrund der 'Haustafeln' des Neuen Testaments," in *Pietas: Festschrift B. Kötting* (Münster: Aschendorff, 1980), 359–68; D. Lührmann, "Neutestamentliche Haustafeln und antike Ökonomie," *New Testament Studies* 27 (1980/81): 83–97; D. Balch, *Let Wives Be Submissive: The Domestic Code in 1 Peter* (Chico, Calif.: Scholars Press, 1981); D. Balch, "Household Codes," in D. Aune, ed., *Greco-Roman Literature and the New Testament* (Atlanta: Scholars Press, 1988), 25–50; See also chapter 4 in Elizabeth Schüssler Fiorenza, *Bread Not Stone: The Challenge of Feminist Biblical Interpretation* (Boston: Beacon Press, 1985); and Clarice Martin, "The 'Haustafeln' (Household Codes) in African American Biblical Interpretation: 'Free Slaves' and 'Subordinate Women,'" in Cain Hope Felder, ed., *Stony the Road We Trod: African American Biblical Interpretation* (Minneapolis: Fortress Press, 1991), 206–31, for feminist/womanist discussion of and literature on the household-code texts; Susan Moller Okin, *Women in Western Political Thought* (Princeton, N.J.: Princeton University Press, 1989), 15–98; Elizabeth V. Spelman, *Inessential Woman: Problems of Exclusion in Feminist Thought* (Boston: Beacon Press, 1988), 19–56.

20. For a feminist discussion of the interplay between language and identity, see, for instance, the contributions in Joyce Penfield ed., *Women and Language in Transition* (Albany: State University of New York Press, 1987).

21. To mark the inadequacy of our language about G*d, I have adopted this writing of the word *G*d*. Because of the "naturalization" and commonsense character of G*d language, I do think it is theologically necessary to destabilize visibly our way of thinking and speaking about G*d.

22. In her Marion Thomson Wright Lecture, given on February 20, 1993, at Rutgers University, Nell Irvin Painter pointed out that Frances Dana Gage published this speech twelve years after the event, in 1864, as a response to Harriet Beecher Stowe's profile article "Sojourner Truth, the Libyan Sibyl," which had appeared in the *Atlantic Monthly*. See Nell Irvin Painter, "The Writing and Selling of Sojourner Truth," in her study packet *An Introduction to Black Women's Studies* (Princeton University, Fall 1993). For further discussion and bibliography, see Nell Painter, "Truth, Sojourner (c. 1799–1885)," in Darlene Clark Hine, ed., *Black Women in America: A Historical Encyclopedia* (Brooklyn, N.Y.: Carlson, 1993), 1172–76; see also Margaret Washington, ed., *Narrative of Sojourner Truth* (New York: Vintage Books, 1993), especially the introduction; and Karen Baker Fletcher, "Anna Julia Cooper and Sojourner Truth: Two Nineteenth Century Black Interpreters of Scripture," in Schüssler Fiorenza, ed., *Searching the Scriptures, vol. 1,* 41–51.

23. Erlene Stetson, ed., *Black Sister: Poetry by Black American Women 1746–1980* (Bloomington: Indiana University Press, 1981), 24–25.

24. Karen Trimble Alliaume, "The Risks of Repeating Ourselves: Reading Feminist/Womanist Figures of Jesus," *Cross Currents* 48, 2 (1998): 198–218.

25. For the elaboration of this expression, see Hazel V. Carby, "On the Threshold of the Women's Era: Lynching, Empire and Sexuality," in Henry L. Gates, ed., *Race, Writing, and Difference* (Chicago: University of Chicago Press, 1986), 301–28. See also the article by Kwok Pui-lan, "The Image of the White Lady: Gender and Race in Christian Mission," in Anne Carr and Elisabeth Schüssler

Fiorenza, eds., *The Special Nature of Women* (Philadelphia: Trinity Press International, 1991), 19–27.

26. See, for instance, her *Household of Freedom: Authority in Feminist Theology* (Philadelphia: Westminster Press, 1978), 71–72; and her *Church in the Round: Feminist Interpretation of the Church* (Louisville, Ky.: Westminster John Knox Press, 1993).

27. Alliaume, "Risks of Repeating Ourselves," 211.

28. For the use of the expression "Africana feminist," see Cynthia Johnson's senior B.A. thesis on the "Women at the Well" (Harvard University, 1996).

29. See Rosemary Radford Ruether, *Sexism and God-Talk: Toward a Feminist Theology* (Boston: Beacon Press, 1983), 137. See also Mary Hembrow Snyder, *The Christology of Rosemary Radford Ruether: A Critical Introduction* (Mystic, Conn.: Twenty-third Publications, 1988).

30. Donna Haraway, "Ecce Homo, Ain't (Ar'n't) I a Woman, and Inappropriate/d Others: The Human in a Post-Humanist Landscape," in Judith Butler and Joan W. Scott, eds., *Feminists Theorize the Political* (New York: Routledge & Kegan Paul, 1992), 90.

31. Eleanor McLaughlin, "Feminist Christologies: Re-Dressing the Tradition," in Maryanne Stevens, ed., *Reconstructing the Christ Symbol: Essays in Feminist Christology* (Mahwah, N.J.: Paulist Press, 1993), 118–49.

32. For a fuller discussion, see my book *Jesus: Miriam's Child and Sophia's Prophet*, 67–88.

33. Since *In Memory of Her* appeared, several important works on Jewish women in the Greco-Roman world have been published. See, for instance, Judith Romney Wegner, *Chattel or Person? The Status of Women in the Mishnah* (New York: Oxford University Press, 1988); Amy Jill Levine, ed., *"Women Like This": New Perspectives on Jewish Women in the Greco-Roman World* (Atlanta: Scholars Press, 1991); Cheryl Ann Brown, *No Longer Be Silent: First Century Jewish Portraits of Biblical Women* (Louisville, Ky.: Westminster/John Knox Press, 1992); Ross Shepard Kraemer, *Her Share of the Blessing: Women's Religions among Pagans, Jews and Christians in the Greco-Roman World* (New York: Oxford University Press, 1992); Sally Overby Langford, "On Being a Religious Woman: Women Proselytes in the Greco-Roman World," in Peter J. Haas, ed., *Recovering the Role of Women: Power and Authority in Rabbinic Jewish Society* (Atlanta: Scholars Press, 1992), 113–30.

34. Dennis Baron, *Grammar and Gender* (New Haven, Conn.: Yale University Press, 1986); Robert H. Robins, *A Short History of Linguistics* (London: Longmans, Green & Co., 1979); Casey Miller and Kate Swift, *Words and Women: New Language in New Times* (New York: Doubleday/Anchor Books, 1977); Gloria A. Marshall, "Racial Classifications: Popular and Scientific," in Sandra Harding, ed., *The "Racial" Economy of Science: Toward a Democratic Future* (Bloomington: Indiana University Press, 1993), 116–27; for a comparison of sexist and racist language, see also the contributions in Mary Vetterling-Braggin, ed., *Sexist Language: A Modern Philosophical Analysis* (Totowa, N.J.: Littlefield, Adams &, 1981), 249–319.

35. For the elaboration of such a "symptomatic reading," see especially the work of Rosemary Hennessy, *Materialist Feminism and the Politics of Discourse* (New York and London: Routledge & Kegan Paul, 1993).

36. Amy Jill Levine, "Who Caters the Q Affair? Feminist Observations on Q Paraenesis," *Semeia* 50 (1990): 145–61.

37. For this concept, see Michel Pécheux, *Language, Semantics, and Ideology* (New York: St. Martin's Press, 1975). In any discursive formation, the preconstructed produces the effect of an "always already given," the "commonsense" meaning, or "what everyone already knows."

38. See, for instance, Bruce Malina, *The New Testament World: Insights from Cultural Anthropology* (Atlanta: John Knox Press), 1981; and Bruce J. Malina and Jerome H. Neyrey, "First-Century Personality: Dyadic, Not Individual," in Jerome H. Neyrey, ed. *The Social World of Luke-Acts: Models for Interpretation* (Peabody, Mass.: Hendrickson Publishers, 1991), 67–96. For a critical assessment, see Mary Ann Tolbert, "Social, Sociological, and Anthropological Methods," in Schüssler Fiorenza, ed., *Searching the Scriptures*, vol. 1, 255–72; for a critical assessment of the anthropological construct of "the Mediterranean," see especially the articles by Michael Herzfeld, "The Horns of the Mediterranean Dilemma," *American Ethnologist* 11 (1984): 439–55, and " 'As in Your Own House': Hospitality, Ethnography, and the Stereotype of the Mediterranean Society," in David Gilmore, ed., *Honor and Shame and the Unity of the Mediterranean* (Washington, D.C.: American Anthropological Association, 1987).

39. See Bruce Chilton and Jacob Neusner, *Judaism in the New Testament: Practices and Beliefs* (New York: Routledge & Kegan Paul, 1995), 10–18, for a critique of E. P. Sanders's construct of a single, unitary Judaism, attested by a coherent canon, in *Judaism: Practice and Belief,* 63 BCE–66 CE (Philadelphia: Trinity Press International, 1992).

40. Elisabeth Schüssler Fiorenza, "Jesus—Messenger of Divine Wisdom," *Studia Theologica* 49 (1995): 231–52.

41. Cf. Barbara H. Geller Nathanson, "Toward a Multicultural Ecumenical History of Women in the First Century/ies C.E.," in Schüssler Fiorenza, ed., *Searching the Scriptures*, vol. 1, 272–89.

42. Jacob Neusner, *Jews and Christians: The Myth of a Common Tradition* (Philadelphia: SCM/Trinity Press International, 1991). See also Arthur Cohen, *The Myth of the Judeo-Christian Tradition* (New York: Harper & Row, 1969).

43. Alan Segal, *Rebecca's Children* (Cambridge, Mass.: Harvard University Press, 1987).

44. For such a (deliberate?) misreading, see Ross Kraemer's reviews of *In Memory of Her* in *Religious Studies Review* 11, 1 (1985): 107 and in *Journal of Biblical Literature* 104, 4 (1985): 722. See also my response to her in the introduction to the tenth anniversary edition of the book.

45. For a comprehensive review of the meaning of this expression in contemporary Judaism, see Anna Maria Schwemer, "Gott als König und seine Königsherrschaft," in Martin Hengel and Anna Maria Schwemer, eds., *Königsherrschaft Gottes und himmlischer Kult in Judentum, Urchristentum und in der hellenistischen Welt* (Tübingen: J. C. B. Mohr [Paul Siebeck], 1991), 45–118. For discussion of the *basileia* discourse in early Christianity, see Helmut Merkel, "Die Gottesherrschaft in der Verkündigung Jesu," in Hengel and Schwemer, eds., *Königsherrschaft Gottes und himmlischer Kult,* 119–61; See also Marinus De Jonge, "The Christological Significance of Jesus' Preaching of the Kingdom of God," in Abraham J. Malherbe and Wayne A. Meeks, eds., *The Future of Christology: Essays in Honor of Leander E. Keck* (Minneapolis: Fortress Press, 1993), 7: "Notwithstanding the intrinsic difficulties in reconstructing Jesus' message concerning the kingdom, there is a surprising consensus" in understanding it as meaning "the time and place where God's power and kingly rule will hold sway."

46. For this expression, see Norman Perrin, *Jesus and the Language of the Kingdom* (Philadelphia: Fortress Press, 1976).
47. For a similar account, see Alan F. Segal, "Jesus, the Jewish Revolutionary," in Charlesworth, ed., *Jesus' Jewishness, 212–14.*
48. Schüssler Fiorenza, *In Memory of Her,* 148.
49. Jacquelyn Grant, "The Sin of Servanthood and the Deliverance of Discipleship," in Emily M. Townes, ed., *A Troubling in My Soul: Womanist Perspectives on Evil and Suffering* (Maryknoll, N.Y.: Orbis Books, 1993), 199–218, and I have problematized servanthood and emphasize discipleship in very similar ways, although we come from quite different social and religious backgrounds. Since Grant does not refer to my theoretical analysis (cf. my article " 'Waiting at Table': A Critical Feminist Theological Reflection on Diakonia," *Concilium* 198 [1988]: 84–94 and my book *Discipleship of Equals: A Critical Feminist Ekklesia-logy of Liberation,* [New York: Crossroads, 1993], 290–306), I feel justified to surmise that a comparable multiplicative analysis of kyriarchy results in coinciding theoretical proposals.
50. Cf. Robert Holst, "The Anointing of Jesus: Another Application of the Form-Critical Method," *Journal of Biblical Literature* 95 (1976): 435–46; Claus-Peter März, "Zur Traditionsgeschichte von Mk 14, 3–9 und Parallelen," *New Testament Studies* 67 (1981–1982): 89–112; for a general bibliography on the passion narratives, see Raymond E. Brown, *The Death of the Messiah: From Gethsemane to the Grave: A Commentary on the Passion Narratives in the Four Gospels* (New York: Doubleday, 1994), 94–106.
51. See, for instance, the fresco at Dura Europos for the importance of prophetic anointing. Cf. Warren G. Moon, "Nudity and Narrative: Observations on the Frescoes from the Dura Synagogue," *Journal of the American Academy of Religion* 40 (1992): 587–658.
52. For a discussion of Mark's account, see Marie Sabin, "Women Transformed: The Ending of Mark Is the Beginning of Wisdom," *Cross Currents* 48 (1998): 149–68; Monika Fander, *Die Stellung der Frau im Markusevangelium unter besonderer Berücksichtigung kultur- und religionsgeschichtlicher Hintergründe* (Altenberge: Telos Verlag, 1989), 118–35; for Matthew, see the excellent analysis of Elaine M. Wainwright, *Towards a Feminist Critical Reading of the Gospel according to Matthew (Beihefte zur Zeitschrift für die neutestamentliche Wissenschaft* 60 (Berlin: Walter de Gruyter, 1991), 252–83.
53. Vernon K. Robbins, "Using a Socio-Rhetorical Poetics to Develop a Unified Method: The Woman Who Anointed Jesus as a Test Case," *Society of Biblical Literature Seminar Papers* 31 (1992): 311.
54. James Brownson, "Neutralizing the Intimate Enemy: The Portrayal of Judas in the Fourth Gospel," in Eugene H. Lovering Jr., ed., *Society of Biblical Literature 1992 Seminar Papers* (Atlanta: Scholars Press, 1992), 49–60.
55. "*Tikkun*—to mend, repair and transform the world" is the programmatic motto of the progressive Jewish journal *Tikkun,* which is published by the Institute for Labor and Mental Health.

11

MENDING OF CREATION

Women, Nature, and Eschatological Hope

Kwok Pui-lan

Turning back to ancient times, the Four Pillars were shattered and the Nine Provinces dislocated. The sky did not cover [the earth] completely; nor did the earth uphold [all of the sky]. Fire roared with inextinguishable flames, and waters gushed forth in powerful and incessant waves. Ferocious animals devoured the good people, and birds of prey snatched away the old and weak. Thereupon, Nu Kua fused together stones of the five colours with which she patched up the azure sky. She cut off the feet of the turtle with which she set the Four Pillars. She slaughtered the black dragon in order to save the Land of Chi. She piled up reed ashes with which to check the flooding waters.

When the azure sky was patched up, the Four Pillars set up straight, the flooding waters dried up, the Land of Chi made orderly and the cunning wild animals exterminated, the good people thrived.[1]

In a popular Chinese creation story, the female mythological figure Nu Kua uses precious stones to mend the sky, thereby stopping the deluge and restoring order from chaos. Nu Kua also creates human beings from yellow earth. Although there are other Chinese creation myths associated with a male figure, it is significant that the saving of human beings and other forms of life from disaster is attributed to a female figure.

In her publications and lectures, Letty Russell often uses the metaphor "mending of creation" to describe the responsibility of women to fight injustice and to restore wholeness in our society. Many years ago, Russell heard Krister Stendahl quoting from a rabbinic saying that theology is worrying about what God is worrying about when God gets up in the morning. Reflecting on this saying, Russell wrote:

> It would seem according to Stendahl that God is worrying about the mending of creation, trying to straighten up the mess so that all of groaning creation will be set free. In order to do this, God has to be worrying about those who have dropped through the "safety net" of society, about those who are victims of injustice and war, and about the destruction of their bodies, their lives, and the environment in which they live.[2]

In her books on feminist liberation theology, on partnership, and most recently on the Christian church, Russell has consistently raised her prophetic voice against patriarchy and other forms of oppression. She offers a theological vision and shares her eschatological hope that women of all colors can feel welcome to table fellowship and to collaboration in the mending of creation. As a tribute to her life and work, I examine some aspects of the current debate regarding women, nature, embodiment, and eschatological hope, focusing on the contributions of indigenous and Third World women theologians. The construction of women's hope for themselves and for nature is largely dependent on their social location and historical background. The questions "Who are the women?" "Whose nature?" and "Whose hope?" must be constantly kept in mind.

This essay consists of two parts. The first part questions the binary construction, "male is to culture as female is to nature" and critiques white women's tendency to homogenize "women" and essentialize "nature." The second part examines the voices of women who have experienced conquest, slavery, and colonization in order to explore their articulation of body, nature, and hope.

BEYOND THE BINARY SPLIT:
MALE VERSUS FEMALE AND CULTURE VERSUS NATURE?

Before Third World feminist theologians can articulate their understanding of women and nature, they must clear a space to think for themselves, because the subject has been worked and reworked by white feminist theorists and theologians. In the 1970s, white feminists noticed that women have been perceived to be closer to nature than are men; and since nature was considered lower than the mind, women were deemed inferior and subordinate to men. The early move was to challenge the connection between women and nature and any forms of biological determinism that contribute to women's subordination. Then, other feminists took another direction, trying to reclaim the positive dimensions of women's embodiment and their closeness to nature.

Sherry B. Ortner published an important essay, "Is Female to Male as Nature Is to Culture?" in 1974.[3] Arguing that female subordination is a universal phenomenon, she discovers what she believes to be a common structure upheld in all human cultures: culture is valued more than nature, and women are seen as being closer to nature than are men. Ortner's definition of culture is Eurocentric, influenced by Enlightenment thought and Western technological advance. She writes: "We may thus broadly equate culture with the notion of human consciousness, or with the products of human consciousness (that is, systems of thought and technology), by means of which humanity attempts to assert control over nature."[4] Her argument that women are seen as closer to nature is based on Simone de Beauvoir's similar observations, on Claude Lévi-Strauss's work in structural anthropology, and on Nancy Chodorow's study of the female psyche and the pattern of mothering. Her essay relies primarily on an analysis of middle-class white society, devoting little space to the discussion of other cultures. Although she acknowledges in the beginning that it is difficult to generalize the position of women within a single country, China,[5] she finds no problem in generalizing their position across all cultures. Writing in the early 1970s, Ortner overlooked differences among women, glossed over the specificity of culture, and provided no nuanced understanding of nature. In short, her essay essentializes "women," "culture," and "nature" in a way that is similar to the works of other early feminists.

Ortner's theory has been quite influential in feminist theological thinking on the subject. Rosemary Radford Ruether, for example, cites Ortner's work in *Sexism and God-Talk* and agrees basically with her argument. Ruether at the same time points out that nature can be seen both as dominated by human beings and as the matrix of life, and that male culture symbolizes control over nature in ambiguous ways.[6] Ortner provides Ruether with a "universal" context and a framework to examine the patterns in Hebrew and Christian traditions, as well as in Greek thought. Ruether notes that the Hebrew Bible does not equate creation or the material realm with evil and that there is no spirit/nature split. But the priestly story in the first chapter of Genesis speaks of human beings as charged to have dominion over the earth, and the Hebrew Bible assumes that women, children, and slaves are to be dominated in patriarchal families by men. Ruether faults the Greek philosophers for creating a more radical dualism between mind and body, wherein women are seen as analogous to matter or body. As an heir to both apocalyptic Judaism and Platonic thought, Christianity perpetuates the pattern of dualistic thinking, reinforced by the misogyny of some church fathers.[7]

To correct the biases against women and nature in these traditions that have shaped Western civilization, some white feminist religious thinkers project their hope through a reclaiming of the body, a revaluation of nature, and an emphasis on women's connection with nature in various ways. Early on in her work within the Christian tradition, Rosemary Radford Ruether offers the metaphor "new women, new earth." Moreover, she links closely the liberation of women from sexism with the renewal of creation.[8] Eschatological hope, for her, lies not in the "salvation of the soul" in some traditional sense but in *metanoia,* or conversion of each person to the earth and to one another.[9] Not until her later work, however, does she focus ultimately on a harmonious union of women and nature.[10] For Ruether, the prophetic tradition is central to the Christian tradition. The prophets emphasize God as the God of history, not only the God of creation. Within history, human beings have a power of agency to change society and the environment, to work therefore for justice.

Another feminist theologian, Sallie McFague, offers the image of the "world as the body of God" to recapture the sacramental dimension of creation in an ecological theology. The body model enables us to honor bodies, our own and those of others; to focus on the basic needs of human beings while respecting the integrity of the earth; and to imagine God as the inspirited body of the whole universe.[11] For McFague, eschatological hope involves the restoration of unity in distinction for all forms of existence, simplicity of living, attention to the physical needs of the earth's creatures, and solidarity with the oppressed.[12]

Other white feminists find their hope in reclaiming the close relationship between women and nature. This is especially true in some forms of feminist spirituality and in the radical feminist philosophy of white women who have come to stand outside the Christian tradition. In her beautifully written book *The Rebirth of the Goddess,* Carol Christ suggests we overcome the mind/body, culture/nature split by practicing "embodied thinking" and by reminding ourselves constantly that we are part of nature. She writes: "The image of the Goddess also evokes the sacredness of nature. This confirms a deep intuition that has been denied in our culture: that we are nature and that nature is body."[13] Starhawk, a post-Jewish peace activist, reclaims the Old Religion of Witchcraft and uses magical formulas and nature-based rituals to evoke the power of the Goddess and the power-from-within.[14] The radical feminist writer Mary Daly uses the term *biophilia* to describe women's inclination toward nature. She speaks of radically self-identifying women as bonding "biophilically with each other, and with the sun and the moon, the tides, and all of the elements."[15]

Not all white women either refuse to connect women with nature or insist on their connection. For example, having learned from the writings of black women, Susan Brooks Thistlethwaite argues that in the racist culture in the United States, the black woman is consigned to signify body and sexuality, while the white woman is the "angel of the home," the soul and spirituality. She claims that "white women in the United States are culture, not nature."[16] Since the "natural" roles of many white women, such as mothering and housekeeping, have historically relied on the exploited labor of black women, white women seek to reunite with nature and see nature as a source of strength. Thistlethwaite argues that white and black women, separated by race and by class, have different experiences of nature; furthermore, the connection between women and nature has been bad for black women. She cautions against a simplified and intuitive understanding of nature without recourse to social and economic analysis.[17]

I have learned much from these white colleagues' works, because they help me understand the cultural heritages of the West. In the end, they make clear the problems with white feminist assessments of the connection between women and nature. Both the binary split and the claims of harmony between women, nature, and body, on the one hand, and men, culture, and mind, on the other, must be subjected to closer scrutiny from cross-cultural perspectives. At least four problems can be identified, each of which follows from the others.

First, Ortner's notion that all human societies devalue nature is far from being true. In the Native traditions of the Americas; in the Asian religions of Buddhism, Taoism, Confucianism, Shintoism, and Hinduism; and in African traditional religion, nature has not been seen as belonging to the lower realm, to be controlled and dominated by human beings. The Western notion of the split between culture and nature must be seen as culturally specific and not generalizable to all cultures.

The second problem emerges because, in the Western imagination of the "primitive" and the "modern," qualities such as "magic, ritualism, closeness to nature, mythic or cosmological aims" are usually associated with the "primitive."[18] White women's new attempts to valorize these so-called primitive qualities can be a way of appropriating the values of other cultures simply to compensate for a lack in one's own. In this way, significant differences between the histories of white women and those of women from other cultures can be glossed over.

This is why, third, Thistlethwaite is right to argue that an abstract and romanticized notion of nature may not be helpful for continued dialogue and solidarity among women. During the colonial days, white men saw land, rivers, and mountains simply as nature, to be possessed without the recognition of national boundaries and respect for people's relationship with their land. White women's limitless reunification with a boundless but abstract nature may fall prey to similar colonial impulses.

Finally, white women's periodic rituals in honor of the earth (however important as ways to value both women and nature) are not radical enough to meet what is needed unless they are joined with concrete social action. While Starhawk links rituals with political demonstrations, many others have conducted such rituals only to ease psychic pain and to search for individual wholeness, but not for the sake of mobilizing communal resources for social transformation.

WOMEN, NATURE, CONQUEST, SLAVERY, AND COLONIZATION

To theorize about women and nature with those who are on the underside of history, we cannot begin by deconstructing Aristotle's philosophy, nor by adopting generalized notions of "women," "nature," and "culture." Instead, we must start with the concrete bodies of women who have experienced conquest, slavery, and colonization in the past and who continue to be subjected to neo-colonialism, militarism, and economic exploitation in the global market. The colored female body is simultaneously "a site of attraction, repulsion, and symbolic appropriation."[19] This body has been consigned to signify nature in demeaning and ambiguous ways.

The brown, black, and yellow bodies of women have been treated as inferior to white bodies in the Western history of domination of the world. During the conquest of the Americas, the Spaniards colonized Native women's sexuality and vented their masculine libido through the subjugation of Native women's bodies. Enrique Dussel has called this colonization of Native women's bodies "erotic violence."[20] During slavery, as Delores Williams has pointed out, black women were indeed treated as animals and their bodies as a "lower order of nature."[21] In what she has called *colorism*, black women's bodies were regarded as less adorable and beautiful than light-skinned women's bodies. Black women were systematically raped to increase the number of slaves for the slave owners, yet they were accused of being temptresses and lustful. Many yellow women today are reduced to sex machines in the sex industry, which turns Southeast Asia into the "brothel of the world." Because of the AIDS epidemic, girls as young as two and three years old are abused to satisfy the sexual cravings of customers.[22]

The bodies of colored women have been and still are subject to severe control and surveillance, often through violent means. The episodes of genocide and forced sterilization of Native women, as well as their relegation to missionary schools for education and discipline, were violent crimes committed against humanity. Branding by fire, forced breeding, and merciless whipping were meant to instill fear and submission in black slave women, so that the lesson could be remembered by the body. If such cruelty is regarded as belonging to a bygone era, we need only look at what happens in the twentieth century. During the Second World War, as many as two hundred thousand Korean, Chinese, and other Southeast Asian women were drafted or kidnapped for sexual services of Japanese soldiers throughout the Asian Pacific region. Beatings and torture were routinely used to subdue the unwilling, while the women were given little food and forced to live in crowded and unsanitary conditions.[23] If we look closer, an international division of labor characterizes our contemporary world economy, with women in Third World countries providing the cheapest unskilled labor. Multinational corporations use "modern" management techniques and technological surveillance to "manage" laborers, in order to increase their productivity.

To remember the atrocities committed against the bodies of colored women is not to generalize all colored women as victims, because some colored women benefit from the status quo and some even collaborate with the oppressors. But the painful and dangerous memories should never be forgotten; we must learn from history to prevent such suffering from happening again. Multiply oppressed women have their history inscribed on their bodies. As Elsa Tamez has asserted, the woman's body is a text to be read:

> Women's bodies, then, can manifest themselves as sacred text setting out their stories to be read and re-read and to generate liberating actions and attitudes. Women's lives enshrine a deep grammar, whose morphology and syntax need to be learned for the sake of better human inter-relationships.[24]

If we theorize about women and nature from the broken bodies of colored women, we can see that the relationship between women and nature is much more complex, ambiguous, and multidimensional than is often assumed. For the sake of clarity, we need to distinguish symbolic and social levels of meaning, although the two are interconnected. In many indigenous traditions and in Asian and African myths and legends, the earth or the land is symbolized by the female. Ancient Chinese people worshiped *timu* (earth mother); the Philippine people venerate Ina; Indians have the feminine principle Shakti; and Native Americans respect mother earth. Although these traditions in general hold nature in high regard, the female symbolization of nature has not been translated into a higher position for women in society. Because I have not found many efforts to explain this, I can only tentatively suggest some reasons.

The symbolic order of any given society may or may not be wholly symmetrical with the social order. Female symbols for nature are often restricted to the reproductive roles of women, such as fertility and nurturance; this, in turn, reinforces the domesticity of women. Thus the female symbols of the goddess or the earth mother may have been incorporated into a male symbolic structure, so that the symbolization of the feminine in connection with nature serves to justify women's subordination. For example, the Goddess of Mercy in popular Buddhism is worshiped because of her alleged capacity to bestow women with sons, all the while losing sight of the fact that in the Chinese legend she is a strong woman who defies her father's will.

Even though women's status was lower than men's in precolonial societies, there is evidence that women still enjoyed relatively more freedom and privilege than in colonial times. During the colonial era, an element was added in the association of women with nature. Here the very ideology of colonization included the symbolization of foreign land as a female body to be possessed and conquered. Catherine Keller's careful reading of Christopher Columbus's descriptions of the Americas shows that he imagined the mysterious land as the lost Eden, having the shape of a pear, culminating at something like the nipple of a woman's breast. The serious measuring and mapping of the nipple of paradise, for Keller, was not just cartography but carto-pornography.[25] She continues: "The continent looms as forbidden fruit, the virgin body ripe for plucking, the mother breast ready to suckle a death-ridden, depressed Europe into its rebirth."[26] The fertile continent was thus imagined to be a dark and wild virgin, lying before the adventurers, waiting to be possessed to give birth to a new people.

Subjugated women were not only used to symbolize the land figuratively, but they were literally treated as part of nature—as beasts and cattle. Although white women have been regarded symbolically and philosophically as close to nature, in modern times they have never been thought to be other than human. This is one of the reasons that anthropological analysis takes a new point of departure in theologies by enslaved and colonized women. Whereas white women differ from white men because of their gender, the black and Native women were regarded as belonging to a different species, occupying a lower rung in the evolutionary ladder. Many black and formerly colonized women observe the white women's rush to reclaim the close connection with nature as full of historical irony.

When we turn to consider the relationship in the Third World between women and nature on the social level, we can also discern ambiguities and uneasy phenomena. Many impoverished women do not have the luxury to seek harmony with nature. Gabriele Dietrich, a feminist theologian who has worked for a long time in India, describes the poverty-stricken Indian communities in this way:

> Ecology then does not come in as a striving force after reconciliation with the earth, honoring cosmic forces and non-human forces of life. It comes in more with a focus on setting ourselves in relationship with one another in the day-to-day survival struggles for water, a piece of land to dwell on, a patch of beach to dry the fish on, the sea as a source of bounty.[27]

Dire poverty and the struggle for survival impose heavy burdens on many women in the Third World, who are responsible for putting food on the table and fetching clean water for the family. Noted Indian eco-feminist Vandana Shiva lifts up Third World women's roles as creative managers of forests, the food chain, water resources, and the whole of a household. "The new insight provided by rural women in the Third World is that women and nature are associated not in passivity but in creativity and in the maintenance of life."[28] Sociologist Sara Mvududu from Zimbabwe also observes that women's knowledge of the environment is more comprehensive than men's because of the diversity of their tasks. Women accumulate great wisdom because they have had to learn how to work with the most unyielding of environments, the result of male migration away from degraded rural areas.[29]

Ironically, while some poor women are creative managers of the environment, others have been forced to abuse the environment for the sake of their own survival and that of their children. In a balanced analysis of women's role in the ecological crisis, Indian theologian Aruna Gnanadason reports: "While women are the worst afflicted by resource depletion, it is also true that because of forces they can scarcely understand, still less control, they are often the agents of their own resource depletion."[30] Although we should not blame the victims of our global economy who have to struggle to obtain even basic necessities, we also should not close our eyes to poor women's capacity to destroy nature.

Given the ambiguity of colored women's relation with nature, what are their hopes and aspirations for the future? Let me highlight several salient aspects of their eschatological hope. First, many Third World and indigenous women believe that their own traditions, where the natural is not separated from the cultural and the spiritual, can offer enormous contributions to saving ourselves and our planet. Victoria Tauli-Corpuz, who comes from the tribal community of the Igorots in northern Luzon, the Philippines, describes her heritage in this way:

> Nature to the indigenous women and men is thought of in spiritual terms. In spite of the aggressive Christianization drive among the Igorots, the majority are still animist in orientation and practice. Nature spirits are revered, respected and feared. Rituals are done to thank or appease nature spirits and ancestors.[31]

While Westernization and modernization are considered irresistible forces of history, indigenous women have persistently pointed us to another alternative. Nobel prizewinner Rigoberta Menchú noted during the Earth Summit at Rio de Janeiro that the conquerors killed Mayan people and put their artifacts in the museum, telling the world that the Mayan culture was long gone. But she pointed out that her people are still alive and still struggling.[32]

Second, colored women's eschatological hope is grounded in their continual struggle and resistance, creating new resources for survival. A reconnection with one's cultural and spiritual traditions does not mean romanticizing the past or overlooking the fact that one's culture has been transformed and appropriated by the political and spiritual conquest of the West. Rather, what is underway is a lifelong process of searching for cultural and spiritual resources to live by in a world dominated by white supremacy, capitalist greed, and patriarchy. This is an effort to create a way out of no way. It is to live under the power of the myth of modernity but refuse to give up resistance. It is to construct cultural hybrids out of fragments that still exist in our collective memory. It is to live to honor our ancestors and to consume as if the next seven generations count.

Third, indigenous women and women of color still hope to work in solidarity with white people, although the latter have exploited them and even stolen their religious symbols. Andy Smith, a member of the Cherokee Nation, observes that many white women are attracted to Native spirituality, especially through the New Age movement. She warns against the "wanting to become Indian" syndrome, in which people want to learn Native secrets and ceremonies without accountability and responsibility for white racism. But Smith and other indigenous leaders look to the day when white people will genuinely respect their cultures and express their solidarity concretely through joining their struggles for land rights, employment, and health care. Mutual trust will be nurtured and acts of solidarity will be accepted on Native terms.[33]

Finally, even in desperate and exhausting situations, women of color believe they do not struggle alone because the tender web of life still holds. Alice Walker, in her recent meditation on life, spirit, art, and her work, discusses her inner spiritual reserve that can be drawn on to face meanness of spirit, racism, sexism, homophobia, hypocrisy, and craziness. The spiritual lessons she has learned include: life is grand, no matter what; suffering has a use; and she and all that she loves are inseparable. Moreover, the universe responds and takes care of us, no matter which god we believe in: Goddess, nature, spirit, mother earth, the universe, or God of the ancestors.[34] When we work intimately with the universe and follow its rhythm, Walker believes, we become most creative. She has a memorable description of her late mother, a woman of modest means, working ecstatically in her garden:

> I notice that it is only when my mother is working in her flowers that she is radiant, almost to the point of being invisible—except as Creator: hand and eye. She is involved in work her soul must have. Ordering the universe in the image of her personal conception of Beauty.[35]

Inspired by Walker's work, Letty Russell, Katie Geneva Cannon, Ada María Isasi-Díaz, and I co-edited *Inheriting Our Mothers' Gardens: Feminist Theology in Third World Perspective*.[36] Working on our book, we soon recognized that as women of different colors, our inheritances are vastly different because our mothers' gardens are not the same. Katie spoke of the awesome task of "surviving the blight," and Ada María had to transplant delicately a "Hispanic garden in a foreign land." My mother has no garden, and I grew up in a land colonized by the British. Letty, by contrast, had her father's victory garden and her grandmother's rose garden as part of her middle-class American inheritance. Letty found it was not easy for her to write about inheriting our mothers' gardens, for she recognized her privileges from her long work promoting global solidarity and network among women:

> I find myself having to confess that as a white middle-class North American woman I have inherited benefits that accrue to me disproportionately because of the social structures of racism, classism, and imperialism.[37]

She said courageously that white women like her sometimes have to reject their mothers' gardens in the struggle for justice. Women of all colors need to search for the liberating fragments in our inheritance so that we can mend the creation for our daughters and their daughters.

NOTES

1. Milton M. Chiu, *The Tao of Chinese Religion* (Lanham, Md.: University Press of America, 1984), pp. 158–60, as quoted in Archie C. C. Lee, "The Chinese Creation Myth of Nu Kua and the Biblical Narrative in Genesis 1—11," *Biblical Interpretation* 2 (1994): 313–14.
2. Letty M. Russell, *Church in the Round: Feminist Interpretation of the Church* (Louisville, Ky.: Westminster John Knox Press, 1993), p. 196.
3. Sherry B. Ortner, "Is Female to Male as Nature Is to Culture?" in *Women, Culture, and Society,* ed. Michelle Zimbalist Rosaldo and Louise Lamphere (Stanford, Calif.: Stanford University Press, 1974), pp. 67–87.
4. Ibid., p. 72.
5. Ibid., p. 68.
6. Rosemary Radford Ruether, *Sexism and God-Talk: Toward a Feminist Theology* (Boston: Beacon Press, 1983), pp. 72, 75–76.
7. Ibid., pp. 75–79; and also her *New Woman, New Earth: Sexist Ideologies and Human Liberation* (New York: Seabury Press, 1975), pp. 187–90.
8. See Ruether, *New Woman, New Earth,* pp. 186–211.
9. Ruether, *Sexism and God-Talk,* pp. 254–56.
10. Rosemary Radford Ruether, *Gaia and God* (San Francisco: HarperCollins, 1992).
11. Sallie McFague, *The Body of God: An Ecological Theology* (Minneapolis: Fortress Press, 1993), p. 22.
12. Ibid., pp. 198–202.
13. Carol P. Christ, *Rebirth of the Goddess: Finding Meaning in Feminist Spirituality* (Reading, Mass.: Addison-Wesley Publishing Co., 1997), p. 8.
14. Starhawk, *Dreaming the Dark: Magic, Sex, and Politics* (Boston: Beacon Press, 1982).
15. Mary Daly, *Pure Lust: Elemental Feminist Philosophy* (Boston: Beacon Press, 1984), p. 311.
16. Susan Thistlethwaite, *Sex, Race, and God: Christian Feminism in Black and White* (New York: Crossroad, 1989), p. 42.
17. Ibid., pp. 58–59.
18. James Clifford, *The Predicament of Culture: Twentieth-Century Ethnography, Literature, and Art* (Cambridge, Mass.: Harvard University Press, 1988), p. 201.

19. Ibid., p. 5.
20. Enrique Dussel, *The Invention of the Americas: Eclipse of "the Other" and the Myth of Modernity* (New York: Continuum, 1995), p. 46.
21. Delores S. Williams, "Sin, Nature, and Black Women's Bodies," in *Ecofeminism and the Sacred,* ed. Carol J. Adams (New York: Continuum, 1993), p. 24.
22. See Rita Nakashima Brock and Susan Brooks Thistlethwaite, *Casting Stones: Prostitution and Liberation in Asia and the United States* (Minneapolis: Fortress Press, 1996).
23. Chung Hyun Kyung, "Your Comfort vs. My Death," in *Women Resisting Violence: Spirituality for Life,* ed. Mary John Mananzan, Mercy Amba Oduyoye, Elsa Tamez, J. Shannon Clarkson, Mary C. Gray, and Letty M. Russell (Maryknoll, N.Y.: Orbis Books, 1996), pp. 129–40.
24. Elsa Tamez, "Women's Lives as Sacred Text," in *Women's Sacred Scriptures,* ed. Kwok Pui-lan and Elisabeth Schüssler Fiorenza (Maryknoll, N.Y.: Orbis Books, 1998), p. 63.
25. Catherine Keller, *Apocalypse Now and Then* (Boston: Beacon Press, 1996), pp. 156–57.
26. Ibid., p. 157.
27. Gabriele Dietrich, "The World as the Body of God: Feminist Perspectives on Ecology and Social Justice," in *Women Healing Earth: Third World Women in Ecology, Feminism, and Religion,* ed. Rosemary Radford Ruether (Maryknoll, N.Y.: Orbis Books, 1996), p. 82.
28. Vandana Shiva, "Let Us Survive: Women, Ecology and Development," in Ruether, ed., *Women Healing Earth,* p. 70.
29. Sara C. Mvududu, "Revisiting Traditional Management of Indigenous Woodlands," in Ruether, ed., *Women Healing Earth,* p. 144.
30. Aruna Gnanadason, "Toward a Feminist Eco-Theology for India," in Ruether, ed., *Women Healing Earth,* p. 76.
31. Victoria Tauli-Corpuz, "Reclaiming Earth-Based Spirituality: Indigenous Women in the Cordillera," in Ruether, ed., *Women Healing Earth,* p. 100.
32. Rigoberta Menchú, in a speech delivered at the World Council of Churches conference on "Searching for the New Heavens and the New Earth," Earth Summit, Rio de Janeiro, Brazil, May 1992.
33. Andy Smith, "For Those Who Were Indian in a Former Life," in Adams, ed., *Ecofeminism and the Sacred,* pp. 168–71.
34. Alice Walker, *The Same River Twice: Honoring the Difficult* (New York: Charles Scribner's sons, 1996), pp. 284–87.
35. Alice Walker, *In Search of Our Mothers' Gardens* (San Diego: Harcourt Brace Jovanovich, 1983), p. 241.
36. Letty Russell, Katie G. Cannon, Ada María Isasi-Díaz, and Kwok Pui-lan, eds., *Inheriting Our Mothers' Gardens: Feminist Theology in Third World Perspective* (Philadelphia: Westminster Press, 1988).
37. Ibid., p. 143.

12

FEMINIST THEA(O)LOGIES AT THE MILLENNIUM

"Messy" Continued Resistance or Surrender to Post–Modern Academic Culture?

Beverly Wildung Harrison

I write on the verge of retirement, a senior academic pondering the current condition of feminist the*a*- (or the*o*-) ethical work, musing on its future. The occasion, writing an essay for a collection honoring an esteemed colleague, Professor Letty Russell, as her seventieth birthday nears, stirs joy. But the fast-approaching terminus to my own formal academic career encourages reminiscence and even a few nostalgic fears about an emerging academic scene that will be going on with far less input from us in the near future. Such moments surely tempt to romanticized memory and even to nostalgic rereadings of the past. So I pause, concerned that voicing worries about the directions of feminist religious/thea(o)logical work as women's religious and ethical scholarship burgeons may reveal nothing more than an anxiety generated by aging. How self-serving and defensive of my own generation's efforts may such an essay seem? I have decided to express my worries, confident that my readers can perfectly well judge for themselves.

In spite of our often-noted similarities of social location, feminist theologians now in our sixties to seventies were, in fact, quite a divergent group, differing in our styles of work, the sources we used, and our accountabilities. Seen now as rather homogeneous and chiefly as "reformers,"[1] what should be at least as notable is this diversity of our voices and of the communities on which we impacted. Even though we mostly engaged existing religious traditions and communities from within and were mostly white and surely not as insightful about white racism, class, or the depth and tenacity of male sex/gender power as we needed to be, we did our work with persistence. When our thealogical and ethical naming overgeneralized our own cultural worlds in ways costly to other women's well-being, we sought to correct our myopias on these matters while we got on with an extraordinary range of constructive work. In retrospect, the rather remarkable array of women who responded is noteworthy, especially given the power of "feminist backlash."[2]

Let it be noted as well that, on the whole, we avoided acrimonious infighting about our disagreements and points of tension. If, in the eyes of many who were to follow, we spoke in styles reminiscent of some of our male academic mentors, we nevertheless forged critical perspectives that fueled rising expectations among women and drew quite diverse groups of women into the enterprise of theological reconstruction.

WERE WE SENIOR FEMINIST SCHOLARS MODERNISTS?

Pondering the relationship of Letty Russell's early work and mine is instructive to me in light of current criticisms of our generation's work. We are both Presbyterians of a rebellious sort, both passionately committed to a continuously reforming theological stance that was, at best, our tradition's rhetorical ideal, even when honored more in the breach than in the practice. Both our efforts have been faulted, not without justification, for language insufficiently reflective of the chasms of difference among women. Neither of us, I am confident, has the least interest in denying the charge that *difference* was not the first word in our early theorizings of women's oppressions, and that we did, at times, speak of wo*men's* "experience" in the singular, without sufficient caution. What is not always recognized, however, is that our assumptions, if not the style of voice we employed, were already *explicitly and subtantively postmodernist* at the methodological level. As I reread the work of my age coterie, (with the exception of the most influential and evocative of us, Mary Daly),[3] the past-sixty crowd of feminist theologians, without exception, *assumed* that theological categories as such are not, nor could they be, ontological in the manner presumed in classical philosophy. To the contrary, all of us began on this side of historicism, recognizing that the foundations of theological claims were not transcendental but were situated, *historical-cultural constructs.* Catholic and Protestant alike among us explictly avoided classical ontological theological approaches. Today, I find that few younger feminist religious theorists recall that Daly's early use of Paul Tillich actually *reinserted* an ontological option into feminist theological discussion, which others of us avoided.

There was, of course, another source of "foundationalist" feminism invoked by those who used a Whiteheadean process approach.[4] Alfred North Whitehead's thought, popular among some feminists, was, if properly understood, a post-modern style of metaphysics—that is, it was scientifically grounded and "speculative" or conjectural, and it did not yield firm or unequivocal knowledge. Nor did most feminists really use Whitehead's cosmological, scientifically based speculation as a *source of theological knowledge.* Historicist perspectives took primacy in feminist work over speculative ones.

Much more could be said about the status of Tillichian and Whiteheadean methods in early feminist theologies in relation to post-modern criticisms of essentialism. Here my point is simple: no theologians in our over-sixty group (nor, as I read the record, any of the now fifty-to-sixty crowd) purported to ground theological claims in philosophically transcendental/essentialist categories or in Enlightenment theories of transcendental reason. Yet the rhetoric of some younger feminist scholars often seems to imply that we worked from such assumptions and that our work is, for that reason, at best deeply flawed, at worst no longer tenable. Though some questions can be raised about what our appeals to "experience" as a source of knowledge really meant, it is far from clear that the most general complaints of post-modernist critique apply. I read our theological anthropologies as rooted basically in historical and cultural claims. Our occasional uses of "ontic categories" that presumed some homogeneity in human identity or constancy of need were derivations from natural or social-science assumptions that are far from being discredited today.

Gender, race, and class were for us "durable inequalities"[5] created through time. The "death of metaphysics" message so dear to current younger feminist theorists had long since reached us, because liberal theology itself had already widely taken a shift toward nonfoundationalism. If we had not been presuming historical malleability, we would not have adopted the theories of social change we embraced. None of us really imagined that the male gender-supremacy mode of quaint and charming nineteenth-century discourse, with its always inadequate abstract term *woman*, was a wise way to talk. If women's experiences were, for us, often analogous and parallel, that was because perduring patterns of male supremacy had taken some definite historical forms.

KEEPING LIBERATIONIST METHODOLOGICAL ASSUMPTIONS ALIVE IN POST-MODERNIST DISCOURSES: PRACTICE AS POLITICS

Today more than ever before, it needs to be remembered that those of us who adopted the term *feminist liberation theology* for our work, did so because we shared the epistemic conviction that theory is a moment *within* praxis, and that theory is to be judged by the practice it engenders. We came to recognize in an urgent way that what was needed was an *academic-political practice of inclusion* that would bring other voices to the academic table as a condition of more adequate knowledge. Our goal was not so much to perfect *our* theories individualistically but to broaden concrete participation in the work of constructing and expanding women's theological "knowledge." In retrospect, I believe this is the important legacy by which subsequent work among us should be assessed. But I am bound to ask, "Is this really the lesson that current academic women, like us still too largely from the tribes of Europe, will carry forward?" Will calls for greater political risk taking and more "messy diversity" continuously emerge in religious studies and theo(a)logical faculties, or will the heavy hand of an ideological consensus that is quietly at home with the academic status quo replace it?

Continuing reflection on the relation of my own work with Letty Russell's is instructive on this point as well. I read (and have always read) Letty's work as rooted in a passionate embrace of human freedom and the continuous need for ecclesial renewal. Most of her readers did not know or appreciate enough of Karl Barth's aim and agenda to understand that his goal was rooted precisely in a militantly anti-essentialist historical political agenda.[6] Some have dismissed Letty's work as "not radical" or "male-dominated" because the innovations of Protestant male voices were sometimes lost on feminists because of *their* gender monism. Because I rejected Barth, I came off better initially among those who were critical. I was unpersuaded that he had found either a satisfactory way beyond liberalism's limitations or a theological method that would make Christian theology genuinely critical enough to escape cultural provincialism. I thought then, and still think, that none of us can afford so wholesale a jettisoning of liberal social, political, and moral theory as Barth attempted, or as post-modernists sometimes call for. So Letty Russell, not Beverly Harrison, deserves credit for taking a path most consistent with post-modernist claims.

Were Letty Russell and I to have an occasion to compare notes on the matter, I expect we would both be amused at the range and convergences of the learnings and unlearnings that each of us has passed through. The solidarity I have with her as a theologian is the havoc we have mutually inflicted on the norm of "decency and order" so valued in our shared Reformed or Calvinist theological tradition. Both of us have frequently referred to our sad little denomination as "God's frozen people,"[7] and we have gotten on with the tasks of encouraging heterodoxy, not for its own sake but because we both find *any* orthodoxy to function as a subtle patriarchal norm. For us, the practice of feminist thea(o)logy aims to give all women the power of their own voices in the naming of diverse visions of sacred power, relations, and healing community. Feminist work envisages no formalized, "fixed" starting point and no final resting place. Such a perspective makes the need for ongoing reformation not a ponderous platitude but an continuing source of theological energy and excitement. It is Letty Russell and Shannon Clarkson, on the occasion of the publication party for the *Dictionary of Feminist Theologies* that they so lovingly edited, whom I quote here: our ongoing work is "the wonderfully messy business of encouraging women's theologies."[8] Are younger feminist theologians as clear as they need to be that this, not the production of "correct" theory, *remains* the ongoing task?

THE NEW SITUATION IN ACADEMIC CULTURE:
NEOLIBERAL ANTIPOLITICS

Unflagging effort to sustain the desire for more messiness is critical in a time when style has replaced depth in academic discernment. Continuous learning of *uncompromising moral/political practices* that encourage and enable alternative lines of departure not aiming at homogeneity will be far from easy. Not only the diversity of sources used and the rhetorical styles and genre to be developed but the constituencies that women in theology and religious studies work among must continue to increase. What "united" us in the past were broadly shared *political* goals—that is, to enhance concretely the range of voices participating in the project of theo(a)logical and moral reconstruction. The cultures and institutional sites that need religious transformation if "women are to count" are innumerable and unending.[9] The currently fashionable "trashes" of "liberationist" approaches to theology, rooted in sometimes subtle and sometimes crass deconstructions of what is and is not possible in our appeals to historicity and our efforts for change, can be dangerous if they celebrate resistance without the determination to *struggle* for such change continuously. Our now-older generation of liberation theologians learned the dialogical style respectful of disagreement, which we practiced in part because we knew the change we sought required a wide range of support systems for diverse constituencies. Our theories may not always have borne the stamp of our diversity concretely enough, but our *practices* encouraging diversity fueled our theoretical learnings directly. Much of the work that we did therefore encouraged a dialogical, not a competitive, ethos.

Today we are living in a hostile, neoliberal climate.[10] The chilling hand of this neoliberalism is contemptuous of any political commitment as "political correctness."[11] This discourages *any practice norm* for defining truthfulness. Neoliberalism is currently working its way into the academic bloodstream so deeply that this point cannot be too much stressed: the lifeblood of feminist religious thought in the late twentieth century has been *resistance* to any episteme of "correctness." Here as in our pragmatic practice, rather than "foundationalist" justifications for religious truth, most feminist theologies have been *appropriately post-modernist,* and in my view far less dogmatic than some current feminist theories that describe any truth claim as "violence."[12]

OTHER ELEMENTS OF OUR LEGACY

In retrospect, the impact of feminist liberation work in the(a)ology has been as dramatic as, from one point of view, it was unexpected. Feminist voices became numerous and posed questions that had to be heard and addressed even in some highly traditional academic and religious circles. The much-remarked massive backlash against feminism is to a considerable extent a measure of the groundedness of our sometimes less-than-elegant-theory in a practice consistent with our intention to *do* "liberating theology." Will setting aside the rhetoric of "doing liberating theology," a prospect that some now celebrate, assure that practices of inclusion remain *the* criterion for whether speech acts may be said to be "truth-bearing?" As one who is not prepared to give up the ongoing search for more or less adequacy in truth claims, I am not optimistic. While it is clear that our task is to accelerate religious and moral movement away from *canonical* readings of religious traditions, treating all *theological* traditions as at best "works in progress" and as completely contestable, we need not eschew the middle ground of "feminist standpoint" theory.[13] Positioning ourselves spiritually for an unending struggle to realign theo-moral resources away from the truth-as-given, most of our work must aim at *creating* "the truths needed" to bring us to a less violent and more cordial common life.

In sum, then, I believe that an important epistemic shift has already occurred, along with the development of the practice of "networking" toward ever new and shifting solidarities. It is a legacy no one should challenge. Networking has been and must continue to be our the(a)ological mode of practice par excellence.[14]

This legacy, especially powerful in light of Letty Russell's work, was also accompanied in our generation by a singular skepticism never much enamored of the standards of pedagogy prevailing in the academy, including academies of theological education. Truth to tell, most of us shared with Letty a willingness to spend perhaps an inordinate amount of our time and energies seeking even *minor* revisions in the curricular, teaching, and institutional practices of the schools where we worked. Few of us gained kudos for the multidimensional involvements we took on. Our research and publications sometimes suffered from our wider investments in academic change, but none of us was or could have been a theorist for theory's sake—if only because all of us understood how much change was needed and knew that *only as we struggled for it* would our theories come closer to adequacy.

In the theological schools where we worked, exploding populations of women presented us with demands that none of us could ignore. In fact, women students, who would often tolerate suffering at the hands of men, invariably expected us, their beloved feminist teachers, "to walk on water."[15] For most of us the workload was unbelievable, and in the face of it we largely proved astonishingly and wonderfully resistant to trying to pull off miracles! Perhaps Letty Russell, better than any of us, modeled a realism in the search for change, all the while being completely persistent in its pursuit. She worked for a revolution of "small changes."[16] It was clear to us that the deconstruction of patriarchy (or "demonarchy," as my womanist colleague Delores Williams has recently taught me to prefer)[17] allowed no superficial commitments to change. If a "liberal" cultural ideology had taught us an overly simple hopefulness that change was possible, our lives as lived out taught us another lesson altogether—a clarity that *nothing* deeply serious for women would happen easily or once and for all, much less in our lifetimes.

Years ago, when Phyllis Trible and I shared an inaugural event celebrating our respective professorships, we received an inspiring reminder of the long-term nature of liberation struggle. Phyllis had come to Union Theological Seminary's faculty as a distinguished scholar from another institution, while I had finally gained promotion from within, after endless battles over my scholarly competence. Because our respective accessions to Union's senior faculty had not been easy, we created an event to mark and celebrate *two* feminist professorial inaugurations. On the occasion, a number of women from Boston Theological Institute faculties made a banner for our respective professorial processions. The banner depicted small drops of water falling on a huge rock and carried the well-known words of a Holly Near song: "the rock will wear away." In the twenty ensuing years, even with all our collective accomplishments, the image of water working ever so slowly, so slowly wearing away stone, remains an apt metaphor for the work women must continue to do.

ONGOING SOURCES OF BACKLASH

It is all too obvious to me that, as we near the millennium, the new Christian Right coalitions command near-monopoly power of interpretation as the sole organized public voice of Christianity. Among us, the wearying organized and systematic discrediting of feminism is taking a toll of ideological fragmentation. Audre Lorde's cautions regarding "the master's tools" of ideological divisiveness are more relevant than ever before.[18] Daily among us, even some of the best insights of postcolonial and gender- and sex-transgressing theories are now *appealed to in order to legitimate* newly "objectivistic" theological strategies. Revival of patriarchal assumptions today takes the form of appeals to Christian cultural particularity and post-modernist communal identity.[19] Now as never before, reaction is able to present itself using the intellectually respectable face and creative style that the postliberal apolitical aestheticism enables. At times I wonder if younger feminists see the dangers of this situation. Personal brilliance, I fear, can sometimes obscure subtle retreats from an uncompromising political practice of advocacy for women.

Given this situation, it is not surprising that there is little clarity or sustained conversation among the growing numbers of women in the academy about the ongoing directions that our feminist religious studies, the(a)ology, and public policy initiatives should take. In the face of this situation, the good news is that our diversity *is* growing, and as noted, the "messiness" of our lives and work is on the increase. Even in the most traditionalist academic enclaves there is now recognition that, whatever the future portends, it should not be shaped exclusively by white, Eurocentric knowledge perspectives. But elitism is also alive and well, and with the growing homogeneity of the antipolitical and aesthetic neoliberal voice, only a few non-Western cultural critiques are given a genuine hearing.[20] These are selected by male Western elites and often feature only elite voices from other cultures. Popular voices, and above all popular and grassroots political movements for change, are invariably excluded.[21] The real virus of Eurocentrism will never be challenged simply by incorporating other cultural elites.

GENUINE CULTURAL DECENTERING: SOME SURPRISES FOR ALL OF US

The full range of the deep epistemic shifts required to accomplish a needed European and North American decentering is bound to require a respectful overturning of many of our attitudes of contempt toward lived-world cultural realities and spiritualities that have sustained those marginalized by dominant Western sensibilities. This includes the religio-political views rejected by most cultural elites and the spiritual practices that sustain the actual resistance of concrete communities. These frequently include cosmological and religious claims that Western and non-Western elites alike frown upon. Even the axioms of post-modernism that I have celebrated here may need to be reviewed.[22]

In a vehemently antipolitical world (the heart of neoliberal polemic), the *practice* of a serious religious feminism is sure to be ever more difficult, postmodernist jargon to the contrary notwithstanding. If concrete practices of resistance flag, the critical consciousness generated by those practices will also wane. For most of my generation, the heart of feminist religio-moral work was lived out and worked out actively between our concrete religious communities and actual ecumenical (that is, planetary) and interreligious networks of women. We measured a postcolonial "decentering" of our Eurocentrism by ongoing involvement in global projects and perspectives. Postcolonialism was far more than an endless set of skeptical questions about problematic truth claims and suspect "manners of speaking." It was through these practical involvements that we discovered the insularity of our own cultures and the need for retheorizing our own cultural understandings and certitudes. Yet, at the moment, trumpet calls to post-modernist feminism seem to me to lead more often to enunciations of what one *cannot* do, say or mean than to interesting re-visioning of what we *can* mean religiously, morally, or even descriptively.

THE COMPLICITY OF ACADEMIC
INSTITUTIONS IN NEO-LIBERALISM

The cultural crisis through which little planet Earth and its dependents are passing also requires all who espouse any version of feminist work to recognize that our academic insitutions themselves are deeply complicit in that crisis, and that they are deeply and profoundly *aligned* with dominant political and economic systems. Those who gain self-esteem through academic achievements are particularly vulnerable to hubris on this point, as Mary Fulkerson has frequently reminded us.[23] The successes of academic feminism in religious studies programs and in theological schools could well lead feminist concern for diversity to be erased by elitist cultural identifications that catch many off guard in the face of an ongoing, grinding pressure for academic conformity. *Nothing that can be "learned" in the present academy can teach any of us what we need to know about political activism.* Grassroots activism together with the rough-and-tumble of actual global networking are the only sources of the knowledge we need. These are the two sites—the only two—where the lessons most needed can be learned. If I am right about this, the taste for the messiness and complexity so much needed to expand the tiny beachheads women in theology and religious studies have gained over the past thirty years depends on concretely maintaining global and local activist contacts. Without them, complacency about a static notion of an already-achieved multicultural sophistication may occur.

All around us, in the midst of turmoil, the newer global political-economic institutions are continuously sponsoring powerful new neoliberal theoretical constructions that legitimate their control.[24] Let no one miss the point that avant-garde feminist literary theory and queer literary theory in particular are at risk for a new captivity because of their overreliance on French philosophical sources and their reaction against the vicious positivism of formerly structuralist historical perspectives. Crass neoliberal calls for the "recovery of cultural values" do not take feminist and queer theorists in, but harder to detect neomodern reinscriptions of postliberal stylistic "traditions of excellence" have an impact on them because style and creativity have become so important in themselves. How will so far achieved commitments to diversity continue to propel us to new coalitions under such circumstances? May we not find ourselves moving down a different road, the one where clever expressionism of fractured subjectivities is ever more cleverly articulated? Emerging feminist theories now being generated in the academy may produce moral and spiritual wisdom sufficient to keep us in touch with concrete longings and yearnings for the changes we need, but they may also deliver us to new games of academic upmanship, poetically expressed.

Current calls for ever more critical and postliberal theory are no substitute for clarification of assumptions and carefully formulated conversations about the possibilities of ongoing feminist theorizing. Too much recent feminist discourse has been dismissive of questions needing ongoing work rather than satirical rejection.[25] To put the point bluntly: too many of us are accepting "the rhetorics of post-modernity" without the depth of textual engagement needed to understand what appeals to post-modernity really propose and reject. Sweeping generalizations about a necessary post-modernity do not suffice. Post-modernist theorizing is "in" for theology and ethics, but post-modernist critics are diverse and varied. Their theses, in my view, have led many to embrace some "misplaced prohibitions" about what thea(o)logians can and cannot claim in our work.

URGENT QUESTIONS, NOT GLIB ANSWERS

Several topics only touched on here need far more careful discussion in current feminist religio-moral theory than they have so far received. Three in particular deserve at least brief further comment here. First, the immense but subtle power of the neoliberal ethos escalates daily in academia, and it is not well diagnosed by most religionists, who imagine that claims of objectivity in knowledge are weakening. To the contrary, ours is a time of unparalleled metaphysical control—albeit a control by neoclassical economic theory, with its withering contempt for "political correctness." In the face of this, it is disastrous for religio-cultural studies to rule out any sources of social-political-theoretical voice, much less to embrace escalating elitism born of the dismantling of opportunities for broad-based participation in higher education. Increasingly, only economic elites who can learn the expressionism of stylistically defined "meritocratic" achievers find their way into places where the most admired religious studies occur. In the universities where elites gather, the economists teach the true metaphyscis and everyone else practices poetic deconstruction of truth claims. As noted, some globally recognized elite intellectuals from outside the "colonial center" are occasionally heard and sometimes even lionized in these elite bastions, but fewer and fewer grassroots voices are being heard there. To forget that the feminisms and feminist theorizings that spawned and fueled our work were generated by women's activism is suicidal. Activism with and for community and against enduring patterns of violence, resistance toward the concrete sources of life threat, the "primary emergencies" that require daily encounter in women's lives, are our lifeblood. These movements, grounded in the discourse of justice and human rights, do not share the total moral and religious skepticism characteristic of Western epistemic skepticism. Certainly, the demand for decentering Enlightenment and Western hegemonic theorizings will require a careful revisiting of epistemic perspectives. This will no doubt include a newly serious interreligious dialogue that involves interrogation of Western knowledge binaries of (among others) spiritual/material and religious/secular.

Second, those of us (myself included) who feel at home in post-modern feminist discourse in North America may be required to recognize that our nearly a priori rejections include the convictions that other cultures value— that is, cosmologies, metaphysics, or inclusive narratives of valuation. The "spiritualities" and the "materialities" (always both) of many non-Western cultures are, by our Western standards, "pre-modern." And the radical *desacrilization* of "reality" underlying our Western binary—secular (or profane) and religious—seems only to grow stronger as enthusiasm for difference and avoidance of any and all essentialisms increases among us. Many of our calls for de-centering involve deep and growing skepticism precisely about the sorts of affirmations that are the heart of non-Western worldviews. Nor dare feminists fail to note that it is a Eurocentered male nihilism that has erupted to declare the death of most Western theoretical traditions. Articulating skepticism about the meaningfulness and adequacy of any and all presumably objectifying discourses does not open the way to the necessary new dialogue. While some of these lines of neopatriarchal analysis have more salience among feminist theorists in other fields of study than they do in religious studies, there is evidence that a new post-modernist religious dogmatism is on the increase. Surely we must ask: Can we celebrate multiculturalism while proclaiming the impossibility of certitudes that are an epistemic bedrock for many non-Western cultural traditions?

In my networking, I have often heard religious women of other cultures express astonishment at the corrosive attitudes toward knowledge that they believe they encounter in Western intellectual traditions. On one occasion, a woman religious educator put the point succinctly: "Your culture seems to look at knowledge *as you look at the world economically*—knowledge, like all other resources you image, is to be understood within the *conditions of scarcity*. You seem to believe that only a few can really possess it. By contrast, in my culture we believe that knowledge is everywhere, that everyone can learn and everyone can share what they know. Truth is inexhaustible. When everyone teaches and everyone learns, only then will we approximate the range of truth we need."[26] I think of this woman when I hear the ever-growing lists of things that the academically sophisticated tell us we cannot claim to know or have no warrant to say. We have, it seems, forgotten even the simpler wisdom of a great post-modernist male philosopher of this century, Ludwig Wittgenstein, who dethroned logical positivism by contending, "It is not the business of the philosopher to tell people what they can and cannot claim."[27]

It is also not for the feminist to replace specific arguments with categorical constraints against certain philosophical claims. So many such a priori constraints have, as I have already noted, derived from French intellectual traditions, above all those bordering on neoliberalisms that have proclaimed the "death" of Marxism. The highly ambiguous legacy of positivist structuralism is obvious, but the "fate" of Marxism in the collapse of French social theory needs a book-length study. Here it can only be observed that the legacy of the "decline" of Marxism in French thought has been a tendency to challenge or dismiss any generalizations regarding the historical character of political economy, labeling all social theory as "master narrative" and "grand theory," though only certain forms of French social theory deserved that characterization. However, the decentering of a few of the worst positivisms created by those Frenchmen who invoked Karl Marx's name has hardly ruled out the growing creativity and persuasiveness of numerous neo-Marxist streams of theory, particularly those addressing cultural formation through a careful analysis of concrete political-economic change. Such theories are gaining even greater attention in the newer global networks of sociopolitical analysis, and those who seek theoretical insights adequate to analyze ongoing events should not ignore this work.[28]

Finally, just as criticisms of grand theory have not discredited sociohistorical perspectives on political economy, so challenges to experience as a suspect concept have not eroded empiricist or pragmatic truth claims. Many of us did not begin with *transcendental* philosophical notions of human identity or privatized views of individuated personhood as the appropriate starting points for human self-understanding or so-called human rationality. "Experience" was never "in" a private arena. In my own view, it is important to continue to invoke experience in order to specify more clearly the *interrelational character* and the *perspectival limits* of what we can claim. Contrary to some, my contention that experience is the crucible from which knowledge claims should be made is rooted in a commitment to perspectival rather than abstract knowledge.

Experiential claims, of course, are not only perspectival but always situated and finite. Whether or how they relate to other subjectivities comes to be known only through the discernments of those "others" who will invoke their own particular horizons of experience. *All testing of truth claims is dialogical,* and important for most of us, narrativity as such is not what we appeal to when we speak of experiential truthfulness. Narrativity plays an important role in "coming to awareness of truth," but while some male theologians appear to have suggested that narrativity produces truth, I have never heard a woman theologian say precisely this. In my view, narrativity feeds the formation of reflexive awareness as an ongoing *source* of self-knowledge. It is not, however, *the* source of our knowledge per se. Without exception, knowledge is relational and grows out of intersubjective confirmations of a variety of sorts. We narrate—that is, we order our experience as subjects—in order to situate our agency, shape it in relationship to others, and to become *subjects to ourselves.* This is a process that is possible only because our subjectivity itself is a *continuous pulling together or gathering-in* (as Whitehead noted) of the blooming, buzzing, and potentially infinite flux, the continous process in which such subjectivity as we may come to possess is embedded. We do not "need" to become fixed or definite subjects, and the subjects we may become are changing, multilayered, and always potentially inexhaustible. Multiple identities indeed!

Like any good post-modernist, however, I (and a lot of feminist liberation thea(o)logians with me) will not readily surrender our rights to claim, albeit relatively, that *through experience we meet endless otherness,* which we come to "know" through the lenses of our theories and their ongoing uses. We will continue to revise those theories as we go, changing them as we encounter dissent to their adequacy, aptness or applicability. Thereby we learn the limits of what we know—when others tell us that their experience is different or our account does not work for them. Thereby our experience teaches us who *we* are at the moment, and thereby we gain further data for reformulating our theory in order to move to another identity. As in the past, I will frequently overstate the meaning, significance, and generalizability of what I know, and happily, I will learn from my mistakes. But I will not deny, not now, not ever, that my experience mediates truth, and that my ongoing search for truthfulness is more than a manner of speaking. Nor will I assume that the truth telling I do out of my life experience will be of no interest or help to another unless that person is like me in most respects. Some very different others have told me that I have helped them understand, and some very different others have enhanced my understanding. I have learned often that others welcome the truth I have to share, just as they evoke learnings in me that I did not expect but need.

Even though all this highly proximate truth seeking and truth telling must go on endlessly, I will not give up the conviction that there are numerous, if partial, procedures for adjudicating between "better" and "worse" claims about what is, what is good, and what is worthy of reverence and devotion. If all this makes me sound "pre-modern" or "modernist," so be it. It surely makes me believe that feminist thea(o)logical work remains a lovely thing to do, and that my longing to stay on the journey home-to-liberation is no colonial impulse or desire for control. Should all talk of liberation thea(o)logies wane as the outmoded dreams of older bourgeoisie like myself? I have been pondering this question for some time now, but the more I do, the more I muse that Letty, following old Karl, had it right, and that I—and yes, everybody else—do best when we live toward freedom, refusing to settle for anything less. This implies that we can discern some dimensions of what authentic freedom is, and we can rule out some pseudo-claims as specious.

NOTES

1. The term *reformist* was first applied to Letty Russell's and Rosemary Radford Ruether's work in the introduction to *Woman-Spirit Rising: A Feminist Reader in Religion*, ed. Carol Christ and Judith Plaskow (New York: Harper & Row, 1979). The term was frequently used to designate any of us who did not characterize our work as post-Christian. I have long protested applying political terms to how feminists position ourselves vis-à-vis our religious communities, noting, for example, that in subsequent discussion Russell, Ruether, and I, among others, have been much more critical of capitalist political economy than many religious feminists who are "post-Christian" and are regularly characterized as "radical."

2. The term became feminist currency with the publication of Susan Faludi's *Backlash: The Undeclared War against American Women* (New York: Doubleday, 1991). See also Carter Heyward, Beverly W. Harrison, Mary E. Hunt, Emilie M. Townes, Starhawk, Anne L. Barstow, and Paula M. Cooey, *Journal of Feminist Studies in Religion* 10 (Spring 1994), pp. 91–111.

3. Mary Daly's important work has had impact beyond the fields of religious studies. Many who have been influenced by her, however, miss the differences between her original, rather more traditional starting point and the starting points of those of us who did not presume we needed foundational warrants for theology resting on a philosophy of Being. Daly's most recent work is *Quintessence . . . Realizing the Archaic Future: A Radical Elemental Feminist Manifesto* (Boston: Beacon Press, 1998).

4. Early feminist discussions of Alfred North Whitehead's work can be found in Sheila G. Daveney, ed., *Feminism and Process Thought* (Lewiston, N.Y.: Edwin Mellen Press, 1981). What needs to be remembered about Whitehead's work is that he did not aspire to do metaphysics as a foundational philosophical enterprise. His was a post-modernist project—i.e., to show that scientific knowledge did not preclude some reflection on general theory. Metaphysics was not, for him, "first knowledge" but rather speculation based on extending empirical knowledges to greater levels of generality.

5. The term is from Charles Tilly, *Durable Inequalities* (Berkeley: University of California Press, 1997). Tilly's notion, which translates "structural inequality" in a less-static direction, is helpful in reconceptualizing "structure" in ways more congenial to social constructionist assumptions.

6. Most followers of Karl Barth in the United States misread his political intent because they overlooked his situatedness in European political debates among left, center, and right. Letty Russell always understood the political-economic significance of Barth's theology.

7. References to liberal protestants as God's "frozen people" originated with Robert McAfee Brown in his "St. Hereticus" columns in the journal *Christianity and Crisis*.

8. Remarks by Letty M. Russell and J. Shannon Clarkson at the publication party for the *Dictionary of Feminist Theologies* (Louisville, Ky.: Westminster John Knox Press, 1996) at the American Academy of Religion meeting, San Francisco, 1997.

9. The phrase "if women are to count" is drawn from an important feminist study in economic ethics by Pamela K. Brubaker, *Women Don't Count: The Challenge of Women's Poverty to Christian Ethics* (Atlanta: Scholars Press, 1994).

10. The term *neoliberal* was self-selected by Reagan-Bush-era theorists whose liberal worldview was reconstituted under the strictures of recent neoclassical economic ideology. Neoliberals accept the defenses of market capitalism generated in the

1980s and consider market captialism the best possible political economy, given the abstract mathematical theories of choice that were generated during that period. Neoliberals accept, usually without historical defense, the thesis that markets are the most "efficient" way to achieve "solutions" to social problems. Neoliberals believe that "politics" can (and should) be rendered obsolete by the successes of an unfettered economy.

11. For an important analysis of the right-wing origins of the term *political correctness*, see Richard Feldstein, *Political Correctness: A Response from the Cultural Left* (Minneapolis: University of Minnesota Press, 1997).

12. The most emphatic theoretical denunciation of "objectivity" claims as "violent" is found in Judith Butler, *Excitable Speech* (Berkeley: University of California Press, 1998).

13. "Feminist standpoint theory" is the epistemic alternative to the sort of anti-objectivism in feminist theory generated by theorists such as Judith Butler and others often closely aligned with French feminist theorists. Standpoint theorists are frequently aligned more with feminist critiques of science than with literary theory. See, for example, Donna Haraway, *Cyborgs, Simians, and Women* (London: Routledge & Kegan Paul, 1991), pp.183–201; and Sandra Harding, *Whose Science: Whose Knowledge? Thinking from Women's Lives* (Ithaca: Cornell University Press, 1991).

14. An excellent theoretical treatment of networking as a goal of feminist political agency appears in Janet R. Jakobsen, *Working Alliances and the Politics of Difference: Diversity and Feminist Ethics* (Bloomington: Indiana University Press, 1998).

15. The phrase is from an important early essay by Jo Freeman in her *Politics of Women's Liberation: A Case Study of an Emerging Social Movement and Its Relation to the Policy Press* (New York: David McKay Co., 1975).

16. The phrase is from Marge Piercy. It was Mary Pellauer, however, who reminded feminist religious thinkers that the needed women's revolution must be "a revolution of small changes."

17. See Delores S. Williams "Black Women's Literature and the Task of Feminist Theology," in Clarissa W. Atkinson, Constance Buchanan, and Margaret R. Milcs, eds., *Immaculate and Powerful: The Female in Sacred Image and Social Reality* (Boston: Beacon Press, 1985) pp. 5–10; and Delores S. Williams, *Sisters in the Wilderness: The Challenge of Womanist God-Talk* (Maryknoll, N.Y.: Orbis Books, 1993).

18. Audre Lorde's canonical essay "The Master's Tools" appears in at least four books. See her famous collection *Sister Outsider* (Trumansburg, N.Y.: Crossing Press, 1984), pp. 110–13.

19. See, for example, the works of John Milbank and Stanley Hauerwas, both of whom celebrate the particularity and uniqueness of Christian theological claims but reclaim the notion of only one, "classical," standard Christian truth as right or "orthodox" (read: patriarchal). Denying the ongoing and continuous contentions among Christians is evidence of pre-modern "post-modernism."

20. Anticolonial thinkers such as Gayatri Spivak and Edward Said often ruthlessly satirize Western colonizing truth claims but also treat the intellectual traditions of anticolonialists like themselves as clear-cut, noncontestable. Many non-Western intellectuals seem to have secularized antireligious biases, rather characteristic of the Western counterparts whom they criticize.

21. The divide between feminist intellectuals who theorize in academic isolation and those who do their work in solidarity and collaboration with grassroots movements of various sorts runs through and across national and global-cultural al-

lignments. Not all critics of Eurocentrism are deeply engaged with concrete communities of struggle.

22. It should be clear that my own theological bias is in sympathy with the assumption of social-constructive historical theory, and that I am skeptical of the sort of metaphysics that characterized "classical" Western philosophy. This makes me comfortable with the consensual Western assumption regarding post-modernity, that metaphysics is suspect as a source of knowledge. However, all of us need to be clear that a genuine cross-cultural global dialogue will require the careful revisiting of even our own most cherished "post-modernist" certitudes. I also want to dissent in the strongest possible way from any readings of post-modernism that do not make a connection between late capitalism and the suppression of normative political and moral categories.

23. Mary McClintock Fulkerson has made this point in several essays and in *Changing the Subject: Women's Discourses and Feminist Theology* (Minneapolis: Fortress Press, 1994); see esp. pp. 133–82 and 355–95 for an excellent depiction of the work of feminist theologies.

24. I believe one of the less-desirable consequences of the numerous and not always carefully constructed lines of post-modernist criticism is already becoming visible in the religious studies literature—i.e., the "blending" of scientific, religious, moral, and political claims, treating each of these as an "equal claimant" to knowledge. The result has been some new interdisciplinary speculations that combine astonishing sense and nonsense. See, for example, Nancy Murphy and George F. R. Ellis, *On the Moral Nature of the Universe: Why Theologians Should Pay Attention to Science* (Minneapolis: Fortress Press, 1996). Murphy and Ellis bring together debatable scientific claims with even more contestable theological assumptions about Christianity. The total erasure of "middle ground" consensus about truth and falsity in historically developed arenas of inquiry hardly constitutes a great gain amid the new dogmatisms of neoliberalism, with its sequestered metaphysic of neoclassical economy.

25. Feminist discussions of the limitations of appeals to experience frequently puzzle me. Some seem to challenge such appeals altogether and to rule out any reference to identity, but then move back to something approaching a "standpoint theory" position. See, for example, Sheila Greeve Daevaney, "Continuing the Story, but Departing the Text: A Historicist Interpretation of Feminist Norms in Theology," in *Horizons in Feminist Theology: Identity, Tradition, and Norms,* ed. R. S. Chopp and S. G. Davaney (Minneapolis: Fortress Press, 1997), pp. 198–214; as well as her contribution to "Round Table Discussion," *Journal of Feminist Studies in Religion* 11 (Spring 1995), pp. 119–23. I agree with much that Davaney says but long for greater specificity as to what methods and claims really meet her criteria for adequacy. I also worry about her following Richard Rorty on epistemic matters.

26. This conversation occurred at a meeting at the University of Zimbabwe in Harare in 1991. Sadly, I never learned the name of the remarkable woman who engaged me in this revelatory exchange about the limitations of Western views of knowledge.

27. Ludwig Wittgenstein, *Philosophical Investigations,* trans G.E.M. Anscombe, 2d ed. (New York: Macmillan Co., 1958).

28. See Ellen Meiksins Wood, *Democracy against Capitalism: Renewing Historical Materialism* (Cambridge: Cambridge University Press, 1995); and Frederic Jameson, ed., *The Cultures of Globalization* (Durham, N.C.: Duke University Press, 1998).

PART 4

LIBERATING ESCHATOLOGY:
The Hope of the Table

13

COMPANIONS IN HOPE

Spirit and Church in the Fourth Gospel

Sharon H. Ringe

Liberating Eschatology

The assumption undergirding this essay is that, chronologically speaking, God has no eschatological word—no λόγος ἔσχατος, in the sense of a *final* word—on the project of creation. Letty Russell has taught me that truth, with her insistence on looking at present glimpses of liberation and wholeness as an "aperitif" of God's intent for us and part of God's eternal truth. Letty also taught me, however, to recognize God's eschatological or *ultimate* word in God's love for the world expressed in God's self-investment in that world. For the Christian church, Jesus Christ is the paradigm and principal (though not sole) locus of that love, bringing community in place of isolation, justice for all who are poor or oppressed, healing for all who suffer, and life so abundant and authentic that death itself cannot stop it.

I would further identify a "liberating eschatology" in the mystery that "Christ has died; Christ is risen," and because Christ is risen, God is still with us—Emmanuel—embodied now in communities of justice and peace and accompanying us into a future that belongs to God.[1] I would be hard pressed to trace that working definition to any specific biblical text or even to a single biblical author or tradition. The reference points of incarnation, community, justice, peace, and divine accompaniment as central to the creative, redemptive, and sustaining activity of the triune God echo throughout scripture. Taken as a whole, the New Testament sustains the tension between present and future as the temporal locus where these reference points can be found in the time since Jesus' life-death-resurrection. I recognize that my formulation of that tension as "accompanying us into the future" emphasizes the present aspect (albeit without fully losing the future affirmation). That emphasis expresses my reaction to the "deferred living" urged by my patriarchal upbringing, which portrayed life as a waiting game—not "real" until some magical future time, which was often tied to the arrival of Prince Charming, a secular redeemer-figure whose kiss would make everything whole. In my experience, such marking time "until . . ." has little in common with the abundant life and "good news" that I understand to be at the heart of the Christian proclamation. Rather, in the embodied reality of divine presence in "Christa community,"[2] the fullness of God's love and will for life in the world is present already, and remains so through the eternity of God's own life.

A Lens on the Fourth Gospel

"Liberating eschatology" seen in this light serves as a lens through which to examine the Fourth Gospel's picture of the figure and role of the "other παράκλητος" (John 14:16, 26; 15:26; 16:7), the "Spirit of truth" (John 14:17; 15:26; 16:13), as the vehicle for the continuing presence of Christ in the Johannine community. Just as the Fourth Gospel presents a narrative portrait of Jesus distinct from that of the Synoptic tradition, so also that Gospel depicts the Holy Spirit in terms found elsewhere in the New Testament only in the closely related 1 John (2:1; 4:6; 5:6). The starting point for the study is the term παράκλητος itself and what is claimed about this figure in the Fourth Gospel. That picture is then contextualized in the larger narrative context of the christological and ecclesiological project of the Fourth Gospel and in what can be known about the historical situation of the Johannine community.

THE παράκλητος, THE SPIRIT OF TRUTH

Word Study

The word παράκλητος is related to the verb παρακαλεω, literally, "call along-side" or "summon," but often with the derivative meaning "comfort."[3] The use of the noun is attested in secular Greek as early as the fourth century B.C.E. to refer to a person called to give assistance. The word seems connected to legal contexts, though it is not a technical term for a court official.[4] Except for two manuscripts that use the word to identify the friends otherwise recognized as "comforters" of Job 16:2, the noun does not occur in the Septuagint. The meaning "comforter," however, deviates from the usual meaning of "advocate" that the word retains in Philo, in early Christian literature outside the New Testament, and where it occurs as a loanword in rabbinic texts.[5] The basic meaning of "advocate" is also reflected in 1 John 2:1, where Christ is portrayed as an advocate with God on behalf of sinning Christians.

That background would lead one to propose the meaning of "advocate" where the word is used in the Fourth Gospel (as is the case in the New Revised Standard Version, Jerusalem Bible, New English Bible, and Revised English Bible), but the history of interpretation and translation has not always supported that choice. Two factors account for the resulting range of translations. First, in the Gospel the term does not carry the intercessory meaning found in 1 John, where the παράκλητος is a mediator between the believers and God in the sense of an "advocate" with God on behalf of sinful believers. Instead, as the discussion below demonstrates, the work of the παράκλητος in the Fourth Gospel is directed toward the believers themselves, or through them toward the hostile world. Second, since the term occurs only in the speech attributed to Jesus on the night of his arrest, and since the principal theme of the speech is the preparation of Jesus' followers to deal with his approaching absence, a number of translators have chosen to direct the meaning of the word toward their pastoral needs ("Comforter" [King James Version], "Counselor" [Revised Standard Version], "Helper" [Today's English Version and New Revised Standard Version note], "Consolador" [Reina Valera]).[6] An examination of the passages where the term occurs is necessary to clarify its meaning in the Fourth Gospel.

The Word παράκλητος in Its Literary Context in the Fourth Gospel

The "farewell discourse" of Jesus in the Fourth Gospel (chaps. 13—17) is a complex tapestry of themes, the various threads of which surface and disappear again in intricate patterns and designs. One's conclusion about the dominant patterns depends on the limits of the section identified for study—how close or how far away one has focused the zoom lens of one's investigative camera. Small sections exhibit their own structure, but then, when the view broadens, parts of the smaller sections turn out to play roles in the larger design in which they participate.[7] This complexity doubtless stems from the interweaving of source materials and their subsequent redactions, through a lengthy process of the Gospel's formation.

For the purposes of this study, I have allowed the four occurrences of the term *παράκλητος* to establish the dimensions of the text being examined. The resulting "unit," then, is 14:15–16:15. In that unit I have identified the following structure:

> A. 14:15–26—First Paraclete Section: Love, Commandment, Presence
> B. 14:27–31—Jesus' Leave-Taking: Assurance for the Community
> C. 15:1–17—Friendship and Accompaniment
> B'. 15:18–25 [16:2–3]—Jesus' Leave-taking: Threat from "the World"
> A'. 15:26–16:15—Second Paraclete Section: Testimony against "the World"

The two sections in which the Paraclete is named set forth that figure's threefold task as providing the believers with assurance of divine presence and peace, teaching the believers and guiding them into truth, and enabling the believers to testify to the world about Jesus.[8] These sections frame and thus define a reflection on how Jesus' followers (and their followers who read this Gospel) are to continue and to further Jesus' "works" after he returns to God who sent him (14:12). The challenge these followers face has two dimensions: their own grief, both at the loss of a friend and companion and at their awareness of all that they still do not understand; and their experience of the hostility of "the world" (15:18–25) and, in particular, of religious authorities (16:2), which they understand to be a consequence of their discipleship.

The First Paraclete Section: Love, Commandment, Presence (14:15–26).

The passage that introduces the Paraclete in the Fourth Gospel is itself in the shape of a chiasmus, as follows:

> a. 14:15–18—The Paraclete, the Spirit of truth: Receive, abide, know
>   b. 14:19–21—Love and keeping commandments
>   c. 14:22—Distinction between disciples and world: Reveal
>   b′. 14:23–24—Love and keeping "words"
> a′. 14:25–26—The Paraclete, the Holy Spirit: Teach, remind

The section is introduced by a saying that links loving Jesus and keeping his "commandments." The content of his commandment (the singular and plural forms appear to be used interchangeably, as do their synonyms *word* and *words*) has been given in 13:34 as loving one another, following the model of Jesus' love for them.[9] The same combination of motifs occurs with various pairs of subjects and objects in 14:21, 23, 24, 31; 15:10, 12. In 14:15, however, these motifs serve as the protasis and the first half of a compound apodosis setting forth a covenant between the disciples and the soon-to-be-departing Jesus, who makes a commitment on God's behalf.

The covenant introduces the παράκλητος, further identified as ἄλλος παράκλητος, which clearly implies that there has been a prior one. The context of the preparation for Jesus' absence posits him as the prototype, and the claims made about this "other's" role confirm that identification. Both are emissaries sent from God (3:16, 17; 5:24, 30, 36; 14:16). Like the Word made flesh (1:11–13), the Paraclete is neither recognized nor received by the world (14:17) but only by those to whom the Sender grants it. Both Jesus and the Paraclete are identified with "the truth" (8:32; 14:6, 17; 15:26; 16:13).[10] The verb μένω identifies "accompaniment" as the basis of their relationship with the disciples (1:38, 39; 2:12; 4:40; 6:56; 11:54; 12:46; 14:10, 17, 25; 15:4, 5, 6, 7, 9, 10, 16). The link between the two figures is made explicit by the first-person singular verbs in 14:18: the one who is speaking and the promised One who is coming speak with a single voice.

Verse 18 gives another important clue to the identity and function of this One who is to come. The assurance that the disciples will not be left "orphans" (ὀρφανούς) applies to them a term common in the Septuagint (most frequently in commandments about protecting "widows and orphans") but occurring only twice in the New Testament. James 1:27 clearly parallels the LXX (Septuagint) usage and appears to refer to the community's responsibility for these potentially most vulnerable members of the society. Here, however, the term is applied to Jesus' followers (whose apprehension at being left alone in the world is suggested narratively by Peter's request to follow Jesus [13:37], Thomas's ignorance about where he was going [14:5], and Philip's request to see God [14:8]), much as it is used among the Greek philosophers to refer to the experience of students bereft of their teacher.[11] In both cases, the emotional sorrow is secondary to the vulnerability and loss of a guiding force that have resulted from the bereavement. More than someone to provide comfort, those left behind in such circumstances need someone to "advocate" on their behalf, like an attorney who can advise them and represent them in their interaction with others. The relationship that they have enjoyed with Jesus prior to his departure results from Jesus' "abiding" with them, and that relationship of accompaniment is now carried forward by the presence of this "other" who is just like him.

The second step of the chiasmus, verses 19–21, develops the theme of assurance of accompaniment that stretches into the future. Key to that assurance is the "knot" of mutual indwelling that integrates Jesus, God, and the disciples (v. 20) and that is linked to their participation in "love" for one another (v. 21).[12] Against our modern association of love only with an emotional connection, here love is connected to their knowledge of Jesus (v. 20) and his self-revelation to them (v. 21), which will be among the tools equipping them for life in the time when the Jesus they have known is absent. The temporal perspective of the entire discourse, and in particular this section, is telescopic, in that the assurance allegedly to Jesus' immediate followers encompasses as well the readers and hearers of the Gospel in subsequent generations. The reason is that the Jesus whom the first disciples *had* known is the same known to subsequent generations in the "other" form of the Paraclete.

The "hinge" or pivot point of the chiasmus, v. 22, underlines the separation between the disciples and "the world," which had already been introduced in v. 17 and which will be developed in 15:18–25. It is that distinction, which moves into separation and finally opposition, that underlies their vulnerability as "orphans" and the necessity for this abiding Advocate.

The chiasmus is completed in two stages. The first takes up again the interrelationship of love and commandment (now called Jesus' "word," given to him from God) and the consequence of divine presence, in verses 23–24. That first step of the chiasmus is then echoed in verses 25–26, where the Paraclete is now identified as the Holy Spirit instead of, as earlier, the Spirit of truth. Once again, the motif of agency is present, as the Spirit is identified as sent by God in Christ's name, and once again the Paraclete has the task of teaching (as also in 16:13) and specifically of reminding them of what Jesus has already taught.

Jesus' Leave-Taking: Assurance for the Community (14:27–31)

The repetitiveness of themes in the "farewell discourse" of the Fourth Gospel is too obvious to require argument. That repetitiveness has led many scholars to suggest that this portion of the Gospel (as well as perhaps larger sections or the Gospel as a whole) has undergone several redactions, as the community reflected in a variety of contexts on the implications of these treasured accounts of words said to be Jesus' final message before his death. The last clause of 14:31 ("Rise, let us be on our way") suggests that at one stage of its development the discourse ended here. The verses that come between the second mention of the Paraclete (in v. 26) and this conclusion (in v. 31c) fit with such a narrative context. They focus on Jesus' leave-taking, with an emphasis on assurance for the disciples about the desirability of this departure for him (his return to his place of origin with God) and them ("Peace I leave with you"). This section draws the hearers in, toward a center that is solid and reliable. God's own faithfulness is affirmed as sufficient for Jesus and for them—an assurance that will stand in sharper relief when the threat against the community from "the world" is identified in the parallel section on Jesus' leave-taking in 15:18–25.

Friendship and Accompaniment (15:1–17)

Between the two sections that focus on Jesus' leave-taking (14:27–31 and 15:18–25) is the central section (15:1–17) of the larger chiasmus that shapes the portion of the Gospel we are examining. It begins with the image of the vine as a figure for the nature and meaning of the relationship between Jesus and his hearers (15:1–11). Themes of love, abiding (μένω), and keeping the commandments are elaborated on in this reflection that echoes and develops sayings of 14:15–26. Verses 12–17 examine even more closely the nature of Jesus' commandment (13:34; 14:15, 21, 23, 24) and link it to "friendship" as the relationship of Jesus to the disciples, and that of the disciples to one another.

Several common motifs link verses 12–17 to the previous two sections of chapter 15. First, the pre-eminence of God (ὁ πατήρ) is affirmed in each (vv. 1, 9, 15, 16). It is God on whom the life of the vine depends, God who initiates the love *for* Jesus (objective genitive) that he passes on to the others (subjective genitive), and God who is the source of all that Jesus makes known to them. Second is the theme of "abiding" (μένω) as a relationship essential to life: the branches must abide in the vine as the disciples must abide or remain in Jesus (vv. 4, 5, 6, 7), and especially in his love as he abides in God's love (vv. 9, 10), in order that their "fruit" also should abide (v. 16). Third is the motif of the "word" or "commandment," which at once gives life and carries its own commission (vv. 3, 7, 10, 12, 14, 17). Finally, the love in which they are to abide is spelled out as also the content of Jesus' commandment to them: they are to love one another as he loved them (with a total identification with their cause, even to the radical step of "appointing" [τίθημι] his life on their behalf), and by participating in this love for one another, they show themselves to be his friends (vv. 12–17).[13]

The love commandment itself depends on the priority of God's love and on the empowering of remaining or abiding in Jesus (and of him in God). It is thus clear that this friendship is contingent not on the disciples' obedience but on God's prior love. Thus "You are my friends" in verse 14 is parallel to "you will abide in my love" in verse 10, and both statements make profound christological claims. Jesus himself embodies friendship, particularly in the approaching passion or "hour" that overshadows the entire farewell discourse. This self-engagement incarnates the life-giving love of God affirmed in John 3:16, and it is the basis for the claim in 1 John 3:16: "By this we know love, that he appointed his life for us—and we ought to appoint our lives for one another" (my translation). More than simply a moral paradigm, Jesus is the lover/friend whose love affects life in the beloved by granting them an intimacy with God that itself can be called friendship with God. The effect of Jesus' love is thus parallel to the work of Wisdom, who "in every generation passes into holy souls and makes them the beloved ["friends," φίλοι] of God" (Wisd. 7:27).[14]

As the climactic point of the "hinge" of the chiasmus within which John's discussion of the ἄλλος παράκλητος is inscribed, 15:12–17 portrays Jesus as one who befriends and calls the followers to be friends of one another and thereby establishes a crucial dimension of the work of this parallel figure who is to come. The Paraclete will continue to enable friendship to be the lifestyle of the community, which sustains them and establishes a mode of divine presence in their midst. This presence not only provides comfort and strength for the community from within but also equips the community as it interfaces with a hostile world (15:18–25; 16:2–3). This "world," in turn, sets the context for the role of the Paraclete set forth in the final section of the chiasmus (15:26–16:15).

Jesus' Leave-Taking from "the World" (15:18–25 [16:2–3])

Warnings about the world's opposition to Jesus have been expressed earlier in the Fourth Gospel (7:7), but there the community was explicitly exempted from that hatred. Now they are warned that they, too, will be its objects if they continue to embody the divine presence as he did, which is precisely what they have been assured will be the case (15:12–17). The world's responsibility for that hatred is linked to their refusal to receive Jesus (a recurring theme since 1:11), just as they also refuse to accept the "other Paraclete" (14:17). The general opposition of "the world" is given sharper focus in 16:2–3, which repeats the threat that they will be declared ἀποσυνάγωγοι (9:22; 12:42). This dire forecast of what lies ahead for the disciples, which presumably the Johannine community would recognize as a depiction of their reality, requires brief elaboration.

The Context of the Johannine Community

Modern readers are confronted with a challenge of weaving a coherent fabric from slender threads of suggestions and clues to the composition and circumstances of this community. For example, the use of the Jewish festival calendar to anchor key events of Jesus' public ministry (5:1, 9; 6:4; 7:2; 12:1) suggests a community with a substantial number of Jewish members for whom these festivals would have been an important point of reference and order in their lives. In contrast, the fact that practices associated with these festivals are explained suggests that some in the intended audience would not be familiar with them—in other words, Gentiles (and on the basis of the account in chap. 4, some would suggest also Samaritans, who would not necessarily have known how the festivals were kept in Jerusalem). Similarly, details of Judean geography suggest a community that would have recognized such points of reference, but their explanation also provides an orientation for persons not familiar with the land.

The language in which the Gospel is written is another thread that provides a clue to the identity of this community. The words in which the Gospel was written are Greek, but the grammar is more like that of a Semitic language (Hebrew or Aramaic, probably). Some words in the old language are used—especially connected to place names in southern Palestine—but they are explained, as though the author could not be sure everyone would get the old references. This type of language testifies to a community living at the edge of an old life left behind and a new one not yet fully embraced. One imagines an immigrant community that with each generation moves further from its language of origin but whose speech retains its flavor, especially when the members are talking among themselves and not deliberately engaging members of the dominant culture.

If these few threads are woven together, the resulting fabric suggests an ethnically mixed though predominantly Jewish community living outside Palestine, in a context where Greek is the dominant language. The role of the festival calendar and the "blended" language suggest a Jewish enclave in a diaspora city, where the religion of their homeland is practiced and its language is still spoken (perhaps especially among the elders), but where the surrounding culture is also making its mark.

We find few, if any, clues to the economic circumstances of the community.[15] As far as the political circumstances are concerned, such clues as Jesus' words about the destruction of the temple in chapter 2, which cast that shadow over the entire Gospel story, suggest that that event was already part of the history with which the community was having to come to terms. There is, however, no suggestion of immediate hostility or persecution that might account for the atmosphere of siege suggested by 15:18–25. Yet scattered through the Gospel are threads that, woven together, suggest enmity between the Johannine Christians and their parent synagogue. For example, throughout the Gospel οἱ Ιουδαῖοι—most often translated into English as "the Jews"—designates persons hostile to Jesus. In fact, that is a misleading translation of the term, for it clearly does not refer to the religio-ethnic group usually meant by that term, since Jesus himself is sharply distinguished from them. Rather, it seems to mean that part of the Jewish community—Jesus' "own"—who do not accept Jesus (1:11) and with whom John's community is in dispute.

The clearest indication of the tension is voiced in the threat that members of the community will become ἀποσυνάγωγοι on account of their faith (9:22; 12:42; 16:2). A near consensus in Johannine scholarship, which I do not share, is that this term implies a decree of expulsion hanging as a threat against any who confessed Jesus to be the Messiah. There is certainly no external evidence of a systemwide decree of that sort in the first century. It may have been a local policy of leaders of this particular synagogue, perhaps in response to the particular Christology of this Christian group that evoked the charges of ditheism mentioned in 5:18.

What seems at least equally likely, however, is a scenario all too familiar to members of Christian congregations (and, I am told by my Jewish friends, to modern-day synagogues as well).[16] In this scenario, one group has a powerful religious experience that leads them to view the symbols and traditions of their religion in a fresh way. When they try to convince the leaders of the congregation to adopt the new way, the leaders may encourage the group to continue their quest, but they do not adopt the new understandings and practices for the whole congregation. Those whose lives have been changed by their new experience feel rejected and even excluded when their way is not embraced by the congregation. They *feel* forced out, banished for their beliefs. The dominant group would probably deny that anyone is being forced out. In fact, they would probably affirm that the congregation is still deeply concerned for the group. But as the dissidents tell the story, yes, they have been banished, and they are the ones who are really faithful to their religious heritage. Over time, they retell the old stories of their faith in ways that make their own interpretation self-evident from the beginning: there is only one "way," and it is now theirs!

Unfortunately, we do not hear the synagogue's version of what happened with the Johannine community, but only how that community experienced the events. It may be that, in time, the leaders responded with condemnation and demands for conformity (that also would not be unknown in our contemporary experience). In the case of John's community, however, there is an important note of dissonance in the Gospel itself that should compel us to rethink the consensus of threatened expulsion. Chapter 11 tells of the death of Lazarus. The family of Bethany—Mary, Martha, and Lazarus—are the only named characters identified as "loved" by Jesus (11:3, 5), making them, I think, the best candidates for the identity of the unnamed "disciple whom Jesus loved" to whom the Jesus traditions underlying this Gospel are attributed in 21:24. As Martha's confession makes clear, they do confess Jesus as Messiah. And yet, after Lazarus's death, οἱ Ἰουδαῖοι have come out to Bethany to console the sisters (11:31). There is no mention of the threatened expulsion, but rather a pastoral call!

I do think there was a rift between the Johannine community and the synagogue, but I think that community exercised considerable initiative in their religious dislocation. From the synagogue's side, they probably could have stayed in the congregation. From the community's side, having decided that maintaining their identification with the synagogue was not a faithful option for them, the experience was one of threat and unmitigated hostility, in which the counsel and testimony of the ἄλλος παράκλητος was their best defense.

The Second Paraclete Section:
Testimony against "the World" (15:26–16:15)

The second introduction of the Paraclete (15:26–16:15) responds to the hostile context sketched in 15:18–25 and 16:2–3 by accentuating the "advocacy" role of the παράκλητος. In that role, the Paraclete both provides direct testimony (15:26) and sustains the members of the community when they themselves must testify concerning the one in whom they believe (15:27). The specific foci of the Paraclete's own testimony are spelled out in 16:8–11, and 16:12–15 addresses the continuing task of the Spirit of truth to instruct them in—or more precisely, lead them into—"all the truth" (16:13). The section as a whole forms yet another chiasmus, as follows:

a. 15:26–16:1—"Testimony" of the Paraclete and the community: To keep them from stumbling
    b. 16:2–4a—Opposition from the synagogue: So that they remember
    b'. 16:4b–7—Jesus' departure: So that the Paraclete will be sent
a'. 16:8–15—"Testimony" of the Paraclete: To convict the world and to guide the community into "all the truth"

Despite the courtroom language and tone of this section, no formal arena of defense is described. Instead, the assumption is that the disciples, and by implication the Johannine community, like John the Baptist (1:15, 32) and those who met Jesus (4:39; 12:17) before them, must become witnesses to Jesus in their own context.

The Paraclete is crucial to the ongoing instruction that is necessary as the time since Jesus' own teaching grows longer, and as the specific circumstances in which the testimony is required change. The assumption is that the basic opposition between the vision or "way" (14:4–6) of Jesus and that of the world will continue, but that the case for the world's error needs to be made in each generation afresh. The dynamic of continuity between Jesus and this One who is to come (emphasized in 16:7, where Jesus himself is the sender of whom the Paraclete is the agent, and not only the one in whose name God does the sending, as in 14:26) and discontinuity of circumstances is conveyed by three temporal indicators in this section. First, we are reminded that those addressed have been with Jesus ἀπ᾽ ἀρχῆς (15:27), and that is why they are called upon to testify. Second, Jesus' presence with them meant that he could not say ἐξ ἀρχῆς what his imminent departure now makes appropriate (16:4). A third moment is indicated when he will still (ἔτι) need to communicate more to them than they can bear at this moment (16:12), and they will be led into that full truth by the very Spirit of truth (16:13–14).

The first section of this passage provides no content to the Paraclete's testimony to the world, but in 16:8–11 the agenda of the Paraclete—sin, righteousness, and judgment—parallels that of Jesus himself in 5:19–47. This agenda is now even more urgent because of "the world's" continued failure to recognize Jesus, despite his return to God (which for the Johannine community is a past event) and his concomitant overcoming of the world (16:33). The testimony of the Paraclete is to "convict" (ἐλέγχω) the world in matters of sin, righteousness, and judgment. In other words, the world itself is to be persuaded of its errors (of which, presumably, the disciples are already convinced). The reasons for the conviction on the first two matters are presented adversatively (μέν . . . δέ). Thus, in the first case (16:9) the ὅτι identifies what the world has done wrong, while the second (v. 10) explains why the Paraclete has the task of convicting the world. The third point (v. 11) is simply appended with no particular link, but in that case, too, the explanation seems to provide the rationale for the Paraclete's action, namely, that the world's judgment against Jesus has been proven wrong by the fact that Jesus has overcome the world (16:33).[17]

In verse 12 the focus shifts back to the disciples and their readiness to assume their own responsibility to testify. Within the story world—at the end of Jesus' life—the disciples have heard all they can "carry" (βαστάζω). The future task of guidance (literally, "leading them into the way [ὁδηγεω] into all the truth" [author's rendering]) will belong to the Spirit of truth (v. 13), thus link-ing once again "way" and "truth," as in 14:6. (Would it not be appropriate to hear in the background echoes of the "life" to which those terms are joined in that verse as well?) In accomplishing these tasks, the Paraclete, the Spirit of truth, once again fulfills the representative role, acting now on behalf of Jesus ("he will take what is mine and declare it to you," v. 14) as well as of God ("All that the Father has is mine," v. 15) to sustain their presence in this community.

COMPANIONS IN HOPE

For the Fourth Gospel, then, the Paraclete is about eschatology, continuing God's ultimate engagement with us into the time beyond Jesus' earthly life, for the respective present times of the about-to-be-bereaved disciples, of the Johannine community, and into the future forever. This παράκλητος—Advo-cate and Spirit of truth—is the form of Emmanuel/God-with-us, the Word now made flesh in communities of those befriended by Jesus and called to be friends of one another. In their friendship and accompaniment of each other, they are accompanied also by God, as they are led into the way where truth/the Spirit of truth itself is known and, in that knowing, becomes the occasion of liberation (8:32).

Themes of justice and peace in the political and social arenas do not figure directly in the language of the Fourth Gospel about the Paraclete. Since at the beginning of this essay I identified them as crucial marks of liberating escha-tology, however, a word needs to be said about them. In our context as citi-zens of the United States at the end of the twentieth century, the testimony to which we are called by a world hostile to the values central to the Gospel, and a world prepared to treat large numbers of its people as expendable com-modities, is precisely testimony to the God who always hears the cry of God's people (Exod. 6:5). The continued "guidance" for which we long from the Spirit of truth is for ways to give structural and institutional expression to the truth we glimpse. That is at the heart of the eschatological challenge we face—one that continues to draw us together into communities of testimony, where God's presence again can become incarnate and where the truth can be known and again set us free.

NOTES

Unless otherwise noted, the translation of the Bible used in this article is the New Re-vised Standard Version. The Greek text is the fifth edition of the United Bible Soci-eties' Greek New Testament.

    1. "Christ will come again," traditionally the third expression of the "mystery of the faith," seems to me to express in the metaphorical language of another era this same affirmation of divine presence that stretches into an eternal future.

2. Rita Nakashima Brock, *Journeys by Heart: A Christology of Erotic Power* (New York: Crossroad, 1988).
3. In the Septuagint (LXX), for example, the verb is often used in that sense to render such Hebrew verbs as נחם (Gustav Stählin, "παρακαλεω," *Theological Dictionary of the New Testament* 5: 776–777).
4. Johannes Behm, "παράκλητος," *Theological Dictionary of the New Testament* 5: 801.
5. Ibid., 801–803.
6. A similar division between the understanding of the word as "advocate" and "comforter" is reflected in early Christian usage of the term and in its historical-religious background (Ibid., 805–812).
7. The overlapping chiastic patterns identified by Wes Howard-Brook demonstrate this aspect of Johannine structure (*Becoming Children of God: John's Gospel and Radical Discipleship* [Maryknoll, N.Y.: Orbis Books, 1994], passim). I began working on chiastic patterns in sections of this Gospel prior to reading his commentary, and while the suggestions presented here derive from my own work, they have inevitably been influenced by his, in ways too subtle to distinguish.
8. Ben Witherington III, *John's Wisdom: A Commentary on the Fourth Gospel* (Louisville, Ky.: Westminster John Knox Press, 1995), 251.
9. The parallels are striking between the commandment of Jesus in John and Deut. 5:10; 7:9; and 11:1, where, in the context of Moses' farewell discourse, loving God is also associated with keeping the commandments. See Howard-Brook, *Becoming Children of God,* 319.
10. The definite article is essential, as "the truth" for John is singular, just as there is only one Messiah (Howard-Brook, *Becoming Children of God,* 321). It is interesting also to note that in Qumran documents, the angelic figure who would lead Israel's final battle against the prince of darkness is often called "the spirit of truth" (Howard-Brook, *Becoming Children of God,* 320, citing A.R.C. Leaney in James H. Charlesworth, *John and the Dead Sea Scrolls* [New York: Crossroad, 1990], 43–44).
11. Heinrich Seesemann, "ὀρφανός," *Theological Dictionary of the New Testament,* 5: 487–488. See also Howard-Brook, *Becoming Children of God,* 321.
12. The location of comfort and assurance as well as the responsibility of discipleship in the life of the community is conveyed grammatically by the second-person plural forms in vv. 15–20, which are joined seamlessly to third-person singular forms (e.g., "the one who . . .") in v. 21.
13. It is important to note that the verb usually translated as "lay down" (one's life) in v. 13 is the same one translated as "appoint" in v. 16. Clearly, the assumption that v. 13 refers to Jesus' approaching death as what he intended as his ultimate salvific act "for his friends" has influenced translators in these different renderings of the same verb in this passage. Translating both occurrences by the same English verb *appoint* changes the emphasis of the first from death as itself the *purpose* to death as the *consequence* of the intended "appointment" or engagement of his life.
14. In the Fourth Gospel, the title "friends" refers to all believers, and not to an elite within the wider Christian community. It was indeed used as an in-group designation among the Gnostics to refer to those united to the Redeemer, to whom he reveals everything, and who were under the obligation to love one another. What distinguishes the understanding of friendship in John from that in Mandaean thought is that in John that designation is based on Jesus' action (15:13) and not on revelation that the believers have received.

15. The careful analysis by Robert J. Karris (*Jesus and the Marginalized in John's Gospel* [Collegeville, MN: Michael Glazier, 1990]) of the role of marginalized persons in this Gospel is not carried over into implications about the Johannine community.
16. I am indebted to Adele Reinhartz for the germ of this proposal, which she suggested in a private conversation. As of this writing, her proposal has not yet appeared in print, and I take full responsibility for the specific terms in which it is developed here.
17. On this point, I disagree with D. A. Carson ("The Function of the Paraclete in John 16:7–11," *Journal of Biblical Literature* 98 [1979]: 547–566), who dismisses the role of the particles and concludes that in all three cases the ὅτι tells why the Paraclete has the particular task.

14

LIBERATING AND ANTICIPATING THE FUTURE

Jürgen Moltmann

Eschatology has to do with "the last things" and, I would argue, with "the first things" too—the end of the system of this world and the beginning of the new order of all things.[1] The subject of eschatology is the future, and more than the future. Eschatology talks about *God's* future, and this is more than future time. It is the future of time itself—time past, time present, and time to come. In God's future, God comes to God's creation and, through the power of God's righteousness and justice, frees it for God's kingdom and makes it the dwelling place of God's glory. In our language, this future in which God comes is described by the word *advent,* and is distinguished from the future time, which we call "future." Advent is expected—future develops. But the future always develops out of what we expect. What comes to meet us determines what we become.[2]

Christian eschatology assumes that the divine future we can expect has already begun with the coming of the Messiah, Jesus. With the coming of the Messiah, the messianic time already begins, the time in which the coming kingdom with its righteousness and justice exerts its power over the present and liberates the present from the powers of the past. In Christ's death on the cross, this world of injustice and violence reaches its end, for his resurrection from the dead is already the beginning of "the life of the world to come." Christian eschatology therefore sees in the end of this world the beginning of the new eternal creation. A saying of Paul gives us the Christian qualification of time: "Let us then lay aside the works of darkness and put on the armor of light" (Rom. 13.12). In this daybreak we experience the end of the past and the beginning of the future.

Christian ethics therefore has this Christian eschatology as its premise and is the response to it in the context of the present world's conditions. In the Hebrew Bible and Judaism we find the same link between God's future and the ethical awakening of the people concerned: "Keep justice, and do righteousness, *for* soon my salvation will come, and my deliverance be revealed" (Isa. 56:1, RSV).[3] And—even more unambiguously—at the end of the book of Isaiah (60:1): "Arise, *become* light, for your light *is coming* and the glory of the Lord is rising upon you." The announcement of God's coming, the coming of God's kingdom, righteousness, and glory, opens up for the people touched by it not just a new future but the way into that future too. A new history and a new "becoming" spring up. So the Christian life and conduct to which Christian ethics are supposed to lead are nothing other than practical eschatology and lived hope.[4]

This practiced eschatology and this lived hope do not exist in a vacuum. We find them only in the real history in which we live. But here "eschatology" has associations that are already fixed, and hope lies crushed under a mass of illusions and anxieties. So the first act of practical eschatology must be to liberate the future from the blockades and repressions of the modern world, and to free hope from the false promises and threats of modern times. "The future must be redeemed from the power of history."[5] It is only then that we can usefully and effectively talk about the possible and necessary anticipations of God's future in the conditions of this world. So we shall look first of all at "the liberation of the future from the power of history" and then, in a second step, go on to consider "the anticipations of the future in the potentialities of history."

THE LIBERATION OF THE FUTURE FROM
THE POWER OF HISTORY

The modern world began with the European seizure of power over the peoples of the world and over nature; and ever since these beginnings, it has been possessed by religious and secular millenarianism. This has meant, on the one hand, expectation of the impending dawn of a golden age, the end of history, and "the third empire of the Spirit"; on the other hand, it has meant the religious and secular apocalyptic of the impending and menacing end of the world. The feeling, thinking, and desiring of modern men and women are dominated by these two eschatological paradigms. Out of the one has developed what we may call here the *conservative syndrome* and out of the other what we shall call the *progressive syndrome*. All the political and ethical decisions of the last 150 years, as of the present day, have been—and still are—determined by one or the other of these syndromes. What we have termed the Christian ethic of lived hope must first of all "free" God's future from these modern syndromes, so that history is once more thrown open and the Christian ethic of hope is again made possible. We cannot combat the one syndrome in the interests of a Christian ethic and in the process fall victim to the other. So the future must first of all be rediscovered and set free.

The Conservative Syndrome

The conservative syndrome in politics and ethics is based on a particular eschatology that can easily be detected at every turn: the fear that the world is about to go down in chaos.[6] There is no escape from this final downfall, for the human being is "chaotic" by nature and, according to the secularized doctrine of original sin, "evil from his youth up." Because of this negative anthropology, the conservative syndrome always and everywhere cries out for "a strong state" and for repressive social institutions. Since human beings are chaotic and evil by nature, they need "a strong hand" that will keep their natural drives in check and their wickedness within bounds. This strong hand is provided by the authoritarian *state*—the country, the "motherland" or "fatherland," which promises identity and requires sacrifice—by the patriarchally ruled *family*, and by the religion of the absolute *fear of God*. It is only when they are in these strong hands that human beings learn to control themselves, to master their drives, to develop the power of their wills, and to become obediently subservient. Monotheism, monarchy, and monogamy, or—to put it more simply—God, king, and family: that is the holy trinity of the conservative syndrome. "I am the Lord thy God," proclaim the priests: "Be subject to the powers that be," demand the political rulers. "I am the master in my own house," claim the fathers. Disobedient and deviant behavior is judged to be a reversion to chaos and presented as an apocalyptic dissolution of order.

The conservative syndrome is, of course, a male syndrome.[7] If someone has been brought up to "be a man," he learns as a result to control the impulses and needs of his body and to suppress the feminine elements in himself. It is only then that he will one day be in a position to dominate the woman. The pathology of the conservative syndrome is at heart a sexual pathology. So domestic "patriarchs" always go in for men's groups—the boys down at the pub, the army mess, or the club, according to social status.

"One people—one emperor—one God" ran the slogan in Wilhelm II's pre-1914 Germany. "One people—one Reich—one Führer!" cried the Nazis in 1933, and they made the Führer their god. In Latin America, "God, family, and country" are values in the name of which protesting land workers and the people's priests have been murdered in the past and are still being murdered today. Marxism and feminism, chaos and the end of the world: These are the specters that these "values" are supposed to put to flight.

The people who preach "family values" today (such as the Promise-Keepers in the United States and the pope in every country he visits) do not just mean the family. In talking about the family, they mean the rights of "the master in his own house" and the subordination of the woman. The person who today begins by preaching publicly the strengthening of these family values will inevitably want "a strong state" as well and will incline to the fundamentalist invocation of divine "authority." But a good marriage and a happy family are gifts of grace, which are destroyed once they are turned into a law and made an instrument of domination.

The conservative syndrome in both its militant and its peaceable guise developed its reactionary form in France, in the struggle of the feudal lords and the clerics of the Roman Catholic Church against the popular revolution of 1789, with its new trinity of "liberty, equality, and fraternity." The political antitype of the authoritarian trinity cherished by the reactionaries was atheistic anarchy, with its slogan "Ni dieu—Ni maitre" (Neither God nor state) and, along with that, the revolutionary attempt to build a truly human society without a state that relies on brute force—a community of brothers and sisters in free association—that is to say, a democracy of "the free and the equal."[8] But in the democratic movement of the nineteenth century and in the emancipation movements of workers, women, and slaves, conservative reactionaries saw springing up only the dragon's seed of the apocalyptic "beast from the abyss," and in the chaos they descried the coming end of the world—which meant the end of *their* world. The democratic, popular sovereignty demanded was thought to be only the devilish antitype to the true state sovereignty by the grace of God. The progressive awareness of liberty in the emancipation movements I have mentioned was denigrated as rebellion against God and an attempt "to wrench oneself out of God's hand"; and it was therefore condemned as the primal sin of blasphemy.

For the conservative syndrome, God has always been solely on the side of order and the authorities, for all authorities on earth are supposed to derive from the sovereignty of God. So wherever that God-given order in state, family, and society is "undermined," "the dams break" and "the red flood," "the flood of immorality" (in the form of pornography, abortion, and homosexuality), and "the flood of unrestricted individualism" bring about the downfall of the world.[9] With the French and American revolutions, the alternatives to the conservative syndrome had become real, possible alternatives; and because of that, the preservation of "the old order" was no longer justified on utilitarian grounds alone but apocalyptically too. But with this justification, the alternatives were forced into an end-time friend–foe relationship, irresolvable by discussion or negotiation but only through Armageddon, the decisive apocalyptic battle. In the ultimate resort, the conservative preservation of order reduces itself to dictatorship, preferably a military dictatorship. And this "ultimate resort" is the political "state of emergency."[10] This expedient has always been potentially to hand since the

French Revolution, and it is declared at every convenient opportunity to be the essential requirement of the moment.

Which eschatology is cultivated in this conservative syndrome? It is the *eschatology of the catechon,* the delay, the holding back.[11] The political and the moral order "hold back the end of the world" and must therefore be preserved under all circumstances and with every expedient. It is characteristic of this negative eschatology that Constantinian Christianity should already have replaced the early Christian prayer "Maranatha, come Lord Jesus, come soon" (Rev: 22:17, 20) and the petition "May thy kingdom come and this world pass away" with the prayer "pro mora finis"—the petition that the end be delayed. This meant that the justification for the Christian ethic changed too: A life in the community of Christ in accordance with the righteousness and justice of God's future world was replaced by the backward-looking transfiguration of the existing political and moral order (which was traced back to the dispensations of creation or to natural law) and therefore by the preservation of its present condition in the spirit of love. The alteration of changeable structures in accordance with the kingdom of God that Jesus preached, and in accordance with the Sermon on the Mount, was superseded by Christian love in structures that were to remain as they were (see the Augsburg Confession, article 16).

But because the restraining powers can postpone the end of the world only for a certain time, in the conservative syndrome the end has to be expected, and preparations for the final struggle must be made. This is the dualistic *Armageddon eschatology.* If one day the power of the state can no longer hold back "the red flood" or the waves of emancipation—then the day of the decisive apocalyptic battle is approaching: "On to the final battle," as the Communists also sang in their "Internationale," though from their opposite viewpoint. This is the appearance of the Antichrist and his annihilation in Christ's parousia (2 Thess. 2:6). This is the clash of good and evil, which will be decided through God's intervention on behalf of the good, as the prophecy about the battle in the valley of Armageddon proclaims (Rev. 16:16).

The expectation that the end will mean the apocalyptic separation of humanity into the good and the evil inevitably means that all differences and conflicts will already culminate here in history in friend–foe relationships and in the demand for uncompromising decision.[12] It is not unifications, compromises, and peace treaties that anticipate the end; it is divisions, severance, and decisions. Anyone who postpones the clarifying end through peacemaking and amelioration of conditions in this world is accounted a heretic—the proponent of an "inner-worldly eschatology"—or a starry-eyed do-gooder who stands in the way of the power struggles among the adherents of Realpolitik by giving them a bad conscience, whereas their own concern is, of course, not to have a conscience at all, for "men of action never have a conscience," as Friedrich Nietzsche said of them.[13]

The Progressive Syndrome

But it is the progressive syndrome that dominates the world of modern times. The conservative syndrome is merely its reverse side and its somber companion. In the progressive syndrome, too, the ruling eschatology is easily detectable. It is the millenarian belief in the progress of humanity and the perfectibility of history. We are already living in "the third stage" of world history as the millenarian Positivist Auguste Comte described it. This is the end-time stage in which history will be consummated.[14] Now, at last, what human beings have sought for from the beginning will be reached, and the desire behind all their struggles will be fulfilled. In this stage of humanity's development, science and technology will spread unhindered; education and prosperity for all will be attained; morality and humanity will grow; but there will be no further qualitative revolutions in history. The first, religious age gave way to the second age of philosophy, and both will be succeeded by the secular and scientific-technological era that is now beginning. Science will now be the vehicle for demonstrating truth. Because humanity has hitherto experienced history as crisis, conflict, and revolution, "the third age" will be "the end of history" and the beginning of eternal peace.

With this age, an era without history begins, the *posthistoire*.[15] Warlike military states will be replaced by the joint administration of the economy. Authorities employing force will be replaced by the free world of responsible, educated people, in which "the free development of each is the condition for the free development of all,"[16] as the Communist Manifesto of 1847 proclaimed, with liberal conviction, in the messianic spirit of enlightened humanism. Human beings are by nature good; if they are bad, it is only bad social conditions that have made them so. Human beings are capable of improved development through upbringing and education. According to the apocalyptic idea, in the millennium the devil will be bound "for a thousand years," so that goodness can spread unhindered.

This positive anthropology was the foundation for anarchist criticism of the allegedly divinely willed authorities in state, family, and nation. These can and will be replaced by "the free association of free individuals." The need for the "state" was justified by the sinful, chaotic nature of human beings. But this no longer applies. It was merely an expression of what Friedrich Engels referred to as humanity's fear of itself. The humanity that has come to itself no longer requires repressive government or its transcendent justification from above. The state based on power gives way to the state founded on a constitution; the sacred family is replaced by a partnership for shared living; and the exclusive nation is superseded by the multicultural society. With this, the different forms of exclusiveness find an end. The human society that is emerging will build a state without wars between the different countries, and therefore without armies or national foreign policies. The foreign policy of the single nation will be replaced worldwide by shared domestic policies. Consequently, politics will no longer be ruled by the notorious friend–foe relationship that Carl Schmitt talks about. Once established, the democratic constitutional states already ceased to wage war against one another. So the vision of eternal peace seems within reach. This, of course, means that previous politics, which worked with the threat of force, will be replaced by the worldwide economy of the multi- and the transnational groups. The economic policies of the single state will be dispersed as the economy is deregulated and its responsibility privatized. A globalized economy will ultimately liberate the politically subjected colonial peoples too and turn their low-wage countries into high-tech locations. The totalization of the economy will put an end to class rule.

A global economy—a global ethic—a global society: that means global peace! This is the golden age, the end of world wars, and hence the end of world history.

In characterizing the progressive syndrome in this way, I have deliberately thrown together utterances made in the eighteenth and nineteenth centuries by Comte and Kant, Marx and Adam Smith, and in our own time by Michel Camdessus[17] and Francis Fukuyama.[18] My purpose in so doing is to show that we modern men and women live, feel, and think in this syndrome as if it were self-evident, and we apparently have no other alternative to hand. Even if the onward march of technology, space travel, and genetic engineering no longer asks for the "faith" required in the nineteenth century, it has nevertheless become the driving force of the system of permanent modernization, to such an extent that we hardly notice it. The "progress" that so fascinated the minds of the ruling Western nations in the nineteenth century has long since become a compulsion toward continually accelerated modernization[19] The new magic word *globalization* is merely a more agreeable way of describing what people in the nineteenth century called "imperialism." For the total commercialization of life, from the private sphere to the care of the old, we have invented the amiable euphemism *privatization*. Wicked old capitalism is now called "the global marketing of everything." Freedom, we are told, grows with the progressive individualization of human beings and with the demolition of the particularist communities that restricted their individual liberties.

If, now that the socialism of the eastern bloc has come to an end, there are no longer any alternatives to this global and total system, then an "end of history" or "the end of a history" has indeed been reached, and with it a "brave new world" without any other threatening options. The millenaristic consummation of history is in sight. In 1989 the most recent secular, right-wing,

Hegelian millenarian, Francis Fukuyama of the State Department in Washington, D.C., proclaimed "the end of history"; and from these viewpoints, he was right.[20] But Karl Marx, too, must posthumously be called correct; for globalized and totalized capitalism conforms precisely to his scenario, with the sole qualification that there is now no transition to a postcapitalist socialism and communism.

Which eschatology is cultivated in this progressive syndrome? The millenarian eschatology dominant here has two remarkable characteristics:

1. The people who know that they are standing at the end of history, or are already in the *posthistoire*, no longer have any future in front of them; instead, they live in a present without any temporal end. What they see ahead of them is not an alternative future; it is merely a prolongation of the present—progress in every direction—improvements wherever possible—expansions unbounded—but without any alternative, because "there is no alternative" to our present condition, as every politician and economist never tires of telling us today at every turn. What was once, in the era of history, "future" no longer exists in the *posthistoire*.

2. When the repressive forces in state, society, and the family end, "God" as their transcendent ground and legitimization ceases to be applicable too. In a world without lordship, "the Lord God" no longer has any place. All people must develop their own possibilities, fulfilling themselves in the process (hetero-, homo-, bi-, or multisexually). Human autonomy no longer permits theonomy. The more the modern millennium becomes anarchistic—that is, democratic—the more the atheism that is practiced simply as a matter of course spreads. It is no longer a militant antitheism, as it was in the nineteenth century. It is merely a theism that has got lost and become superfluous. If every effort for "fulfillment" is directed toward nothing other than the self, then the self is, to all intents and purposes, the human being's God and Lord—if that human being has a self and does not fall into the vacancy of everything possible, like Robert Musil's *Man without Qualities*.[21] This was at one time called pantheism, or to be more precise, anthropotheism. But today, many people are losing even this ancient overvaluation of the self, and both theism and atheism are being replaced by a cheerful nihilism or a trite complacency about things as they simply happen to be, and by the self's hollow emptiness. We were once promised the fulfillment of historical hopes; but all that remains is the impression of a helpless lack of alternative. The *posthistoire* is as tranquil as it is tedious.

The Liberation of the Future

The liberation of the future must lead to a new opening up of history, with its alternative possibilities to the present. The conservative syndrome blocks every alternative future because it immediately identifies the new possibilities and changes with the dreaded downfall of the world. Because the authoritarian powers of history only "hold back" the end, they make it impossible for new possibilities to arrive. This conservative blockade of the future is matched in the progressive syndrome by the repression of all alternative future possibilities through the extension of the present and its prolongation. The end of history that is "progressively" sought is, as we have seen, always the desired "end of the future" too.

To gain space for innovative action in history, every Christian eschatology must critically address and challenge both the conservative *blockade* of the future and the progressive *occupation* of the future. Christian eschatology assumes that future issues from God's creative energy and therefore expects that the historical future of the world will acquire its openness, its potentialities, and its alternatives in the coming of God. For this eschatology, the creative expectation of God's coming is founded on creation's openness to the future, on Israel's history of promise, on the raising of the crucified Christ, together with the outpouring of the creative energies of God's Spirit, which is bound up with raising. For the people affected, these recollections of "future" neither terminate history nor do they put it out of commission; they throw it open afresh. In these recollections, the end is not "held back"; it is "at hand," as the New Testament stresses throughout. But because the coming kingdom of God and God's righteousness and justice are already near, they can and must already, as far as possible, be "anticipated" today.

But is the future that is an alternative to the obstructing or extending system of life in the present, and that is actualized in the Jewish and Christian history of promise, really desirable? If we already exist in the final world or in the best of all possible worlds, an alternative future is unwelcome. But if the contradictions are continually growing, and if the victims of the present system of living are becoming more and more numerous, we are bound to look around for alternatives. The people who control the present system, and the system's beneficiaries, always have only a conservative interest in its preservation or a progressive interest it its expansion. But the victims can survive solely by virtue of the hope for an alternative future. The victims of the present system are:

1. Unemployed "surplus people," whom nobody wants and nobody needs. Automated industries and digital communications no longer merely exploit; they also produce more and more of these surplus people.
2. Future generations, which will have to pay off the mountains of debt that present generations are heaping up so that they can enjoy their own existence.

3. Nature, which is being driven into ecological catastrophe and left "without form and void."

4. The present system itself, which is going to founder on the contradictions it produces and will annihilate the human race unless history is opened up afresh and real alternatives emerge that make this system reformable.

Today, the modern capitulation of politics before the globalized economy is already destroying the human community and is ruining public finances. An economic system that produces ever-greater inequalities between people destroys political democracy.[22] The participatory democracy which was the original goal is then replaced by an apathetic absentee democracy. When men and women are de-politicized from above they respond from below with disinterest in politics. People can withdraw into private life and pursue their own interests without having to fear intervention by the state.

ANTICIPATIONS OF GOD'S FUTURE IN HISTORY

Where can this future of God's be experienced in the midst of human history, so that it can be anticipated and lived by men and women? The answer is simple. It can be experienced wherever this future *happens* in history—wherever, that is, God gives his future of the kingdom *in advance*. According to the Jewish idea, this future of God's occurs *discontinuously* in time on the sabbath, in the sabbath year, and in the Year of Jubilee and will one day be present *continuously* in the messianic time.[23] On the sabbath, God "interrupts" the purposeful working time of human beings and makes this interruption the place of his presence in time. The sabbath is the temporal place of his indwelling (his Shekinah). That is why in the sabbath time the laws of this world are suspended and only the righteousness of God counts. Fleeting time makes people restless; the sabbath gives rest in the happiness of the presence of the Eternal One. Work allows people to exist in their own world; the sabbath rest leads them into God's creation again, and into God's pleasure in themselves. On the sabbath, the future redemption of the world is celebrated, for the sabbath rest is already a foretaste of the redeemed world. Consequently, in Israel the sabbath has always been especially close to God's expected Messiah: "The sabbath is a sixtieth of the coming world." "If Israel were to keep one single sabbath rightly, the Messiah would immediately come.[24]

In this way, the sabbath festival links Israel's particular experience of God with God's general presence in creation and with the general hope of redemption for this unredeemed world. The sabbath rest links the experience of God *in* history with the messianic hope in God *for* history. The laws about the sabbath in the Old Testament must therefore be viewed as the special form of the redemptive righteousness of God's kingdom in the midst of history. They become a pattern for the messianic form of the righteousness and justice of the kingdom in the midst of history, the righteousness and justice that Jesus proclaimed in the Sermon on the Mount.

We shall look at the laws about the sabbath with reference to (1) social justice for human beings and (2) ecological justice for the earth. And we shall look at both in their reference to the messianic righteousness and justice of redemption.

Social Justice for Human Beings

The first thing we notice about the sabbath laws is *the principle of equality.* The sabbath rest and the presence of God that can be experienced in it are given to all equally and suspend the privileges that otherwise obtain. Men don't rest at the expense of women—parents at the expense of their children—one's own people at the expense of strangers—human beings at the expense of animals. All are meant to come to rest together. Moreover, because the sabbath applies to all equally, all have the same right to rest on that day. The enjoyment of the same divine grace has as its corollary the equal rights of human beings and animals.

The sabbath principle of equality returns in the principle of equality in Christ Jesus. In him "there is neither Jew nor Greek, there is neither slave nor free, there is neither male nor female; for you are all one in Christ Jesus . . . heirs according to the promise" (Gal. 3:28, 29, RSV). The one same justification of sinners gives the one same right to inherit God's coming kingdom. The seal of this is the one same baptism in the one divine Spirit (Eph. 4:4–5). It follows from this community between men and women, Jews and Gentiles, masters and servants, that they are equal in their present endowment with the Spirit and equal in their rights to God's future. Here, too, the social, religious, and sexual privileges of the one and the corresponding oppressions and belittlements of others are done away with. A messianic community of "the free and the equal" is created; and through that community, God's future dawns in human history.

The Spirit-filled community of Christ lived this sabbath and messianic equality by setting aside the order of private property: "Now the company of those who believed were of one heart and soul, and no one said that any of the things which he possessed was his own, but they had everything in common. . . . There was not a needy person among them" (Acts 4:32–35). In a world in which the possessors are becoming ever richer and the have-nots are suffering more and more privation, a community that lives in solidarity like this really is the beginning of a divine future that endures in a world of inequality—a world that will pass away because it has no permanent durability. It has no permanent durability because it is unjust. The Christian religious orders of nuns and monks and the communities living in radical discipleship of Christ have always lived this community of possessions.

The second thing we notice about the sabbath laws is that the liberation of prisoners from their enslavement and debtors from the burden of their debts is in the foreground. Because injustices always arise in the course of six years of labor and commerce, in the seventh year the original, divinely promulgated justice is to be restored. The person who has been enslaved because of his debts "shall go out from you . . . and go back to his own family, and return to the possession of his fathers" (Lev. 25:41, RSV). There must be neither usury nor profiteering (Lev. 25:36).

The freeing of prisoners and the remission of debts return in the messianic works from which we are supposed to recognize Israel's Redeemer. "To proclaim liberty to the captives and the opening of the prison to those who are bound": that is the charge given to the Messiah who proclaims the time of the messianic sabbath (Isa. 61:1, RSV). That is why Jesus' first sermon in Nazareth after his endowment with the Spirit (Luke 4:18–19) begins with his reading of this Isaianic prophecy, and his explanation: "Today this scripture has been fulfilled in you hearing" (Luke 4:21, RSV). Remarkably enough, according to Luke, after Jesus has proclaimed "the acceptable year of the Lord" (that is to say, the messianic sabbath era), he leaves out the Isaianic phrase "and the day of vengeance of our God." The liberation of prisoners and the remission of debts are also the prophetic proposals for the season of fasting and the "day acceptable to the Lord" (Isa. 58:5, RSV). "On that day God will act to loose the bonds of wickedness, to undo the thongs of the yoke, to let the oppressed go free . . . and share bread with the hungry" (Isa. 58:6–8, RSV). This is the true worship in the world of everyday. It is only this sabbath and messianic activity that make "your righteousness . . . go before you, and the glory of the LORD . . . your rear guard" (Isa. 58:8, RSV). The petition in the Lord's Prayer, too, "Forgive us our trespasses as we forgive those who trespass against us," doesn't mean moral guilt or religious sins, as we generally think: It is talking about remission of debts in the sabbath righteousness of the messianic era, which begins with Jesus' coming.

Not least important: The sabbath year is intended for the well-being of Israel's poor and for the benefit of foreigners in Israel: "The seventh year you shall let [the land] rest and lie fallow, that the poor of your people may eat" (Exod. 23:11, RSV). "The sabbath of the land shall provide food for you, for yourself and for your male and female slaves and for your hired servant and for the sojourner who lives with you; for your cattle also and for the beasts that are in your land" (Lev. 25:6, RSV). Here again we find the principle of equality and the preferential option of the divine sabbath justice for the poor and the asylum seekers, who are otherwise disadvantaged. Here, too, we can point to Isaiah 61 and to Luke 4.18–21. This divine sabbath justice is "the gospel for the poor," for according to Jesus' promise, it is to the poor that God's coming kingdom belongs.

Ecological Justice for the Earth

According to the sabbath laws, God's righteousness and justice are not confined to human society. They also embrace the community shared by human beings *and the earth*. Exodus 23:10–11 provides a social reason for the sabbath year: "so that the poor of your people may eat." But in Leviticus 25:1–7 we find an ecological justification: "so that the land may keep its great sabbath to the Lord" (RSV). The sabbath year is not just a festival for human beings. It is the festival of the whole creation. In the seventh year *the land* "celebrates." That evidently presupposes a covenant made by God with his land, a covenant that, when they enter the country God has promised them, the people must respect by leaving fields and vineyards uncultivated and unharvested every seventh year. That the land should rest every seventh year is God's blessing for the land. It is to lie fallow so that it can recover from human exploitation and can restore its fertility. Israel, it is true, rejected the fertility cults it found in the Canaanite country, but instead it introduced the fallowing principle of the sabbath year: "You shall make for yourselves no idols. . . . You shall keep my sabbaths" (Lev. 26.1–2, RSV). If the people respect the sabbath worship of the earth, they will live in peace and enjoy the blessing of the land. If they disregard the earth's sabbath, "I will devastate the land, so that your enemies who settle in it shall be astonished at it. And I will scatter you among the nations . . . and your land shall be a desolation, and your cities shall be a waste. . . . Then the land shall rest, and enjoy its sabbaths" (Lev. 26:32–34, RSV). The explanation 2 Chronicles 36:19–21 gives for Israel's Babylonian captivity is that the people had disregarded the sabbath of the earth. The land "kept the sabbath to fulfill seventy years" (RSV).

Inherent in this sabbath law for the land is the ancient ecological wisdom of the fallowing principle, which agricultural societies have always observed. If the land is the system that sustains life, then the times required for its regeneration must be observed. Once the land is exhausted, the people are forced to emigrate. Only the great world empires have exploited the fertile regions to feed their great cities and armies, turning these fruitful lands into deserts through uncontrolled overgrazing and overcropping. If, today, the expanding human population continues to exploit the earth nonstop by way of monocultures and chemical fertilizers, the deserts will grow, and one day human beings will disappear from the earth, so that God's earth can "celebrate" its sabbath.

The earth will survive. We humans won't. That is the warning of the Old Testament story about "the sabbath of the earth."

The divine justice that the Messiah is to bring will take possession of the land, too, and make it fertile, according to Isaiah 32:15–18: "When the Spirit is poured upon us from on high the wilderness will become a fruitful field and the fruitful field will be deemed a forest. Then justice will dwell in the wilderness, and righteousness abide in the fruitful field. And the fruit of justice will be peace . . . " (RSV). That reads like a sequel to the Christian community's Pentecost experience, according to which the Spirit of life is "poured out upon all flesh"—which means not just on human life but on all the living. But in the New Testament, only very little is said about the sabbath of the earth and its salvation in the messianic time. It is only in "the new heaven and the new earth" (Rev. 21:1) that the paradisal fertilities will return, when the eternally living God comes to rest in God's creation, and everything God has created arrives at its peace in God.

Guidelines for a Christian Ethic

The guidelines for an ethic in the community of Christ follow on the ideas about the messianic righteousness and justice that we find in the Prophets and on Israel's laws about the sabbath, and they take these ideas up. As we have seen, in both these forerunning concepts, it is no longer a matter of equalizing justice (*iustitia distributiva*). This is the justice that redeems—frees—from misery, brutality, and guilt. It is the justifying justice of God (*iustitia iustificans*), which puts things to rights and creates justice. When the biblical traditions talk about "justice and righteousness," as they do again and again, it is this creative justice of God they mean, the justice that gives human laws their justification and at the same time relativizes them.[25] Faithful observance of the established law and the demand for better justice then make of the prevailing human legal system a process that points toward the future. In this process that is aligned toward God's coming and his redeeming righteousness, human institutions are what Wolf-Dieter Marsch refers to as institutions in transition. This is also true of the Christian ethic itself. It is not a catalog of eternally valid, unchangeable dispensations given at creation, targeted at the chaos of human caprice, as it were. Nor is it a carte blanche for personal "decisions of conscience" that no one is permitted to judge. A Christian ethic is an ethic of lived hope and is hence related to the horizon of historical change that is open to the future. It is not an "ordering" ethic, nor is it a situation ethic. It is an ethic of change, like the Jewish Tikkun ethics. To do what is good means asking about what is better. For this ethic of change we need guidelines instead of laws and regulations. These act as signposts, steadily oriented toward the future, and offer changing responses to the challenges of history. Every *theologia viatorum* demands an *ethica viatorum*.

In the ecumenical discussions of the last thirty years, three guidelines of this kind have crystallized and point the way toward hope in action: (1) the anticipation of God's future; (2) the preferential option for the poor; (3) correspondence and contradiction in history.

1. *To live in anticipation* means letting one's own present be determined by the expected future of God's kingdom and God's righteousness and justice. In 1968, the General Assembly of the World Council of Churches in Uppsala, Sweden, provided the classic formulation: "We ask you, trusting in God's renewing power, to join in the anticipation of God's Kingdom, showing now something of the newness which Christ will complete on his day.[26] The anticipation of the kingdom of God is not yet the kingdom itself, but it is a life determined by that hope. It is a historical form of God's kingdom.[27] Here God's righteousness appears in the conditions and potentialities of history, not yet in its own new world. This difference in the anticipation makes the second part of the formulation clear too. There is already a new creation here and now, for there is already here and now a rebirth to a living hope; but it is related to, and differentiated from, the hoped-for new creation of all things that is to come to pass on the day of Christ's coming in the glory of God.

Life and action in *anticipation* of God's future is like life and action in the *Advent* that leads up to Christmas. It is a life in the community of Christ, following the guidelines of his Sermon on the Mount. As in the peace movement of 1979–1981, this means "peace is possible" in the midst of a time when missiles are being stationed in a mutual threat of universal annihilation.[28] It also means that righteousness which redeems, puts to rights, creates justice and justifies, is possible in the midst of a world where evil is "justly" requited with evil. But to requite evil with good is the idea behind a penal law based on resocialization, such as was introduced in Germany by Gustav Radbruch, who appealed to the Sermon on the Mount. Of course, in each individual case we have to ask: "What is objectively possible?" so that we don't chase after unreal dreams. And we have to ask too: What can I, or the community concerned, do subjectively, so as not to come to grief on the tremendous requirements? But even more important is the question: Cui bono? For whom and in whom is the divine righteousness to be anticipated? And this brings us to the second guideline.

2. The preferential option for the poor goes back to Latin American liberation theology and found a place in the official documents of the Latin American bishops' conference in Medellín (1968) and Puebla (1979).[29] It has become a component in Roman Catholic social doctrine. This option corresponds (1) to the sabbath laws in Israel, (2) to the messianic justice of the prophets, (3) to Jesus' gospel to the poor, and (4) to the judgment of the Son of Man and universal Judge: "as you did it to one of the least . . . , you did it to me" (Matt. 25:40, RSV). What is new about the option for the poor is that

the poor are no longer the object of Christian charity. They are taken seriously as determining subjects among Christ's people (*ochlos*). The church will become the church of the poor for Christ's sake, for in the poor we find Christ's real presence. And society's poor, exploited, and humiliated people, who today have been made "surplus," belong together with the other victims of modern civilization—exploited and despoiled nature, and the coming generations at whose expense present generations are increasingly living.

The preferential option for the poor is not just an ethical guideline for Christians. It is a daily experience among Christian communities that serve as contact addresses or drop-in centers for the long-term unemployed, the homeless, and the abandoned. In Christian soup kitchens, shelters, and emergency accommodation and in the agencies and organizations of Christian diaconal services, the victims of the free-market economy and its wintry social climate gather together. The more the churches live in the presence of this society's victims, the more they have the right to challenge prophetically the consciences of that society. If they simply restrict themselves to ministering to the poor, they become the accomplices of the ruling society. If they simply confine themselves to prophetic declarations, no one listens. Every declaration on social conditions made by the churches, and every "report," must be legitimated by the churches' work for this society's victims. But in the name of these victims, the unjust conditions in society must be publicly indicted as well. The option for the poor and criticism of the brute and violent anticipate the coming kingdom and the coming judgment, and with that the righteousness of God, which will put things to rights.

3. In every sphere of life there are conditions that are in accord with the awaited kingdom of God, as it is present in Jesus' life and teaching, and conditions that are in contradiction to it. The kingdom of God isn't indifferent to prices on the world market, because the survival or starvation of millions of children depends on them. That doesn't mean that just prices in international trade are already the kingdom of God itself; but for all that, they correspond to the kingdom more closely than unjust prices. There is no identity between the divine justice of the coming kingdom and the human justice of conditions in our world. Even the best of all the possible worlds open to us is still a human world and won't become a divine one, for what is divine is not an enhancement of what is human.

But this qualitative difference between divine and human justice is not all. Between the similarity and the difference we find *the historical parables* of the coming kingdom. That is the way in which Karl Barth defined the relation between divine and human justice in the conflicts and contradictions of the Hitler dictatorship; and in doing so, he was picking up the ideas of Zwingli and Calvin (though not those of Luther and Melanchthon).[30] Parables or images correspond to the thing imaged in different material: "The kingdom of

God *is like* a grain of mustard seed." In this way the images, for their part, make the other material open to parable and in need of parable. So politics can be a parable—and needs to be a parable—for the coming kingdom of God if we use a political vocabulary in talking about that "kingdom" and its "citizens." The same may be said about the economic sector, the lives we live together, and our culture. These "parables" are correspondences in the sphere of what doesn't correspond—or simply liberations in this unredeemed world and acts of human justice on the foundation of the approaching justice of God: "do righteousness, *for* soon my salvation will come" (Isa. 56:1, RSV).

But whereas the concept of *parable* presupposes an enduring qualitative difference between earth and heaven, the idea of *anticipation*, which we used before, belongs to the difference between history and eschatology. What we ought to do and can do is to correspond to the future of the coming God. And this future "is at hand" and "will reveal itself"; and thus *it thrusts us forward* to do what is right, and toward the actions that correspond to God's future in this present world, which is otherwise in contradiction to that future.

In Christian ethics, earthly justice is not just intended to *correspond* to the heavenly justice of God. It should also *prepare the way* for God's coming kingdom.

Christian ethics are eschatological ethics. What we do now for people in need we do filled with the power of hope, and lit by the expectation of God's coming day.

(Translated by Margaret Kohl)

NOTES

1. Jürgen Moltmann, *The Coming of God: Christian Eschatology*, trans. Margaret Kohl (London: SCM Press; Minneapolis: Fortress Press, 1996).
2. Jürgen Moltmann, "Hope and Planning," in *Hope and Planning*, trans. Margaret Clarkson (London and New York: Harper & Row, 1971).
3. B. Klappert, "Auf dem Weg der Gerechtigkeit in Liebe," in *". . . und hätte die Liebe nicht." Texte vom Mülheimer Symposium*, ed. Evangelische Kirche im Rheinland (Düsseldorf, 1997), 23–114.
4. This has been brought out best and for many people with convincing force by G. Gutierrez, *Theology of Liberation*, trans. C. Inda and J. Eagleson (1973; reprint, Maryknoll, N.Y.: Orbis Books, 1988).
5. Moltmann, *Coming of God*, p. 45: "The messianic interpretation of the experience of the moment that ends and gathers up time is the *redemption of the future* from the power of history. The power of history is exercised by the mighty. They have to extend their victorious present into the future in order to augment and consolidate their power. *Their* future is without an alternative, and devoid of surprises."
6. The theological side of this conservative syndrome has been excellently described by R. Strunk in his *Politische Ekklesiologie im Zeitalter der Revolution* (Munich: Chr. Kaiser Verlag, 1971). The thesis of the pietistic theologian Gottfried

Menken was "All revolutions are contrary to the kingdom of God" (102). The influential church politician and Prussian statesman Julius Friedrich Stahl believed, "Only the church can heal the nations from the sickness of revolution" (154). And for the Hessian traditional Lutheran August Vilmar, the church's "torch" "shone there ahead of the returning Lord Christ, and here in the face of the Antichrist" (230).

7. This is shown by N. Sombart's brilliant account *Die deutschen Männer und ihre Feinde. Carl Schmitt—ein deutsches Schicksal zwischen Männerbund und Matriarchatmythos* (Munich: Hanser, 1991). The neoconservatives of the Reagan era in the United States, such as Norman Podhoretz, Michael Novak, Irving Kristol, and Peter Berger, in spite of all the differences among them, seem to be at one in their anticommunism and antifeminism. See G. Dorrien, *The Neoconservative Mind: Politics, Culture, and the War of Ideologies* (Philadelphia: Temple University Press, 1993).

8. M. Bakunin, *God and the State* (New York: Dover Publications, 1970).

9. This is the substance of the famous Stone Lectures on "Reformation against Revolution" given by the Dutch theologian and statesman Abraham Kuyper at Princeton Theological Seminary in 1900 (*Reformation wider Revolution. Sechs Vorlesungen über Calvinismus,* translated into German by M. Jaeger [Berlin, 1904]). Kuyper was the leader of the "antirevolutionary people's party" in Holland and the founder of the Free University in Amsterdam.

10. This is the fundamental idea of the disputed German constitutional lawyer Carl Schmitt in his book *Die Diktatur. Von den Anfängen des modernen Souveränitätsgedanken bis zum proletarischen Klassenkampf* (Berlin, 1921), with its appendix: "Die Diktatur des Reichspräsidenten nach Art. 48 der Weimarer Reichsverfassung." The thesis of his *Political Theology: Four Chapters on the Concept of Sovereignty,* trans. George Schwab (Cambridge, Mass.: MIT Press, 1985) is that "one is sovereign who can declare the state of emergency"—which is simply to say, sovereign is the dictator who proclaims dictatorship. He argues, theologically, that in a situation of radical evil, dictatorship is the only choice"—as if dictatorship itself were not the "radically evil" thing in politics!

11. This apocalyptic eschatology goes back to 2 Thess. 2:6–8: "And you know what is now restraining him, so that he may be revealed when his time comes. For the mystery of lawlessness is already at work, but only until the one who now restrains is removed. And then the lawless one will be revealed, whom the Lord Jesus will slay him with the breath of his mouth, annihilating him by the manifestation of his coming" (RSV). In his life, Carl Schmitt was fascinated by this "catechon" and was concerned to uphold it. Cf. H. Meier, *Die Lehre Carl Schmitt. Vier Kapital zur Unterscheidung Politische Theologie und Politische Ethik* (Stuttgart and Weimer: Klett-Cotta, 1994), 243–253. Conservative circles thought that the United States was this catechon when it entered the Vietnam War and were afraid that the "hindrance" would cease to exist when the United States was unable to win this war against "the red flood."

12. This dualistic apocalyptic about the struggle between Christ and Antichrist can be detected in the biblical writings. But is it Christian, in the christological sense of the word? It seems to reflect Manichaean influence, rather than to be an expression of the hope founded on the raising of the crucified Christ.

13. Friedrich Nietzsche, *Genealogy of Morals: A Polemic.* trans. Horace B. Samuel (New York: Macmillan Co., 1924).

14. Auguste Comte, *System of Positive Polity: Treatise on Sociology*, vol. 4, Research & Source Works Series 125 (London: Burt Franklin, 1877).
15. L. Niethammer, *Posthistoire: Has History Come to an End?* trans. P. Cammiller (London and New York: Verso, 1992). This is an exposition of the French tradition. Cf. Also the earlier study by R. Seidenberg, *Posthistoric Man* (Chapel Hill: University of North Carolina Press, 1950).
16. K. Marx, *Die Fruhschriften*, ed. S. Landshut (Stuttgart, 1950), 548.
17. M. Camdessus is the director of the International Monetary Fund. His lecture on "The Market and the Kingdom of God in the Globalization of the World Economy" is critically commented on by F. J. Hinkelammert in *Orientierung* 60 (15 May 1996): 98–102 and *Orientierung* 60 (31 May 1996): 115–119.
18. Francis Fukuyama, *The End of History and the Last Man* (New York: Free Press, 1992).
19. W. Stahel, *Die Beschleunigungsfalle oder der Triumph der Schildkrote* (Stuttgart: Schäffer-Poeschel, 1995).
20. Francis Fukuyama, "The End of History," *National Interest* 16 (1989): 3–18.
21. Robert Musil, *Men without Qualities* (Mann ohne Ergenschaflen), trans. Eithne Wiekens and Ernst Kaiser, 1st American ed. (New York: Coward-McCann, 1953).
22. H. P. Martin and H. Schumann, *Die Globalisierungsfalle. Der Angriff auf Demokratie und Wohlstand* (Hamburg: Rowohlt, 1996) ; cf. also Marion Grafin Donhoff, *Zivilisiert den Kapitalismus* (Stuttgart: Deutsche Verlags-Anstalt, 1997).
23. Cf. A. Heschel, *The Sabbath: Its Meaning for Modern Man*, 7th ed. (New York: Farrar, Straus & Giroux, 1981); J. Moltmann, *God in Creation: An Ecological Doctrine of Creation*, trans. Margaret Kohl (London and San Francisco: SCM Press, 1985), chap. 11, "The Sabbath: the Feast of Creation," 276–296; E. Spier, *Der Sabbat* (Berlin: Institut Kirche und Judentum, 1989).
24. Midrash Rabbah: Exodus 25. 12. Cf. here F. Rosenzweig, *Der Stern der Erlösung. Dritter Teil. Erstes Buch*, (Heidelberg: Suhrkamp, 1959), 69 (English translation: *The Star of Redemption*, trans. W. W. Hallo, 2d ed. [Boston: Beacon Press, 1972]); J. Moltmann, *The Way of Jesus Christ*, trans. Margaret Kohl (London: SCM Press, 1990), 116–136.
25. W. Huber, *Gerechtigkeit und Recht. Grundlinien christlicher Rechtsethik* (Stuttgart: Chr. Kaiser Verlag, 1996); H.-R. Reuter, *Rechtsethik in theologischer Perspektive* (Gütersloh: Chr. Kaiser Verlag, 1996).
26. Cf. N. Goodall, ed. *The Uppsala Report, 1968* (Geneva: World Council of Churches, 1968).
27. Jürgen Moltmann, *Creating a Just Future: The Politics of Peace and the Ethics of Creation in a Threatened World*, trans. John Bowden (London: SCM Press, 1989).
28. Jürgen Moltmann, ed., *Friedenstheologie—Befreiungstheologie. Analysen, Berichte, Meditationen* (Munich: Chr. Kaiser Verlag, 1988); idem, "Political Theology and the Theology of Liberation," in *God in the Project of the Modern World* (*Gottim Projektder modernen Welt: Beiträge zur öffentlichen Relevanz der Theologie* [Gütersloh: Kaiser, 1997], English trans. forthcoming).
29. Cf. Second General Conference of Latin American Bishops, Medellín, *The Church in the Present-Day Transformation of Latin America in the Light of the Council*, 2 vols. (Bogota: General Secretariate of Conference del Episcopado Latinoamericano, 1970). See J. Eagleson and P. Scharper, eds., *Puebla and Beyond*

(Maryknoll, N.Y.: Orbis Books, 1979). This gives a history of events preceding the conference, a conference report, and the official English translation of the final document.

30. See K. Barth, "The Christian Community and the Civil Community," in *Against the Stream* (New York: Philosophical Library, 1954), as well as the comment in J. Moltmann, *The Crucified God,* trans. R. A. Wilson and J. Bowden, 6th ed. (London and New York: Harper & Row, 1984) and 9th ed. (New York: Harper & Row, 1991), chap. 8, "Ways towards the Political Liberation of Mankind," 317–338.

15

A SACRED HOPE AND SOCIAL GOAL

Womanist Eschatology

Joan M. Martin

My Lord, what a mornin',
My Lord, what a mornin',
My Lord, what a mornin',
When the stars begin to fall.

You will hear the trumpet sound,
To wake the nations underground,
Looking to my God's right hand,
When the stars begin to fall.

You will hear the sinner mourn, . . .

You will hear the Christian shout, . . .

—*Traditional Negro Spiritual*

Singers of this spiritual are familiar with the fact that it can be sung with two word variations, that is, *mornin'* and *mournin'*. "The songs," according to Sweet Honey in the Rock founder Bernice Johnson Reagon, "are free, and they have the meaning placed in them by the singer. . . . They are about things that happen to people everyday. A lot were about stating a worldview and positioning yourself in the world. They could be applied to everyday, practical situations."[1] As a young child, however, I did not know or care about such things. When I first learned "My Lord, What a Mornin'," I simply remember loving its beautiful word-pictures and melody. In my child's imagination, the conjured sight of stars falling in the emerging dawn sky made me think of comets in the heavens. The blaring of trumpets reminded me of pictures of the angel Gabriel I had seen in Sunday school and on Christmas cards. Moreover, the only "underground" to me was the caves my brother and I made from large cardboard boxes. And, Christians "shouting" was a regular experience in Sunday worship! Little did I know then of the ancient biblical world's cosmology. Nor did I know much about the world of my enslaved forebears. Nor was I a student of worship expressions of the black religious tradition. Only later, after growing up during the Civil Rights movement, after a seminary education taught me the words *eschatology* and *apocalypticism,* after pastoring African American churches and performing ministry within a university context, after doing issue advocacy, and after intentionally exploring and meditating on the narratives of enslaved blackwomen[2] for more than ten years, did I *know deeply* the truth of Reagon's words. Reagon was right: the meaning comes from living out life's everyday situations and taking a stand from the perspective of one's own worldview.

In our contemporary world, we generally do not construct our worldviews, our prophecies of the future, or our liturgical expressions on the cosmology of either the ancient biblical world or the nineteenth-century world of chattel slavery. Nevertheless, African Americans, people of color, poor people, women and children of diverse cultures and social status domestically and globally, still suffer under the legacies of racism, classism, and misogyny from earlier eras. Many of us remain Christian. Those of us who claim the liberating and sustaining power of God—the reign (kingdom) of God in Jesus Christ—as a support in our struggle against forms of oppression are forced to face the historical and contemporary experience of human injustice and to examine our continuing grounds for faith and action. Confronted with this, what meanings do I and my communities make, and what insights into how I should act do I derive from Christian eschatology, especially when it is seen from a womanist perspective? What meanings do I give to the spiritual's "mornin'" or "mournin' "? What time is it eschatologically?

This essay attempts to address these broad questions first and foremost for myself as a womanist[3] Christian liberation ethicist. Thus the first person, "I," represents the confessional and intellectual nature of the questions. That is, I own the questions, I ask them of myself. Second, these are also questions in the womanist activist-scholar community and African American Christian faith community, and I try to address them as such. The nature of Christian community today for me, a late-twentieth-century African American woman, is deeply ontologically bound to the women and faith traditions that have gone before me. My faith and my actions are lodged in historical and contemporary contexts. Third, these questions are individually appropriated and shaped, yet they contain the "relational" foundations and "spiritual" questions of African American communities. They concern the past, present, and future form and quality of life of our peoples. This essay is therefore part of an ongoing conversation—provisional in nature—about accountability in *faith, action, hope,* and *history*. How are we—African-American women Christians—account-able in the struggle to be fully human in a world where some humans create unjust structures of oppression for other humans and the earth?[4]

The starting point of womanist thought is not an idea or a value, not even a set of ideas, religious or philosophical truth claims. It does not emerge from a canon of "great books" (Western philosophical, literary, or scientific texts), nor from a dominant group with gendered and racial military, economic, and political power. Rather, the starting point is the spiritual and the religious, the historical and the economic, the social and the cultural, the personal and the diverse, the complex and the simple experience of African American women. This experience, critically and constructively reflected on, is central for our un-derstanding of what it means to be human and how to act so that we reach our full humanity. As Alice Walker defines the womanist, an individual woman is also communal, respectful of self, of blackwomen, and of the entire people, male and female. Her being, her activity, her goal is love in its fullness—bold, courageous, and compassionate. Womanist thought, therefore, takes seriously blackwomen's lives in such a way that they become valid for theological and ethical reflection on the nature of God, humanity, and the world.

The context of critical theological thinking about blackwomen's experi-ence from a womanist Christian perspective is the black religious experience, and not solely the black church. Like the gospel, black religious experience is larger than what is contained in any particular ecclesial structure.[5] Black-women's experience and its attending womanist thought move beyond church community to faith community, beyond racial (and racialized) com-munity to human community. Further, womanist ethics is specifically about blackwomen's agency of love. Its ethical reflection is about God, humanity, and the world, and it takes place in communities of faith and spiritual move-ments for humanness and against racism, sexism, classism, heterosexism. It resists the internalization of these dominant forms of oppressions. Wom-anist ethics confronts blackwomen's prescribed nonbeing and invisibility in the world constructed by patriarchal, racist, and imperialist forces; it discerns the ethical nature and action of God in the world and responds to the ques-tions "Who am I *really?*" and "What am I to do?" In the words of Delores S. Williams, the task of womanist ethics is nothing less than a "revaluing of values in the world which has caused black women to be engaged in a most fierce survival struggle that seems to have no end."[6] Positively said, woman-ist ethics is about moral agency centered in relationality and community for the reign of God.

My interest and training is in Christian ethics, specifically Christian social ethics. Yet I still congregationally sing such spirituals as "My Lord, What a Mornin' " and attempt to live within the reign of God. Further, I dare to learn about and teach Christian moral agency as a spiritual practice and as a web of social relations. Both of these together suggest that eschatology is an ethical issue for consideration. So what do I mean by eschatology?

THE MEANING OF ESCHATOLOGY

Under the rubric of eschatology, the "doctrine of last things," the church has reflected on issues in the Bible and Christian tradition regarding death and eternal life, heaven and hell, and the destiny of the material world. But eschatology therefore includes presuppositions about the divine origin of time, history, and humanity, that is, "first things." The language of eschatology is theological talk about " 'last things' in light of 'first things' . . . a commencing of the end," as the black liberation church historian Gayraud Wilmore maintains. "This is in light of Christianity's central claim that Jesus Christ is [t]he Word of Life spoken at creation [and] is the Word of Life spoken at the *eschaton*."[7] Hence, eschatology addresses the power that participates in the shaping of all history, past, present, and future. It asks the meaning of history, and it culminates in its attempt to understand the biblical drive for ultimate hope. Eschatology therefore takes into account two basic perspectives: the *prophetic* and the *apocalyptic*.

Prophetic eschatology is an eschatology that recalls the prophetic judgments and promises of God in the Hebrew scriptures. It anticipates, on the one hand, the "day of the Lord," one in which there is "darkness, and not light, and gloom with no brightness in it" (Amos 5:20). Yet it looks, on the other hand, to a vision of justice in the earth: "Let justice roll down like waters, and righteousness like an ever-flowing stream" (Amos 5:24). In the African American tradition, we can say that prophetic eschatology is the ability of "some Christians . . . to look upon the world with new eyes. . . . The social, economic, and political structures that order our lives, justly and unjustly, the environment that sustains us in abundance and scarcity, are not devoid of the sign which Jesus called to the attention to John's disciples":[8] "the blind receive their sight, the lame walk, the lepers are cleansed, the deaf hear, the dead are raised, and the poor have good news brought to them" (Matt. 11:5). Prophetic eschatology culminates in the restoration of human and earth community through the historical transformation promised to God's entire "groaning creation."

Apocalyptic eschatology embodies a different, "highly imaginative and symbolic form in which eschatological hopes are expressed in the Bible and then decoded and elaborated by every generation."[9] It hopes in the end of history itself. Here is the belief that history will be not redeemed by God but in fact destroyed by God. In theories of dispensationalism and in basic, though diverse, forms of millennialism, apocalyptic eschatology is consumed by the finality of otherworldliness. It looks to the end of reigns of earthly injustice, to catastrophic tribulations destroying the earth and humanity, to cosmic struggles between good and evil, to the Christ and Antichrist, and finally to "a new heaven and earth, the new Jerusalem."[10] While such eschatology is evident in Hebrew scripture (Daniel, for example), the New Testament book of the Revelation to John serves as the quintessential apocalyptic text.

In either form of eschatology, the meaning of history is central, wherein the understanding of the past and the anticipation of the future form the practices of the present. Thus, Wilmore can comment that what Christians believe about eschatology influences how they, like other people concerned with such ultimate notions, may live their lives in the world. Here, where people's beliefs about eschatology influence how they live, we can begin to understand a womanist ethical perspective.

WOMANIST ETHICS AND ESCHATOLOGY

There is a relevant, more general feminist approach that is useful as a background for a womanist approach. Catherine Keller, for example, writes that "Eschatology—[is] a clumsy nineteenth century term from systematic theology mean[ing] 'teachings about end things' and referring to the larger doctrinal category of which apocalypse is an instance. *Eschatos* originally means either a spatial or a temporal end, or edge." Keller sees the apocalyptic as "a spiritual boundary, an edgy and porous one . . . a horizon that always recedes again into a 'not yet' that 'already is,' or is nothing at all."[11] She notes that "apocalypse . . . did not originally or solely mean cataclysm or end. The Greek word *apokalypsis* meant to unveil, to disclose, to reveal . . . "[12] For Keller, eschatology generally and apocalypse specifically are sites of enactment—a situatedness within our subjectivity and a situatedness of external historical-social habits that operate with a certain objectivity. Both are the result of the biblical and the European Christian tradition's impact on the West. In postmodern language, our individual and cultural-historical narratives are "performed" within and are affected broadly from without by notions of eschatology and apocalypse. Like Wilmore, Keller, too, recognizes that within our cultural context how we act, our values and beliefs, is shaped profoundly by our formative story.

Here are the overarching elements in the African American "formative story." All are relevant to the cosmology of our womanist eschatology. First, blackwomen are part of a worldwide diaspora of people who have, over the span of four centuries, transformed our African heritage into tools for survival and quality of life.[13] Such tools include our spirituality, our kinship and familial community structure and sensibilities, our art and music, and our economic-marketplace leadership. For example, social constructs of "time," "space," and "cosmos" are related elements of spirituality that influence African/African American existence.[14]

Second, blackwomen share a heritage of brutal and violent racism, misogyny, and classism. Originally organized as chattel slavery and perpetuated later as white supremacy, this has been an intentional cornerstone of American (colonial and U.S.) society since its inception. The blackwoman has been systematically oppressed in a demonizing equation: skin color equated with race equated with negative character (black/blackness/evil); geographic origins equated with negative genetic traits (African primitive/heathen/biologically and intellectually inferior); race equated with oversexualization (animalistic/female gendering); and race and gender equated with property (*partus sequitur ventrem*—the child follows the condition of the mother). This schematic set of equations has had historical specificity in the different periods of white supremacy and yet has returned with a chilling and pernicious sense of déjà vu throughout the development of the United States.

The third part of African American women's story is its ongoing struggle in resistance to, and for freedom from, patriarchal and maternalistic white supremacy and class relations. On the one hand, enslaved resistance and black abolitionism, the creation of self-defense and internal community "sanctuary," and formal civil rights movements in each era demonstrate the struggle against oppression. Simultaneously, on the other hand, there has been constructive engagement in the creation of an authentic African American culture, in the struggle for survival, and in the betterment of our quality of life. The blackwomen's spiritual movements and church leadership in the antebellum period, the Black Women's Club movement of the late nineteenth and early twentieth centuries, and blackwomen's blues and jazz creations exemplify just a fraction of the blackwoman's cultural production. None of the three parts of African American women's story should be viewed romantically or triumphalistically. Yet together they offer a unique perspective on eschatology.

WOMANIST APOCALYPTIC SENSIBILITIES
AND ESCHATOLOGICAL HOPES

From a womanist standpoint, one lives the reign of God, in part through having apocalyptic sensibilities and by nourishing and being nourished by eschatological hope. This was deeply true for our enslaved foremothers who created in community the spiritual "My Lord, What a Mornin'." Essayist Sterling Brown commented, "In the wake of the Union Army and in the contraband camps, spirituals of freedom sprang up suddenly. The grass was ready for the quickening flame."[15] Imagine an enslaved woman seeing the stars of the Confederate flag as it fell to the ground in retreat, surrender, and defeat. From the depths of her soul and out of her untied tongue leapt the words "My Lord, what a mornin' . . . when the stars begin to fall." In her way of figuring, she had just witnessed part of the great battle between good and evil, had just beheld the disclosure of justice triumphant over injustice, had sensed the answer to her perpetual prayer "How long, oh Lord, 'til freedom?" This enslaved woman, mother of children sold into further bondage, could picture in her mind the runaways emerging from the concealed caves and could see the hiding places of the Underground Railroad fling open their doors! The bugle call of the Union troops signaled advancing legions of liberated brothers and sisters, and the shouts of battle had become

> *Oh Freedom! Oh Freedom!*
> *Oh Freedom, I love thee!*
> *And before I'll be a slave,*
> *I'll be buried in my grave,*
> *And go home to my Lord and be free!*
>
> —*Traditional Negro Spiritual*

Such a scene is not limited to the imagination of a womanist ethicist. One has only to read the testimonies of black Union soldiers and the narratives of enslaved blackwomen and to listen to the spirituals to know the historical possibility of apocalyptic sensibility and eschatological hope within "slave religion"—that is, to know that death is not the ultimate evil, and that there is a trustworthy source for the meaning of being human and being known as human.

The Shaping of Hope

The apocalyptic sensibilities and eschatological hope of such an enslaved woman would have emerged from several sources. One source would have been the Bible and its rich ancient cosmology of the struggle between good and evil. The Revelation to John comes to mind, particularly chapter 8, in which the images of trumpeting angels and falling stars appear. A crucial point is made by womanist ethicist Emilie M. Townes: womanist apocalypticism is "not an apocalyptic of gloom and doom. It does not exhort a kind of fascination with utter destruction that simply begets a passivity of inaction, and worse indifference. It poses the question of Micah, 'Is it not for [us] to know justice?' . . . It is, as the tradition from Isaiah to 2 Peter to Revelation suggests, a new heaven and a new earth. One in which the dominant norms are challenged and debunked . . . "[16]

Another source would have been the enslaved woman's immediate and historical context of chattel slavery, in all its dehumanization. To her, slavery was evil, plain and simple. Enslaved woman Elizabeth Kleckley wrote, "When the war of the Revolution established the independence of the American colonies, an evil was perpetuated, slavery was more fully established." She continued, remarking how the evil of slavery was like a plant, growing in stages as do all plants, little noticed until it ripens into monstrous proportions that over-shadow important interests, and must be destroyed.[17]

Rather than an apocalyptic "vision," Kleckley offers an apocalyptic "metaphor": evil (i.e., slavery) is like a plant. Her words speak prophetically, discerning the contradiction in the actions of those who launched a revolution for their freedom and then, in turn, further reinforced an unjust and evil sys-tem of enslavement for others. Kleckley's metaphor judges what finally hap-pened: even the best of seeds can grow dangerous awry. At the very least, it exposes the complacency in human behavior that cannot confront human in-justice; people let things go until they are out of control or jeopardize their own interests. Positive action must be taken to destroy evil. Destruction of hu-man evil is the responsibility of humans in sociohistorical reality

Yet a third source for African American women's apocalyptic sensibilities and eschatological hope emerged from the transformative integration of African heritage and Christian faith. In the slave narrative *Incidents in the Life of a Slave Girl: Written by Herself,* Harriet Jacobs prepares for her final escape attempt from Edenton, North Carolina, after hiding for nearly seven years in the crawl space of her grandmother's home:

> Perhaps this is the last day I should ever spend under that dear, old shelter-ing roof! . . . Perhaps it was the last time I and my children should be to-gether! Well, better so, I thought, than that they should be slaves. I knew the doom that awaited my fair baby [girl] in slavery, and I was determined to save her from it or perish in the attempt.[18]

She returns to "the burying-ground of the slaves . . . in the woods" beside "the old meeting house." She had frequented the stop before, but for the first time she notices the sacredness of the place where her father and mother were buried. "I knelt down and kissed them, and poured forth a prayer to God for guidance and support in the perilous step I was about to take. As I passed the wreck of the old meeting house, where, before Nat Turner's time, the slaves had been allowed to meet for worship, I seemed to hear my father's voice from it, bidding me not to tarry till I reached freedom or the grave. I rushed on with renovated hopes."[19]

This is the cultural site of empowerment in the midst of the ancestors—deceased parents and generations of enslaved women and men—as well as the religious site of ritual prayer. The Christian God and the revered ancestors to-gether strengthen Jacobs in the quest for both physical and spiritual freedom from enslavement. Sterling Stuckey has reminded us that such sites are spirit filled, conjuring or mediating spaces of empowerment between the living and the dead.[20] The apocalyptic sensibilities reside in the rootedness of movement between and within African and African American sacred cosmologies and history, peopled with the moral authority of ancestors' spirits, of God, of one's offspring (vital for the past in what they carry of the ancestors and for the future of free African American people), of justice, and of life and death. Herein also lies the source of eschatological hope.

Womanist ethics, then, must sustain the dynamic relationship between belief in the God who acts in human history through personal and communal human agency, in the God who is known in the past and present of the inclusive African cosmology of time and spirits, and in the God who is known in apocalyptic struggles for life now, as well as in the future. Eschatology and apocalypse in this sense are not transhistorical or ahistorical. Rather, they are dimensions of the religious landscape of life in every era—they have to do with moments of faith and action in times of crisis and judgment and which are simultaneously positive opportunities and fulfillment of God's promise. This sets African American womanist theo-ethical thought, action, and critical reflection apart from the other eschatologies related to the biblical texts and to the Western Christian tradition.

Shaping and Reshaping Hopes

All three sources for womanist eschatology and apocalypticism influenced the form that apocalyptic sensibilities and eschatological hopes were to take in the years after Emancipation and Reconstruction. As the historical context changed, so the sensibilities and hopes modified. After all, the apocalypse was not yet here, nor the was eschaton yet realized. History moved on, and not necessarily with the transformations that had been hoped for. For example, at the close of the Reconstruction era emerged a spiritually sobering new apocalyptic sensibility and eschatological hope. In retrospective analysis of Reconstruction and the work of the Freedman's Bureau, W.E.B. Du Bois wrote "Of the Dawn of Freedom," the second essay in his collection *The Souls of Black Folk*. Like all the essays of *Souls*, "Of the Dawn of Freedom" begins with a musical epigraph, indeed, with the refrain from "My Lord, What a Mornin'." In the post-Emancipation and Reconstruction periods, and in the dawning resurgence of white supremacy in *de jure* segregation, Du Bois's essay is both an apocalyptic lament and a prophecy. The "falling stars" of the spiritual may signify the variant rendering "mournin'."[21] African Americans experienced systematic re-exploitation in the neoslavery of economic existence, and Jim Crow characterized the South while *de facto* segregation existed in most areas of the North. In many ways the reintroduction of systematic oppression was cataclysmic, swift in nature, the new arrival of pernicious human evil. Du Bois, in the opening and closing sentences of the essay, reiterates his lament and prophecy for the situation in which the United States still lives: "The problem of the twentieth century is the problem of the color-line."[22]

In the years after Emancipation, blackwomen's collective existence changed very little in terms of material conditions. Angela Davis illustrates blackwomen's predicament:

> Vast numbers of Black women were still working in the fields. Those who made it into the "big house" found the door toward new opportunities sealed shut—unless they preferred, for example, to wash clothes at home for a medley of white families as opposed to performing a medley of household jobs for a single white family. Only an infinitesimal number of Black women had managed to escape from the fields, from the kitchen or from the washroom.[23]

Davis goes on to relate the specific forms of oppression blackwomen experienced in the decades after Reconstruction, oppression that structured itself on the patterns of social relations from chattel slavery. Jim Crow laws governing the civil and legal rights of blacks replaced the former body of antebellum state laws called Black Codes. Sharecropping or contract peonage often left black families, who had mortgaged large percentages of hopeful harvests to white landowners, in perpetual debt for the rent of farmland, living quarters, and basic staples purchased on credit at white-owned stores. Whether as sharecroppers, farm workers, or tenant farmers, just "as during slavery, Black women who worked in agriculture . . . were no less oppressed than the men alongside whom they labored the day long."[24]

Blackwomen employed in white homes as domestic servants were still the targets of sexual abuse by the white patriarch (or his sons) and of physical and emotional abuse by the white female householder and her children. Domestic service was remunerated at exceedingly meager levels, and further exploitation was incurred either through the long hours of work or the "live-in" demands of employers. Clearly, the pattern of slavery was being repeated: blackwomen were forced to provide domestic service for white families, particularly in but not limited to the South, as a major means of economic survival and employment. This employment pattern would not significantly change until the early 1960s,[25] and it is but one example of a 350-year struggle for womanhood and peoplehood.

According to historian Deborah Gray White, "The victimization of black women continued for over seventy-five years after emancipation. For African Americans these years were not characterized by optimism. Hopes were cautious. They were sobered by an uphill struggle for literacy, jobs, and the franchise."[26] The terrorism of lynching and rape and the destruction of African American economic initiatives for independence and autonomy from whites replaced the terrorism of sale and family breakup, the whip and the chains, and the bondage for life that been characteristic of antebellum slavery. The journalistic investigations and reporting of Ida B. Wells in the closing decades of the nineteenth and beginning of the twentieth century document the vulnerability of all African American women, men, and children—regardless of class or social status—to white supremacist violence and repression, particularly in the South. Wells, who herself carried a pistol for protection against racists, documented the increasing systematic violence of the lynching of blackmen and the rape of blackwomen in Southern cities and the significant numbers of interracial liaisons, which fueled white male rage against blacks. As a result of her editorials, the newspaper of which she was part owner, *Free Speech*, was looted and burned to the ground while Wells was out of town. Her co-workers barely escaped the mob, and her own life was threatened were she to return to Memphis. Tirelessly she not only sought to expose the false negative stereotyping of blackmen in the cause of white racial terrorism but was adamant about challenging the false social assumptions regarding blackwomen's immorality and promiscuity.

Violence of another type also adversely affected the African American community. The health and physical welfare of the community was precarious. At an 1899 Atlanta University conference, and again at a convention of the Alabama Teachers Association, it was reported that the living conditions and health of much of the state's black population put the African American community's actual survival in jeopardy. Inadequate diet, economic want, and lack of health education were seen as paramount concerns for the church, educational institutions, and social organizations in the community.[27] In response to this crisis, the Black Women's Club movement, in locales throughout the South, Midwest, and East, sought to establish nurseries and kindergartens for early childhood education and child-care facilities for working mothers.

These organizations, while attacking the living conditions of African American women, men, and children, also strove to address the particular plight of blackwomen, especially poor blackwomen, through advocacy and social reform. The Black Women's Club movement and the church sought to raise the standard of living within the blackcommunity in the midst of an economic, political, social, and theological milieu that caught blackwomen's realities in a web of contradictions. Christian moral perfection, uplift of the race, freedom, and equality were the themes and the goal of Christian life from the perspective of the black church and black organizations. Yet the socioreligious ideologies of womanhood and moral reform placed blackwomen in a catch-22 situation. In general, women were seen as the moral guardians of society in their familial roles as mothers, caretakers of households, and childbearers—the cult of true womanhood. But blackwomen were still plagued by constructions of their sexuality and breeder status that had carried over from enslavement. Blackwomen were in this sense excluded from the definition of "womanhood."[28] As women in the church and club movements organized for social reform, the religious affirmation of woman's moral role in society through the family, the internalization of the negative stereotypes of the "black woman," and class differences among blackwomen often came into tension in the theo-ethical perspectives and the social reforms sought by these women.[29] Yet blackwomen would not allow such tensions to deter their religious faith, their gifts and talents, or their hope for freedom and human dignity. The eschaton may have seemed farther away, but eschatological hopes for change within history remained.

Sustaining Hope

In the decades after Du Bois penned the problematic of the twentieth century as the problem of the color line and Ida B. Wells began her activist anti-lynching and antirape crusade, the black church and Black Women's Club movement focused on securing basic education, health care, food, clothing, and shelter for blackwomen and the blackcommunity. For women, emerging issues even included birth-control advocacy, reproductive choices, and welfare policy. For example, African American history of the 1920s through 1940s suggests that birth-control education and advocacy for reproductive choice were issues alive and well in communities within the traditional Southern "Black Belt" and, as a result of the Great Migration, in Northern cities as well. In many instances, birth-control discourse was related to economic issues of family survival, as well as to the changing gender roles of African American women.[30] Black male and female leadership, community based as well as national, argued intensely both the conservative and the progressive viewpoint. Historian Jessie M. Rodrique illustrates the role of blackwomen's organizations and the church:

> In 1918 the Women's Political Association of Harlem, calling upon black women to "assume the reins of leadership in the political, social and economic life of their people," announced that its lecture series would include birth control among topics for discussion . . . [and] William Lloyd Imes of the St. James Presbyterian Church [Harlem] reported that he had held discussions on birth control at his church . . . and at another meeting . . . announced that if a birth control pamphlet were printed, he would place it in the church vestibule.[31]

Prior to the Great Depression (and during it as well), black male and female sociopolitical organizations and associations, along with the black church, provided the overwhelming amount of welfare aid to the African American community. On the one hand, political scientist Barbara J. Nelson demonstrates, blackpeople were systematically prevented from utilizing the emerging public welfare aid through the development of a two-channel welfare state in the first quarter to third of the twentieth century. "Workmen's [*sic*] Compensation was a program developed for the white northern men employed in heavy industry, even though it always covered some female workers." White working-class men were the first beneficiaries of "judicial, public, and routinized" public policy aid. On the other hand, "Mothers' Aid was originally designed for the white impoverished widows of men like those eligible for Workmen's Compensation. It set the tone for the second channel of the welfare state, which was female, administrative, private, and nonroutinized in origin."[32]

In the face of such brutal class-stratified racism, the Black Women's Club movement and women of the black church often joined forces in local communities in addressing the needs of the poor in the blackcommunity. The Phyllis Wheatley Club and literary Lit-Mus Club of 1922 in Buffalo, New York, were second in their efforts only to the women's missionary societies and auxiliaries of the churches, such as the Bethel AME Church and its Josephine Hurd Women's Mite Missionary Society, founded in 1915.[33] By the time of the 1929 depression, such groups provided aid in the form of fuel and appliances as well as food, shelter, and clothing.

The socioreligious movements in which African American women are today engaged are both ancient and new, seemingly "timeless" yet "timely." The work begun when white supremacy shut down Reconstruction sustained itself for more than a half century, blossoming in the blackwomen's club movements, women's church and missionary auxiliaries, suffrage movements, the labor movements of the 1920s and 1930s, legal rights struggles of the immediate post–World War II era, and the Civil Rights movement of the 1950s and 1960s. These were years of grief, of lament, and of somber expectation. Apocalyptic sensibilities and dimmed eschatological hope expressed the realization that the dream of a new postbellum nation awakening and emerging as a sign of God's justice and rule had become a "false dawn."[34] The world, in which "mornin'" followed the night and in which stars yielded to the sun as a source of joy and promise, became a bleak gray of "mournin'." Apocalyptic sensibilities and sobered eschatological hope now fit the distorted nature of the world, still maimed by the reconstruction of white supremacy, economic exploitation, and gender violence. From the perspective of the spiritual "My Lord, What a Mo(u)rnin,'" such a world was and is contrary to the way God intends the world to be. A womanist eschatological reading sees the times as a resubversion of the freedom that God's world holds out for those whose lives are oppressed by the human constructs of race, economic and political power, and gender.

Yet a womanist reading is also a recognition of the grief and lament that "airs" the renewed call for hope-filled spirits. The spirits are those souls who are not dead but who will continue the struggle. Howard Thurman recalled a spiritual that is reminiscent of just this sentiment:

Oh, He's going to wake up the dead,
Going to wake up the dead,
God's going to wake up the dead.
One of these mornings bright and fair,
God's going to wake up the dead.[35]

—*Traditional Negro Spiritual*

According to Thurman, such religious expression has served first to strengthen the perseverance of the faithful "in the face of those facts that argue most dramatically against all hope and to [encourage them] use those facts as raw material out of which they could fashion a hope that the environment with all its cruelty, could not crush." It served, second, "to not paralyze action [or] make for mere resignation. On the contrary, it gave the mind a new dimension of resourcefulness."[36] Womanists affirm that such apocalyptic sensibilities and eschatological hope provided a "new dimension of resourcefulness" in the struggle for freedom against the neoslavery of U.S. racism, sexism, and class oppression.

THE BATTLE BETWEEN SYMBOLS
OF HOPE AND DESPAIR

The signs and symbols of the spirituals function broadly to form and to sustain apocalyptic and eschatological hopes. But they also provide alternative normative principles of theo-ethical and social criticism, an insight revealed by black theologians and ethicists, including womanists.[37] Apocalyptic sensibility and eschatological hope hold within them an alternative normative conviction that full human identity is not found in the social constructs of race or gender, nor in economic and political fortune. Rather, human identity, for those judged through oppression to be less than human, finds its definition and ground in the God who is free, the ultimate Judge of freedom, creation, humanity, death and life. The very concept of an alternative source for defining humanity and freedom, a source that a community can come to know and by which a community can be known, enables radical resistance to the falsehood embodied in oppression. It opens up the possibility of a history mediated in and by the actions of African Americans.

This alternative normative view, then, holds together belief in a God who works to free all people and the need for people to work for freedom in their own history. It generates principles that challenge the drive of the forces of injustice to naturalize, essentialize, what are constitutionally human sociohistorical constructions. When social and historical constructs are rendered as "ontological," they mask the "design, building, and maintenance of such systems to serve the special interests of some at the expense of others."[38] One set of symbols struggles against another. African American women from Elizabeth Kleckley and Harriet Jacobs to the women of the Josephine Hurd Women's Mite Missionary Society have affirmed that the worlds of enslavement, of Jim Crow, of the cult of true womanhood, and of the "welfare queen" of the 1980s and 1990s are contrived worlds, worthy of notions of neither objectivity nor truth. As humanly contrived and constructed, they can be discredited and destroyed.

Voices of lament, grief, and renewed call, however, are necessary to "wake the nations underground" to engage sustained moments of prophetic and apocalyptic eschatological action. Enslaved women and their communities were caricatured as "happy" and "content" in their enslavement by those invested in the perpetuation of slavery. First-generation freed bondpersons had their constitutional rights adjudicated under the white supremacist legal theory of "separate but equal." Lynching and rape were intended to intimidate, terrorize, and silence struggles by blacks for their democratic and human rights. Blackwomen such as Ida B. Wells could not be quieted or silenced, nor could the instruments of their voices. The alternative normative principle of the vocalized lament, grief, and renewed call is powerfully evoked by blackwomen of every faith generation and community, perhaps by none more forceful in this generation than Audre Lorde:

> My silences had not protected me. Your silences will not protect you. . . . Within this country where racial difference creates a constant, if unspoken distortion of vision, Black women have on one hand always been highly visible, and so, on the other hand, have been rendered invisible through the depersonalization of racism . . . we have had to fight, and still do, for that very visibility which also renders us most vulnerable, our Blackness. For to survive in the mouth of this dragon we call america [*sic*], we have had to learn this first and most vital lesson—that we were never meant to survive. Not as human beings. . . . We can sit in our corners forever mute while our sisters and our selves are wasted, while our children are distorted and destroyed, while our earth is poisoned; we can sit in our safe corners as mute bottles, and we will still be no less afraid.[39]

To grieve, to lament, and to renew the call to action is to "value." Valuing, or "revaluing" in the words of Delores Williams, noted earlier in this essay, is an alternative to the attempt by the dominating culture and society to *de*value "othered" existence as less than human and less than fully historical. Through our own historical valuing of our communal and individual selves and our actions, we determine, in part, the significance of life and the valid expectation for what is based on "the evidence of things not seen, but hoped for."

The post-1950s and -1960s Civil Rights era has striking parallels to the post-Reconstruction period of the nineteenth century. This makes this time potentially one of renewed apocalyptic sensibilities and eschatological hope from a womanist ethical perspective. There is great resistance in the dominant society, culture, and church to egalitarianism, full personhood, and earth community. Past history makes current legacy. The fundamental questions of basic economic and social resources for a common good that is inclusive rather than exclusive are symptomatically disguised in anti–affirmative action attacks, in so-called welfare reform and workfare, in anti-immigration legislation, in privatization of public education, and in the lack of political will to provide anything other than drugs and prisons for those who are structured out of the common good.

Those who sing, "My Lord, What a Mornin'/Mournin' " take our cue from the knowledge that "judgment is personal *and* cosmic so that even the rocks and mountains, the stars, the sea are involved in so profound a process."[40] A womanist apocalyptic sensibility and eschatological hope affirms the words of Bernice Johnson Reagon: "I really see an immense struggle taking shape in our communities . . . people trying to claim them as places where human beings can develop and grow. That struggle might make the Civil Rights Movement look like a picnic. So the songs in our current crisis and challenge must 'express your need to change your situation'."[41]

NOTES

1. Bernice Johnson Reagon, "The Songs Are Free," with Bill Moyers (New York: Mystic Fire Videos, Inc., 1991). Reagon is the founder, lead singer, and artistic director of the vocal group Sweet Honey in the Rock; she is also a curator of African American history and culture at the Smithsonian Institution, Washington, D.C. Reagon holds a Ph.D. in American history.
2. *Blackwomen* is a more accurate term than *black women,* expressing the social construction of race and gender of African American women, i.e., contextuality, skin color, etc. I first used this term in my essay "The Notion of Difference for Emerging Womanist Ethics: The Writings of Audre Lorde and bell hooks," *Journal of Feminist Studies in Religion* 9, 1–2 (Spring–Fall 1993): 39–51.
3. For the definition of *womanist,* see Alice Walker, *In Search of Our Mothers' Gardens: Womanist Prose* (San Diego: Harcourt Brace Jovanovich, 1983), pp. xi–xii, 81.
4. See the discussion of the "slave poet," creator/singer of slave spirituals, and her use of the spiritual "I" both for individual self-reliance and self-responsibility and for the "person-in-relation-to-community" in John Lovell Jr., *Black Song: The Flame and the Forge* (New York: Macmillan Publishing Co., 1972), pp. 274–281; John Lovell, "The Social Implications of the Negro Spiritual," in *The Social Implications of Early Negro Music in the United States,* ed. Bernard Katz (New York: Arno Press, 1969), p. 136; and Bernice Johnson Reagon, "Songs Are Free."
5. See Delores S. Williams, *Sisters in the Wilderness: The Challenge of Womanist God-Talk* (Maryknoll, N.Y.: Orbis Books, 1993), pp. xii–xiii, 204–228, and 242n. 4.
6. Ibid., pp. 175 and 271n. 44.

7. Gayraud S. Wilmore, *Last Things First* (Philadelphia: Westminster Press, 1982), pp. 23–24.
8. Ibid., p. 59.
9. Ibid., p. 41.
10. Catherine Keller, "Eschatology," in *Dictionary of Feminist Theologies*, ed. Letty M. Russell and J. Shannon Clarkson (Louisville, Ky.: Westminster John Knox Press, 1996), p. 86.
11. Catherine Keller, *Apocalypse Now and Then: A Feminist Guide to the End of the World* (Boston: Beacon Press, 1996), p. xiii.
12. Ibid., p. ix.
13. Williams articulates her womanist theological and ethical principle as one focused on "survival and quality of life."
14. For further discussions of these constructs, see Wilmore, *Last Things First*, chapter 6; and John S. Mbiti, *New Testament Eschatology in an African Background: A Study of the Encounter between New Testament Theology and African Traditional Concepts* (London: Oxford University Press, 1971), pp. 24–32.
15. Sterling Brown, "Negro Folk Expression: Spirituals, Seculars, Ballads, and Work Songs," *Phylon* 14, 1 (1953): 445–61.
16. Emilie M. Townes, *In a Blaze of Glory: Womanist Spirituality as Social Witness* (Nashville: Abingdon Press, 1995), p. 122.
17. Elizabeth Kleckley, *Behind the Scenes, or Thirty Years a Slave and Four Years in the White House*, ed. Henry Louis Gates Jr., reprint by the Schomburg Library of Nineteenth-Century Black Women Writers (New York: Oxford University Press, 1988), pp. xii–xiii. Elizabeth Kleckley was an enslaved woman who, after being emancipated, served as a seamstress for Mrs. Lincoln in the White House.
18. Harriet Jacobs, *Incidents in the Life of a Slave Girl: Written by Herself*, ed. L. Maria Childs; ed., with a new introduction, Jean Fagan Yellin (Cambridge, Mass.: Harvard University Press, 1987), p. 90.
19. Ibid., pp. 90–91.
20. Sterling Stuckey, *Slave Culture: Nationalist Theory and the Foundations of Black Nationalism* (New York: Oxford University Press, 1987), pp. 12–14, as quoted in Joan M. Martin, "A Womanist Investigation: The Work Ethic of Enslaved Women in the Ante-Bellum, 1830–1865, and Implications for Christian Social Teachings on Work and Human Meaning" (Ph.D. diss., Temple University, 1996), pp. 167–168.
21. For an in-depth discussion of Du Bois, the spiritual "My Lord, What a Mornin'," and the impact of African American culture on American culture, see Eric J. Sundquist, *To Wake the Nations: Race in the Making of American Literature* (Cambridge, Mass.: The Belknap Press, 1993), introduction and chap. 5.
22. W.E.B. Du Bois, *The Souls of Black Folk* (1903; reprint, New York: Vintage Books, 1986, 1990), pp. 16, 35.
23. Angela Y. Davis, *Women, Race, and Class* (New York: Random House, 1981), p. 87.
24. Ibid., p. 88.
25. Bonnie Thornton Dill, "Making Your Job Good Yourself: Domestic Service and the Construction of Personal Dignity," in *Women and the Politics of Empowerment* (Philadelphia: Temple University Press, 1987), p. 51, n. 3. Dill states that between 1890 and 1960 a higher percentage of blackwomen were employed in private domestic service than in any other single (broad) occupational category. By 1960, 60 percent of blackwomen were employed in service occupations, but only

37 percent were in private domestic service, with 23 percent in other service work. By 1970, only 18 percent were in private domestic work and 27 percent in other service.

26. Deborah Gray White, *"Aren't I a Woman?" Female Slaves in the Plantation South* (New York: W.W. Norton & Co., 1985), p. 163.
27. Paula Giddiness, *When and Where I Enter: The Impact of Black Women on Race and Sex in America* (New York and Toronto: Bantam Books, 1984), p. 99.
28. Hazel Carby, *Reconstructing Womanhood: The Emergence of the Afro-American Woman Novelist* (New York: Oxford University Press, 1987), pp. 23–31.
29. For in-depth discussions of these issues, see historian Evelyn Brooks Higginbotham, *Righteous Discontent: The Women's Movement in the Black Baptist Church, 1880–1920* (Cambridge, Mass.: Harvard University Press, 1993); and womanist ethicists Marcia Y. Riggs, *Awake, Arise and Act: A Womanist Call for Black Liberation* (Cleveland: Pilgrim Press, 1994); Emilie M. Townes, *Womanist Justice, Womanist Hope* (Atlanta: Scholars Press, 1993); idem, *In a Blaze of Glory;* and Williams, *Sisters in the Wilderness.*
30. Jessie M. Rodrique, "The Black Community and the Birth Control Movement," in *"We Specialize in the Wholly Impossible": A Reader in Black Women's History,* ed. Darlene Clark Hine, Wilma King, and Linda Reed (Brooklyn, N.Y.: Carlson Publishing Co., 1995), p. 508.
31. Ibid., p. 511.
32. Barbara J. Nelson, "The Origins of the Two-Channel Welfare State," in *Women, the State, and Welfare,* ed. Linda Gordon (Madison: University of Wisconsin Press, 1990), p. 133. Nelson reports that Mothers' Aid was not a federal program but began at the state level in 1911 in Illinois. By 1919, thirty-nine states had passed similar laws. In a 1931 study by the U.S. Children's Bureau, it was noted that only 3 percent of Mothers' Aid clients were blackwomen, with certain areas such as Washington, D.C., and Ohio having higher proportions of aid going to blackwomen (p. 139).
33. Lillian S. Williams, "And Still I Rise: Black Women and Reform, Buffalo, New York, 1900–1940," in *"We Specialize in the Wholly Impossible,"* ed. Hine, King, and Reed, pp. 528–529.
34. Sundquist, *To Wake the Nations,* p. 2.
35. Howard Thurman, "Deep River: Sorrow Songs—The Ground of Hope (I)," in *For the Inward Journey: The Writings of Howard Thurman,* ed. Anne Spencer Thurman (Richmond, Ind.: Friends United Meeting, 1984), p. 217.
36. Ibid., pp. 215, 216.
37. See the works of scholars such as Howard Thurman, James Cone, Peter Paris, Cheryl Kirk-Duggan, Karen Baker-Fletcher, and Delores S. Williams.
38. Walter Brueggemann, *Hope within History* (Atlanta: John Knox Press, 1987), pp. 20, 24.
39. Audre Lorde, *Sister Outsider: Essays and Speeches* (Trumansburg, N.Y.: Crossing Press, 1984), pp. 41, 42.
40. Thurman, "Deep River," p. 217.
41. Reagon, "Songs Are Free."

16

MUJERISTA NARRATIVES

Creating a New Heaven and a New Earth

Ada María Isasi-Díaz

There is something disturbing about hearing the "new heaven and new earth" of Revelation 21:1 referred to as "a new world order." What today is called a new world order usually refers to the kind of society being shaped by neoliberal forces that endorse unbridled capitalism and a kind of economic globalization that favors the haves at the expense of the have-nots. No matter how much I want to believe that those of us who try to be justice-seeking people can influence this so-called new world order, the forces defining and shaping it do not seem to be animated by a commitment to liberation, by a commitment to "a society in which all can fit."[1]

In contrast to my despondence about the apparent impossibility of influencing the priorities of the United States and other societies responsible for this so-called new world order was the utter elation of four Indonesian women taking a course on women's ethics I was teaching recently in Manila, at the time of the student demonstrations in Indonesia that forced President Suharto to step down. One day I adjourned class early so these women and their friends from Bangladesh, Korea, and the Philippines could go to a demonstration outside the Indonesian embassy. Off they went, in a suffocating heat, convinced not only that they had to be present but that their very presence at that demonstration was a needed element in the struggle for justice. Are they not right in claiming that they contributed to this one tiny step taken in Indonesia that may bring about opportunities, absent until now, for justice to flourish in the so-called new world order?

I have what I consider to be a healthy obsession with how to influence what is normative in society, how to bring to the attention of those who control the so-called new world order the voices of the poor and the oppressed who struggle for liberation, particularly the voices of my own community of accountability, grassroots Latinas. This drive has led me to reflect on biblical eschatology, more precisely, on prophetic eschatology.[2] Undoubtedly this biblical tradition can encourage us to continue our struggle for justice by giving us a deeper understanding of the responsibility we have not only for what exists but also for the "new heaven and new earth" that we believe lies somewhere in our historical future.

PROPHETIC ESCHATOLOGY: HISTORY COUNTS!

Prophetic eschatology is concerned with ending situations of oppression that are happening in the here and now of history.[3] It points to and calls for radically different times within history. It is a perspective that makes us turn toward the future, a future that will have "a sort of social and/or cosmic arrangement fundamentally different from that which currently exists."[4] A text that makes clear the historicity of the new heaven and new earth, and thus a text that is central to prophetic eschatology, is that of Isaiah 65. This text makes clear that the inequities that offend Yahweh are committed in the hills and the mountains (v. 7), in actual geographic space, and that Yahweh's reward will also happen in geographic space, the here and now of Israel: "Sharon shall become a pasture for flocks, and the Valley of Achor a place for herds to lie down, for my people who have sought me" (v. 10). It is this-world life that will be radically changed for the people: they will eat and drink, they will rejoice and sing (v. 13), they will build houses and live in them, they will plant vineyards, they will not labor in vain but shall enjoy the work of their hands (vv. 2 2–23).

Because prophetic eschatology is related to history, the solutions it offers are directly related to the concrete crisis it referred to originally and are not necessarily transferable to present-day situations. But the vision that guides the solutions offered in prophetic eschatology can indeed be of use to us today. The vision is one of righteous living, of justice among all peoples, a justice that is not possible without a commitment to protection of the weak (the widows, the slaves, the foreigners of the biblical world) and to restoration of right order in nature and the cosmos. The vision is best captured in the biblical shalom, in the embrace between justice (righteousness) and peace (Psalm 85) necessary for the creation of a truly new heaven and a new earth.

In all eschatology, apocalyptic as well as prophetic, God is in ultimate control of history. But at least in prophetic eschatology, God's role does not exclude or excuse human participation from averting or remedying the crisis at hand. The prophets never grew tired of denouncing the attitudes and actions of the people, particularly the religious and political leaders who were responsible for the crises Israel suffered. This is precisely why, to overcome any and all kinds of crises, the people had to repent (*la-shuv* in Hebrew, as Jeremiah 8:4–12 indicates). "The most prominent and most significant" meaning of repentance in the Bible is that of "repentance in the ethico-religious sense, turning away from sin and back to God."[5]

The ethical implications of repentance indicate the responsibility of people for the situation that somehow they have had a hand in creating, whether by commission or omission. Of course, insistence on human responsibility for bringing about radical change does not mean this whole process happens apart from God. However, the fact is that it is not given to us humans to know how God participates in personal lives and in human history. Most of us believe in a mixture of determination and free will, of destiny and personal responsibility, of luck and hard work. Therefore, in *mujerista* theology—a theology emerging from the lived experiences of grassroots Latinas—because human beings do not have any responsibility for God's role in history and can do nothing about it, we believe that what we need to concentrate on is using "our temporal life span to create a just and good community for our generation and for our children."[6] Do our actions have any implications beyond our limited historical horizon? "It is in the hands of Holy Wisdom to forge out of our finite struggle truth and being for everlasting life . . . [we] trust Holy Wisdom will give transcendent meaning to our work, which is bounded by space and time."[7]

Apart from emphasizing the importance of personal responsibility for our world, two other elements are needed if prophetic eschatology is to become a liberating eschatology. First, we need to realize the enormous urgency to bring about a real new heaven and new earth for the women, children, and men around the world who are living in the worst of conditions and are dying precisely because of the present world order. Because of this reality, the prevalent understanding of Ecclesiastes that nothing happens outside God's will is not acceptable. To believe there is a time for everything, including a time for war, a time to break down, a time to kill, is not acceptable because, among other reasons, it promotes an erroneous way of understanding suffering as good in and of itself. It also "uses" the idea of a reward in the "next world" as a consolation for the poor and the oppressed, as a way of discouraging them from demanding their rights and struggling for their liberation. Second, we need to flesh out the shape of the kind of new heaven and the new earth for which justice-seeking people hunger and thirst. Actual strategies and tactics to accomplish this result are beyond the scope of this essay. I suggest, however, that the designing of the new world order and of the strategies to be used to bring it about has to start with and take always into consideration the understandings of the poor and the oppressed.

To be able to act responsibly, to respond to the urgent need for change, and to create an efficient way of bringing about a just new heaven and the new earth, we need to put aggressively into practice what many of us have mouthed but have not done: we must privilege the lived experiences and visions of the poor and the oppressed. The last four decades of the twentieth century have shown us that trying to work out of some a priori idea of society, whether based on the free market and private property or centralized markets and socialized property or some other organizational principle,[8] brings about a social order that is not good for even half of humanity. It is time, therefore, to turn to the understandings of the poor and the oppressed and to their everyday experience of struggle for survival. I believe that we need to provide opportunities for grassroots people to share their stories, hopes, and expectations, from which emerge new narratives capable of providing specifics as to the shape and content of a truly new heaven and new earth.[9]

MUJERISTA NARRATIVE: SOURCE FOR A NEW HEAVEN AND A NEW EARTH

In *mujerista* theology, in our search for what is required of us as justice-seeking people, we have turned to the voices of grassroots Latinas who struggle for liberation. Their lived experiences constitute the source of *mujerista* theology, while our criterion is a holistic understanding of liberation-salvation that includes social, psychological, and spiritual perspectives.[10] We privilege Latinas' lived experiences not because grassroots Latinas are morally better or holier than others but because we believe that since they do not profit from the present situation, they are capable of imagining a radically different future. They can do this better than those who benefit from current structures and who are, therefore, tempted to protect them.[11]

The sharing by grassroots Latinas of their lived experiences yields rich narratives that need to be taken into consideration in the development of a really new world order, in which no one will be excluded. Four elements emerging from these narratives are particularly important. First, a narrative is a tool one uses to organize lived experiences into meaningful episodes. "Narrative displays the goals and intentions of human actors; it makes individuals, cultures, societies, and historical epochs comprehensible as wholes; it humanizes time; and it allows us to contemplate the effects of our actions and to alter the directions of our lives."[12] Narratives allow us to link the distinct events of our lives by making us note that something is but a part of something else and that it is cause and/or effect of something else. Personal narratives, then, are stories of one's life that make it possible for the person to give meaning to her life and to interpret it within its historical and cultural context.

Second, it is obvious to *mujerista* theologians that unless Latinas have a narrative of our own, a narrative in which we can see ourselves as moral agents, as subjects of our own history, we will not be able to conceive and work toward our liberation-salvation, toward the creation of a new heaven and a new earth. A narrative of our own makes it possible for us to give meaning to our lives. We consider emerging Latinas' narratives "new narratives" because they help us imagine ourselves in a new way, and to imagine ourselves in a new way is to know ourselves in a way different from the way in which the dominant group knows us. A *mujerista* narrative will help us "read" ourselves differently because it talks to us about what we have not been able to see in ourselves, about what we have ignored in ourselves.

Third, it has become clear that we need to insist on what the writers of the Gospel stories knew long ago: people do not live or die for creeds or for beliefs that are expressed only in rational dicta. Large-scale social changes that make liberation possible necessitate changes of heart and mind that are not possible on the grounds of reason alone. People need a story. A story puts sinews and flesh on the dry bones of reason and creed. People need a story—a narrative— that sets before us situations and understandings "by means of which we learn to join the ethical aspect of human behavior to happiness and unhappiness, to fortune and misfortune."[13] Discovering the stories of Latinas and elaborating a *mujerista* narrative is important not only because it helps us conceive a new and just world order but also because it motivates us remain faithful to the struggle to make this a reality.

Fourth, Latinas' narratives are an important way of making obvious to those who are willing to see and to understand what it is that has challenged the hegemonic Western male center; what has called into question the different forms of oppression, such as ethnic prejudice, racism, classism, sexism and heterosexism; what challenges the present world order. It is not the theories of the academy that call into question and challenge. It is the struggles of marginalized and oppressed peoples. What has erupted and threatens to dislodge the subjugating aspects of the rationality of modernity is not the theories of the academy, the debates about postmodernity, but the insistence of subjugated people on being subjects of their own histories, on being central characters in their own narratives. Latinas' narratives weave into subversive stories the subjugated knowledge of Latinas, and they can produce "epistemological earthquakes and psychic shocks,"[14] capable of dislodging the present world order and of becoming intrinsic elements of new canons that are multiple and remain open and are at the heart of all attempts to imagine and to struggle to bring into existence a really new heaven and a new earth.

In elaborating *mujerista* theology, as we have listened to grassroots Latinas, we have been aware of how eager they are not only to share with us what has happened to them but also to interpret for us what has occurred to them.[15] We have noticed repeatedly that telling their stories helps the women give shape to their lives. They might start by relating only what has happened to them, but after a while they are explaining the meaning of what they have experienced. Furthermore, as time goes by, the women begin to make more and more explicit the conditions under which they have lived, the conditions that have helped them or have kept them from doing what they wanted. Some of them have gone even further, identifying the conditions under which they would have been able to accomplish what they have not been able to do.

In other words, the women have not only revealed the facts of their lives; they have not only allowed us to come to know their world. These women have indeed constructed a narrative: they have fashioned a certain story of their lives, with those with whom they have interacted as characters and themselves as protagonists of their own stories. The link that seems to connect the lived experiences they have shared with us about themselves is not a theme or a linear time concept but the character they have created for themselves, an exposition of how they understand themselves. The characters they create for themselves are ones that lead to and/or emerge from their present self-understanding. The characters of themselves they create are very influential in determining what they are willing to share, what they communicate to others.[16]

Through their narratives, Latinas have shared their understandings of how their gender impinges on their lived experiences, on who they are, on who they have become. They have explained cogently through their stories how different prejudices about women and the systems based on these prejudices have come together to affect their lives. Their narratives have indeed shown how they have been conscious of often having to adapt and pretend in order to survive, and how, in some circumstances, they have been unwilling to compromise because to do so would have been a betrayal of who they were/are. In her narrative, each Latina makes obvious

> her heroic attempt to respond to her situation in a positive way and create a . . . [person] that can confront the conditions of her life. This attempt is not a misrepresentation, nor is it trivial conceit. It is the self-expression of a woman who is doing what we all do: struggling to make sense of events that are beyond her control and to establish a place for herself in terms of the things that are within her control, and doing so not only through her actions but also through her representation of those actions via language.[17]

These narratives are subversive in nature because they unveil what has been suppressed or ignored by society and by the academy: they reveal how Latinas consciously adapt and pretend, how they do not think or feel or act the way they are "supposed to." They are subversive tales, then, because they are "counter stories—narratives of resistance and insubordination that allow communities of choice to challenge and revise the paradigm stories of the 'found' [dominant] communities in which they are embedded."[18] The narratives are "sources of counterhegemonic insight" because they expose how the understandings of the dominant ideology are not universal; because they reveal lives that defy or contradict the rules;[19] and because they uncover quiet but effective forms of resistance.

The effectiveness of these narratives may not be immediate; Latinas have not yet been successful in challenging the dominant community in a signifi-cant way. But these subversive narratives begin to break the hegemonic dis-course by insisting that Latinas' lived experiences and the narratives woven with them are legitimate sources of knowledge. As such, they pass on from generation to generation understandings that make it possible for us to live with a modicum of self-definition. These subversive narratives are full of in-stances of counterhegemonic insights that help Latinas redefine ourselves and the social institutions of society.

Here is an example of a subversive narrative that emerged from a group re-flection on the topic of embodiment and sexuality. While discussing her sex-ual experience, one of the women said that at times she pretends to experience orgasm for the sake of her husband, so he will not feel bad; "el pobre" (the poor man), she said, to punctuate why she does it. Other women joined the dis-cussion, most of them tacitly or implicitly indicating that they had done like-wise. Only one strongly indicated that she had not pretended and would not pretend in this regard.

At first this narrative might appear to indicate how women are oppressed by men. Certainly, if the women continue to be in a situation that limits their options, the kind of power available to them is limited. Nonetheless, the women are indeed exercising power, power understood not as a "thing" but as a process of decision making in which they can have a say.[20] This narrative is subversive because it shows that, even in a situation not of their making, Lati-nas have found a way to have some control of the situation: none of the women thought she was obliged to pretend to have an orgasm. Their reasons for pretense or its lack clearly show that they are aware of what they need to do to be able to live in situations they cannot or do not want to leave. The ones who pretended did so to gain the goodwill of their husbands or out of pity or "para que me deje en paz" (so he will leave me alone). None did it out of a con-viction that she was obliged as a woman to make her husband believe her own sexual performance was adequate. The women certainly did not blame them-selves for not having an orgasm. They pretended for their own sake, just as did those who would not pretend. From this perspective, one can reevaluate the perception that women who pretend to have orgasms are afraid of or con-trolled by their male partners. Instead, does it not show that Latinas claim the truth of their lives, that they act to protect themselves, they act for their own sake, and do not see themselves as failures because they do not have orgasms, even if they are aware of other versions of what the sexual performance of women should be? This narrative shows that Latinas are critical of "officially condoned untruths" because they consider them an injustice.[21]

This narrative is subversive because it shows that these women are able to analyze their reality and to translate it into the basis for liberative actions. This and other Latinas' narratives are windows into the conscience of Latinas indicating their criteria and method for choosing and deciding. The decisions that this narrative about Latinas' sexual experiences highlights indicate that the objectification of their bodies and the lack of importance the dominant ideological system has given to their own desires and pleasure have not impacted Latinas' consciences. In *mujerista* theology and ethics, we believe that it is precisely at the level of conscience that important battles against oppression are waged. Oppression and domination depend on how much they are enthroned in the conscience, in the feelings and thought processes of grassroots people. This is important in the struggle for liberation, because it is at the level of our consciences that life is determined.[22] Conscience is what becomes the determining element in all social processes and must, therefore, be taken into consideration as a key component of the process of liberation. Narratives like this one are subversive because they show that those who suffer under oppression and poverty and imperfect systems can still manage to save or create small spaces where they can operate according to their own criteria. This is important because as long as people are self-defining, even in a reduced capacity, they are capable of being agents of their own history, capable of imagining and working for an alternative system.[23]

The validity of this and other Latinas' narratives is "not dependent on the approval of the established regimes of thought."[24] A *mujerista* narrative is made up of insights that the dominant group has "disqualified as inadequate . . . or insufficiently elaborated" or "beneath the required level of cognition or scientificity."[25] In reality, however, a *mujerista* narrative shows the deficiency of "the centralizing powers which are linked to the institution and functioning of an organized scientific discourse within a society."[26] It also questions the methods used in setting such a discourse. In questioning the methods, it questions the content.[27]

The narratives of these Latinas are subversive because they show that the image the women have of themselves is different from that of the dominant culture. Satisfaction with their body size and weight is a good example of this sort of "independent thinking" in Latinas. At one of the reflection weekends, I shared my struggle to keep a positive self-image in spite of my big size. The women in the group immediately reacted in what could be considered a very pastoral way and repeatedly affirmed me by saying I looked "wonderful." During the breaks, the women continued to tell me that I should not have a negative view of myself because "en nuestra cultura" (in our culture) my body size would not be considered unsightly. These Latinas were not simply trying to make me feel good, even at the price of a half-truth. Rather, they offered me a different truth, based on a Latina interpretation of body and size.[28]

The ability of Latinas to see the differences in how big women are viewed in Latino as opposed to Euro-American culture reveals how conscious Latinas are of the meaning of their experiences and of the social conditions in which those experiences take place. It is precisely from the coming together of their lived experiences and the social conditions in which they live that Latinas draw their sense of reality.[29] Their narratives, moreover, reveal aspects of the human condition that are true not only for Latinas but for other women, if only the latter are willing to recognize that we can be mirrors for them. Being open to Latinas and to our world will help others to lay aside prejudices and to embrace differences.[30]

The narratives point to different elements of the social context of Latinas' lives, a context which "is not a script. Rather, it is a dynamic process through which the individual simultaneously shapes and is shaped by her environment."[31] Perhaps the most obvious influence is the interpersonal one. Latinas' lives are shaped and even made possible by their relationships with others.[32]

> This reliance may well be a function of women's relative powerlessness, their lack of access to more formal and institutional routes to influence, and as such a survival strategy shared with other relatively powerless groups. While it must be acknowledged . . . that the relationships which contextualize the lives of the women in question are forged, negotiated, and experienced within the framework of larger social-structural forces and factors, the significance of such relationships is *seldom revealed* in the analysis of social structure per se, nor can they be explained through a focus at that level. It is in looking directly at women's lives that relationships come to assume contextual importance and interpretative power.[33]

Interpersonal relationships are a key element in the Latina social context, for we come from a culture that continues to function in a very personalized fashion. By this we mean that Latina culture has not been extensively bureaucratized: we do not operate according to rules and regulations most of the time but rather at the level of knowing someone who can help or who knows someone else who will find a way of assisting. In Latina culture a network of relationships is essential for any person to survive and develop fully. This is why, for Latinas, individualism is the antithesis of a true sense of community, without which we could not survive as a marginalized group and without which we could not conceptualize liberation and struggle for it. Understanding ourselves always within an interpersonal context, then, helps us grasp the power dynamics that exist in society despite the myth that anyone, no matter who she or he is, can be materially successful in this society. The fact is that it does matter who you know; it is not only a matter of how good you are at what you do or how hard you work. The importance we give to the interpersonal helps us see that central to societal structures are networks of people who vouch for one another, who help one another, and who do all they can to keep the benefits of society in the hands of those who belong to "their kind."[34] This helps to demythologize structures, the level at which the so-called political works, making clear that its elements and processes are not so different from those that are present at the personal level. The differences between the two are more at the level of scale and accumulation of causes and effects.

The second element of context to consider is the intersection in Latinas' lives of their socioeconomic-political situation, the ideology of the dominant culture in which we live, and the Latino culture and ideology that also frames and informs our daily living. In the narratives of Latinas, it is noticeable how they are able to juggle two cultural-ideological frameworks. Latinas' lives and understandings of ourselves point to what is called "situational ethnicity," in which cultural change and ethnic persistence occur simultaneously.[35] To understand how Latinas deal with the cultural-ideological frameworks in our lives, it is best to consider a "multidimensional model of cultural change and persistence . . . [which takes into consideration] the study of the interrelationships of cultural, social and structural factors in historical perspective."[36] This means that for Latinas "the acceptance of new cultural traits and the loss of traditional cultural traits varies from trait to trait," some traditional traits being retained, some new traits being adopted.[37] In other words, what Latinas do is pick and choose from each culture whatever is beneficial to them, depending on, among other *things,*[38] in which of the two "worlds" we are operating. It is precisely this picking and choosing that gives birth to "new cultural and social patterns created by migrants and ethnic minorities in the new society,"[39] which we Latinas call *mestizaje* and *mulatez. Mestizaje* and *mulatez* shape our most immediate context; they refer to Latinas' condition as racially and culturally mixed people; our condition as people from other cultures living in the United States; our condition as people living between different worlds.[40] *Mestizaje* and *mulatez,* for Latinas, are not givens but a conscious choice, made obvious in how we move in and out of Latino and Anglo-American culture according to need and desire.

The third element that we consider part of Latinas' social context because of its influence is the expectations that Latinas have of themselves and their lives, expectations that often shape how they understand their life stories.[41] These expectations lead them to choose this or that point of reference for telling their stories, according to the meaning they are giving their lives. By "expectations" here we do not refer only to those a person may have had when she did or experienced something or when she has reflected on it in the past. We also mean her intentions for sharing her story, the way in which she views herself when she is sharing her story, how she perceives her narratives will be used, what she believes her story has to contribute, and how she thinks sharing her story will benefit others.[42]

Two examples make this point clear. Cuquita participated in one of the first reflection groups we had. She is a sixty-year-old woman born and raised in Mexico, with no home of her own. She works as a maid, and from what she said, we gathered that she lives in the homes where she works, yet keeping a room in one of her children's homes where she stores "mis cosas" (my stuff). Her full name is María del Refugio Quevedo, Cuquita being her nickname. She had compelling reasons for not wanting us to use a pseudonym for her. When she was young, she fell in love with a man who, after traveling to Texas, returned to their village. He was in love with her, but he was financially better off than she was. Cuquita says that "no fue lo suficiente hombre" (he was not man enough) to go against his parents' wishes and marry her. She eventually left the village and married another man, but she never has forgotten the man from Texas with whom she has always been in love. She keeps hoping she will find him. At the end of our time together, when we were explaining to the participants that if we quoted them directly we would use a pseudonym, Cuquita told us in unequivocal terms that we were to use her true name. "Maybe my love will read this book and he will come for me."

Since this was at least one of the reasons Cuquita shared her story with us, it has to be taken into consideration in analyzing her interpretation of herself and her life. Throughout, she presented herself as someone who always has been and is sexually passionate. We do not believe she invented her story, and nothing Cuquita said led us to believe it was not true. But we do think that her self-portrayal in this regard is linked to her desire to find the man she always has loved. How conscious she is of this motivation is not possible to tell, but we believe that her confessed desire to use this opportunity to find him points to an important expectation that we think is a key element in the way she understands herself and the meaning she gives to her life story.

Another example concerns one of the 120 Latinas with whom we worked in this project on embodiment. Only two said they were not comfortable with recording the sessions, although they allowed it. One woman, Rosario, came to see the importance of the project not only for herself but for Latinas in general, so in spite of her initial reticence, she would lean into the microphone to be sure that what she was saying would be adequately recorded. Is it unreasonable to believe that what she shared was in part shaped by her desire to help other Latinas? We venture to say that this expectation probably led her to a deeper reflection and analysis of her experiences, and even to a shaping of the experience in a way that she thinks would be positive for other Latinas. Wanting to help others by telling her story probably also gave her an added sense of confidence in herself and in her ability to relate her experiences in a meaningful way.

We consider these two narratives to be subversive because they uncover understandings Latinas have about themselves and their actions that contradict the passive image of Latinas that the dominant culture has. Both Cuquita and Rosario show how intentional Latinas can be about what they do. Their stories clearly indicate that they see themselves as creating meaning for themselves and as capable of contributing to better their lives and that of other Latinas. Both narratives show their self-awareness and, therefore, their ability to create their own identity.[43] Cuquita's insistence on naming herself is indeed an indication of her power; Rosario's belief that her story can make a difference shows the power that Latinas find in doing for others, in relationships and mutuality—a way of being that the dominant group, with its pervasive individualism, sees as obstructive to one's well-being.

CONCLUSION

The interests of *mujerista* theologians who facilitated the reflection weekends at which the narratives were gathered and who elaborate *mujerista* theology play a role in the development of *mujerista* subversive narratives.[44] Therefore, these interests must be taken into consideration when analyzing the results. What are our intentions and our ideology? Our programmatic worldview?[45] Undoubtedly, our own interests, our prodding questions, the stories of our own lives that we shared with the different groups of Latinas with whom we met—all of this influences the development of these narratives.

Our intention is not only to provide opportunities for personal growth for particular Latinas—opportunities to review their stories, evaluate them, and be intentional about future actions—but also to enable the development of a subversive, community narrative, a *mujerista* narrative, that will make public the values, norms, and ethical criteria of Latina culture. Our purpose is to see emerge not a grand narrative but rather a contextual narrative that weaves together Latinas' lived experience in the United States in the closing years of the twentieth century. Our purpose is not to help evoke the past for the past's sake; our purpose is to provide an opportunity for Latinas to interpret their experiences so they can value them and learn from their past in order to look confidently into the future. One of our main goals has been to provide opportunities for the development of Latinas' "communities of choice," so that being Latina can become something intentional, something more than being members of an ethnic community because of who our parents are.[46] We have wanted the reflection weekends for Latinas that we have facilitated to function as a moral space in which Latinas can analyze their identity, place, and actions, within the Latino community and within society at large. Communities of choice also provide a safe space for differences among Latinas to emerge and for the participants to deal with those differences. It has not been easy. Often we have not gotten much beyond the mere airing of those differences. Other times we have moved to an acknowledgment of respect for differences, and once in a while a given group has been able to understand that to embrace differences, they have to be open and allow those differences to impact on them. To encourage groups to become communities of choice, we have intended these reflection weekends to make it possible for Latinas to understand themselves as challenging the dominant group within which our communities are embedded.[47] To do this, they have to understand that their life stories are linked to the possibility for social action that leads to social transformation.[48]

Another hope of ours is that a *mujerista* narrative that gathers and weaves together Latinas' stories can be instrumental in creating a "cosmos of meaning" from which new consciousness and creativity can rise.[49] It is our belief that by enabling the emergence of a collective identity, a *mujerista* narrative will contribute to form a vision of a new heaven and a new earth for Latinas and our communities and motivate all of us to action.[50] A *mujerista* narrative can emotionally bind people together who have a shared experience, for "whether in touch with each other or not, the collective story . . . provides a sociological community, the linking of separate individuals into a shared consciousness."[51]

Our goal is to make known Latinas' narratives so that our beliefs and understandings can give theological meaning to and transform societal and church institutions.[52] We are convinced that Latinas' narratives, already recognized as a primary source for *mujerista* theology, make explicit the modes of thought and subjectivity of Latinas. They offer a specific historical analysis that "explains the working of power on behalf of specific interests"[53] that do not include Latinas, as well as reveal opportunities for resistance against such exclusion. The *mujerista* narratives point to the fact that "subjectivity and consciousness, as socially produced in language, . . . [are] a site of struggle and potential change." Latinas' narratives indeed suggest that meanings are social constructs, and that

> language is not an abstract system, but is always socially and historically located in discourses. Discourses represent political interests and in consequence are constantly vying for status and power. The site for this battle for power is the subjectivity of the individual and it is a battle in which the individual is an active but not sovereign protagonist.[54]

Latinas' narratives are still not powerful discourses because they are not known and/or lack firm institutional basis. We trust, though, that because of the important role of Latinas in our culture and the rapid growth of our communities in the United States, a *mujerista* narrative will begin to challenge understandings, practices, and forms of subjectivity that at present are staunchly supported by society even if they are oppressive. We continue to gather and circulate Latinas' narratives, convinced of their value and the need that exists to recognize them as key elements in the development of a new heaven and a new earth, of a real new world order that can indeed make way for the fullness of the kin-dom of God.

240   Ada María Isasi-Díaz

NOTES

1. This is a phrase used by the Zapatistas in Chiapas, México.
2. Prophetic eschatology shares many elements with apocalyptic eschatology. The main difference is that unlike prophetic eschatology, apocalyptic eschatology makes God and the kin-dom of God totally transcendental, requiring complete discontinuity from history. I use *kin-dom* instead of *kingdom* because the latter is a sexist and elitist concept, a time-bound image that I do not think portrays today what the Gospels intended.
3. My main conversation partners in this exploration of eschatology, particularly of prophetic eschatology, have been J. J. Collins, *The Apocalyptic Imagination: An Introduction to the Jewish Matrix of Christianity* (New York: Crossroad, 1984); Rosemary Radford Ruether, "Eschatology and Feminism," in *Sexism and God-Talk* (Boston: Beacon Press, 1983), 235–258; and Armando J. Rodriguez, a Ph.D. candidate at Chicago University and fellow Cuban living in the United States. His M.A. thesis at Garrett-Evangelical Theological Seminary, "Birth-pangs of an Age to Come: In Search for Links between Apocalyptic Eschatology and Ecology"; his presentation at the Hispanic Theological Initiative the spring of 1998; and several conversations we have had have been very instrumental in helping me frame the discussion presented here.
4. David L. Petersen, George W. E. Nickelsburg, D. E. Aune, "Eschatology," in *Anchor Bible Dictionary*, vol. 2 (New York: Doubleday, 1992), 575.
5. W. A. Quanbeck, "Repentance" in *The Interpreter's Dictionary of the Bible*, vol. 4 (Nashville: Abingdon Press, 1962), 33–34.
6. Ruether, "Eschatology and Feminism," 258.
7. Ibid.
8. Franz Hinkelammert, "Una sociedad donde todos quepan: De la importancia de la omnipotencia," in José Duque, ed., *Por una sociedad en donde quepan todos,* Cuarta Jornada Teológica de CETELA (San José: Editorial DEI, 1996), 361–377.
9. I have chosen to focus this essay on the creation of new narratives as a key element in living a prophetic sense of eschatology, for this is what Letty Russell has made and continues to make possible in very specific ways. Letty has been adamant about providing opportunities for racial/ethnic women theologians to bring to the theological forum the voices of our communities of accountability. She has provided opportunities for racial/ethnic women theologians from around the world to meet each other, to share understandings, to engage each other. She also has been relentless in creating opportunities for and pushing first-world theologians to meet and dialogue with U.S. racial/ethnic women theologians and those from the third world. No one more than Letty has shown us that, instead of attempting to deny the privileges we academicians in the first world enjoy, what we need to do is to use those privileges on behalf of the poor and the oppressed. It is an honor to call Letty Russell a friend, a sister in the struggle. *Ad multos años,* Letty.
10. As a Latina, in my work as a *mujerista* theologian I am an insider/outsider, sometimes speaking in the first person, sometimes in the third. In other words, my own lived experience is part of the source used in elaborating *mujerista* theology. It is part of the shared experiences that constitute the subversive *mujerista* narratives to which I refer in this article. I also refer to other Latinas' experiences when I speak broadly about Latinas. This leads at times to the use of "I," at times to the

use of "we," which refers to other *mujerista* scholars who participate with me in the gathering of narratives and the elaboration of *mujerista* theology or to Latinas more broadly speaking. Other times I use "they," referring to Latinas who have shared their stories with us.

11. José Míguez Bonino, "Nuevas tendencias en teología," *Pasos* 9 (January 1987): 22.
12. Laurel Richardson, "Narrative and Sociology," *Journal of Contemporary Ethnography* (April 1990): 117.
13. Paul Ricoeur, *A Ricoeur Reader: Reflection and imagination* (Hertfordshire, England: Harvester Wheatsheaf, 1991), 428.
14. This is a phrase that I heard from Elizabeth Minnick at a conference.
15. Since Latinas' lived experience is the source of *mujerista* theology, we do our research by gathering with groups of no more than ten Latinas for weekends of reflection. Though we have focused on different aspects of their religious understandings and practices, the reflection weekends always start with a long session in which the women share their life stories. Those of us who facilitate the weekends also share our stories.
16. Daphne Patai, *Brazilian Women Speak* (New Brunswick, N.J.: Rutgers University Press, 1988), 1–35.
17. Ibid., 33.
18. Hilde Lindemann Nelson, "Resistance and Insubordination," *Hypatia* 10, 2 (1995): 24.
19. The Personal Narratives Group, *Interpreting Women's Lives* (Bloomington and Indianapolis: Indiana University Press, 1989), 7.
20. Elizabeth Janeway, *Powers of the Weak* (New York: Alfred A. Knopf, 1981), 20. Janeway's thesis, which has greatly influenced me because it has been confirmed by grassroots Latinas' lives, is that the view of power from below is not less real than the view from above, that power is grounded on relatedness, and that what we need to do for power from below to gain importance and momentum is to stop thinking of it as unimportant.
21. Personal Narratives Group, *Interpreting Women's Lives* 7.
22. The material world can indeed coerce us to act against our consciences, and the material world is an intrinsic element of reality. However, though material needs can coerce us, they cannot convince us, and as long as we are not convinced that things are the way they should be, then we will find ways of struggling against oppression.
23. Isabel Rauber, "Perfiles de una nueva utopía," *Pasos,* 72 (July–Agust, 1997): 15–25.
24. Michel Foucault, *Power/Knowledge,* ed. Colin Gordon, trans. Colin Gordon, Leo Marshall, John Meplam, and Kate Soper (New York: Pantheon Books, 1980), 81.
25. Ibid., 82.
26. Ibid.
27. In this we disagree with Foucault, who sees subversive knowledges as not being primarily opposed to the prevalent methods and content but to how they are used. See ibid., 84.
28. See Christy Haubegger, "I'm Not Fat, I'm Latina," in *Reconstructing Gender: A Multicultural Anthology,* ed. Estelle Disch (Mountain View, California: Mayfield Publishing Co., 1997), 175–176.
29. Personal Narratives Group, *Interpreting Women's Lives,* 14.

30. María Lugones, "On the Logic of Pluralist Feminism," in *Feminist Ethics*, ed. Claudia Card (Lawrence: University of Kansas Press, 1991), 41–42.

31. Personal Narratives Group, *Interpreting Women's Lives*, 19.

32. The elaboration of the first three elements is based on those (more than three) identified in Personal Narratives Group, *Interpreting Women's Lives*, 20–23. We gained further insight into these three elements from reading Ricoeur, *A Ricoeur Reader*, 425–437.

33. Personal Narratives Group, *Interpreting Women's Lives*, 20. Emphasis added.

34. For us Latinas, what makes community and relationships so important is survival and fullness of being, not *exclusion* of those who are not like us.

35. Susan E. Keefe and Amado Padilla, *Chicano Ethnicity* (Albuquerque: University of New Mexico Press, 1987), 191.

36. Ibid., 195.

37. Ibid., 16.

38. Ibid., 18.

39. Ibid., 18.

40. Ada María Isasi-Díaz, *Mujerista Theology: A Theology for the Twenty-first Century* (Maryknoll, N.Y.: Orbis Books, 1996), 64–66.

41. Ibid., 22–23.

42. Marjorie Mbilinyi, " 'I'D HAVE BEEN A MAN'—Politics and the Labor Process in Producing Personal Narratives," in Personal Narratives Group, *Interpreting Women's Lives*, 204–227.

43. Janeway, *Powers of the Weak*, 22–35.

44. My other two colleagues in this project are Sister Yolanda Tarango, CCVI, director of Visitation House, a shelter and program for homeless women in San Antonio, Texas; and Milagros Peña, a sociologist of religion who teaches at the New Mexico State University in Las Cruces. Helping us facilitate the weekends of reflection were Adele González, of the Office of Lay Ministry of the Archdiocese of Miami; Carmen Torres Reaves, a community activist in New York City; and Josefina Durán, an American Baptist laywoman who is an educator and church activist.

45. We use *ideology* here in the sense used by the Sri-Lankan theologian Aloysius Pieris. See Aloysius Pieris, SJ, *An Asian Theology of Liberation* (Maryknoll, N.Y.: Orbis Books, 1988), 24–31.

46. See Marilyn Friedman, "Feminism and Modern Friendship: Dislocating the Community," *Ethics* 99, 2 (January 1989): 275–290.

47. See Nelson, "Resistance and Insubordination" 33–38.

48. Richardson, "Narrative and Sociology," 128.

49. David T. Abalos. *Strategies of Transformation toward a Multicultural Society* (Westport, Conn.: Praeger Publishers, 1996), 7–19. Abalos's work gives great importance to stories, though he relies on literary fiction and uses as his lens, almost exclusively, the theory of transformation developed by Manfred Halpern.

50. Ibid., 30. Our educational/research project was not set up to organize the women for action. Several of the groups wanted to find ways to keep meeting, and at least three are ongoing groups that we hope will factor this experience into their future projects. It was important and interesting to us that a major foundation seemed willing to give us a large sum of money for our project if we would turn it into an ongoing one. They told us that they saw this kind of project as being capable of becoming a social movement. We are sure they are right!

51. Richardson, "Narrative and Sociology," 128. She talks about "same experience" instead of the expression we use, "shared experience." See also Nelson, "Resistance and Insubordination," 28.
52. This is what Michel Foucault called a *discursive field*. We are indebted here to the presentation of his ideas made by Chris Weedon, *Feminist Practice and Poststructuralist Theory* (Cambridge, Mass.: Basil Blackwell Publisher, 1987), 35–42, 107–135.
53. Ibid., 41.
54. Ibid. Note that we are not saying that it is only in language that subjectivity and consciousness are socially produced.

BIBLIOGRAPHY OF WORKS BY LETTY M. RUSSELL

1960

"Daily Bible Readings." East Harlem Protestant Parish, New York, 1960–1968.
"The Family and Christian Education in Modern Urban Society." *Union Seminary Quarterly Review* 16 (November 1960): 33–43.
The City—God's Gift to the Church. Co-edited with Clyde Allison and Daniel C. Little. New York: United Presbyterian Church U.S.A., Board of National Missions, Division of Evangelism and Department of the Urban Church, 1960.

1963

"Equipping the Little Saints." *World Christian Education,* 4th quarter (1963): 124–26.

1966

"Changing Structures in the East Harlem Protestant Parish." *Union Seminary Quarterly Review* 21 (March 1966): 333–38.
"Christian Education and the Inner City," pp. 267–77 in *An Introduction to Christian Education,* edited by Marvin J. Taylor. Nashville: Abingdon Press, 1966.
Christian Education Handbook. New York: East Harlem Protestant Parish, 1966.
"The Cost of Missionary Action," pp. 215–18 in *Planning for Mission: Working Papers on the New Quest for Missionary Communities.* United States Conference for the World Council of Churches, 1966.

1967

"A Case Study from East Harlem." *Ecumenical Review* 19 (July 1967): 297–301.
Christian Education in Mission. Philadelphia: Westminster Press, 1967.

1969

"Renewal, Rapidation and Future." *Risk* 5 (1969): 60–69.
"Tradition as Mission: Study of a New Current in Theology and Its Implications for Theological Education." Th.D. diss., Union Theological Seminary, New York, 1969.

1970

"Church and Future: An Educational Perspective." *Colloquy* (October 1970): 32–34.
"Education in Action." *Manhattan College Magazine* (December 1970): 1–5.
"Shalom in Post Modern Society." *Colloquy* (December 1970): 21–25.
"Tradition as Mission." *Study Encounter* 6, 2 (1970): 87–96.

1971

Women's Liberation in a Biblical Perspective. New York: Young Women's Christian Association, National Board, 1971.

1972

"Celebrating World Community." *YWCA Magazine* (June 1972): 22–26.
"Christianity," pp. 10–14 in *According to the Scriptures: The Image of Women Portrayed in the Sacred Writings of the World's Major Religions,* ed. Stanley Samartha. Geneva: World Young Women's Christian Association, 1972.
Ferment of Freedom. New York: Young Women's Christian Association, National Board, 1972.
"Human Liberation in a Feminine Perspective." *Study Encounter* 20, 8 (1972): 1–12.

1973

"Soromundi." *YWCA Magazine* (March–April 1973): 12–13, 32.
"Unfinished Dimensions in the YWCA." *YWCA Magazine* (January 1973): 10–11, 33.

1974

Human Liberation in a Feminist Perspective. Philadelphia: Westminster Press, 1974.
"Impossible-Possibility." *Duke Divinity School Review* 39 (Spring 1974): 73–78.
"The Road to Freedom." *Sexism in the 1970's* (1974): 89–93.
"Women and Ministry," pp. 47–62 in *Sexist Religion and Women in the Church: No More Silence!* ed. Alice L. Hageman. New York: Association Press, 1974.

1975

"Ferment of Freedom." *Les Chiers du grif* (1975): 23–31.
"The Freedom of God." *Enquiry* 8 (September–November 1975): 27–48.
"Journey toward Freedom." *Lutheran World* 25, no. 1 (1975): 73–81.
"Letting Down the Clergy Line: Ministry Isn't Just for Ministers." *United Methodist Today* (May 1975): 16–19.
"Liberation Theology in a Feminist Perspective," pp. 88–107 in *Liberation, Rev-*

olution and Freedom: Theological Perspectives, ed. Thomas M. McFadden. New York: Seabury Press, 1975.
"Symposium on the Hartford Declaration." *Theology Today* 32 (July 1975): 186–87.
"Women: Education through Participation." *Religious Education* 70 (January–February 1975): 45–53.
"Women in the WCC: Participating in a Symphony of Groaning." *Midstream* (January 1975): 11–22.

1976

"Feminist and Black Theologies." *Reflection* (November 1976): 14–16.
"Theological Aspects of the Partnership of Women and Men in Christian Communities." *Pro Mundi Vita* 59 (March 1976): 4–10.
Editor. *The Liberating Word: A Guide to Nonsexist Interpretation of the Bible.* Philadelphia: Westminster Press, 1976.

1978

"Called to Account." *Ecumenical Review* 30 (October 1978): 369–75.
"Doing Liberation Theology with All Ages." *Church Educator* (February 1978): 1–4.
"A Feminist Looks at Black Theology," pp. 247–66 in *Black Theology II: Essays on the Formation and Outreach of Contemporary Black Theology,* ed. Calvin E. Bruce and William R. Jones. Lewisburg, Pa.: Bucknell University Press, 1978.
"Liberation and Evangelization—A Feminist Perspective." *Occasional Bulletin of Missionary Research* (October 1978): 128–30.

1979

"Clerical Ministry as a Female Profession." *Christian Century* (February 1979): 125–26.
The Future of Partnership. Philadelphia: Westminster Press, 1979.
"Handing on Traditions and Changing the World," pp. 73–86 in *Tradition and Transformation in Religious Education,* ed. Padraic O'Hare. Birmingham, Ala.: Religious Education Press, 1979.
"Partnership and the Future." *Bangor Alumni Bulletin* (Fall–Winter 1979): 19–27.
"Partnership in Educational Ministry." *Religious Education* 74 (March–April 1979): 143–46.
"The Role of the Church in the City," pp. 3–10 in *A Workbook for Urban Strategies.* Urban Minister's Network, United Methodist Church, (Fall 1979).
"Universality and Contextuality." *Ecumenical Review* 31 (January 1979): 23–26.
"Women and Freedom," pp. 234–46 in *Mission Trends No. 4: Liberation Theologies in North America and Europe,* ed. Gerald H. Anderson and Thomas F. Stransky. New York: Paulist Press, 1979.

1980

"Beginning from the Other End." *Duke Divinity School Review* 45 (1980): 98–106.
"Bread instead of Stone." *Christian Century* 97 (January–June 1980): 665–69.
"Education as Exodus." *Midstream* 19 (January 1980): 3–9.

1981

"The City as Battered Woman." *Cities in Transition* (Fall 1981): 20–21.
"Education for Partnership." *Reflection* 78 (Spring 1981): 13–16.
Growth in Partnership. Philadelphia: Westminster Press, 1981.
"The Role of Lutheran Colleges in Human Liberation: Education as Exodus."
    Academy (Summer 1981): 120–36.
"Women and Unity: Problem or Possibility." World Council of Churches, *Faith
    and Order Document* 81, 11 (1981): 37–43.

1982

Becoming Human. Philadelphia: Westminster Press, 1982.
"Ecumenical Implications of Feminist Theologies." *Ecumenical Trends* (October
    1982): 136–39.
"Feminist Critique: Opportunity for Cooperation." *Journal for the Study of the Old
    Testament* 22 (1982): 67–71.
"A Hard Word about Adultery," pp. 105–11 in *Proclaiming the Acceptable Year; Ser-
    mons from the Perspective of Liberation Theology,* ed. Justo Gonzalez. Valley
    Forge, Pa.: Judson Press, 1982.
"Refusal to Be Radically Helped." *Reflection* (November 1982): 7–8.

1983

"Forms of a Confessing Church Today." *Journal of Presbyterian History* 61 (Spring
    1983): 99–109.

1984

"Changing My Mind about Religious Education." *Religious Education* 79 (Win-
    ter 1984): 5–10.
Imitators of God. New York: United Methodist Church Women's Division, 1984.
"Partnership in New Creation." *American Baptist Quarterly* 3 (June 1984): 161–71.
"Women and Ministry: Problem or Possibility?" pp. 75–92 in *Christian Feminism:
    Visions of a New Humanity,* ed. Judith L. Weidman. San Francisco: Harper &
    Row, 1984.

1985

"The Church and Feminist Theologies," pp. 98–104 in *Korean American Women:
    Toward Self-Realization,* ed. Inn Sook Lee. Mansfield, Ohio: Association of
    Korean Christian Scholars in North America, 1985.

"A First World Perspective," pp. 206–11 in *Doing Theology in a Divided World*, ed. Virginia Fabella and Sergio Torres. Maryknoll, N.Y.: Orbis Books, 1985.

"Inclusive Language and Power." *Religious Education* 80 (Fall 1985): 582–602.

"Partnership in Stewardship: Creation and Redemption," pp. 2–8 in *Teaching and Preaching Stewardship: An Anthology*, ed. Nordan C. Murphy. New York: National Council of Churches of Christ, 1985.

Editor. *Changing Contexts of Our Faith*. Philadelphia: Fortress Press, 1985.

Editor, *Feminist Interpretation of the Bible*. Philadelphia: Westminster Press, 1985.

1986

"Authority in Mutual Ministry." *United Methodist Quarterly Review* 6 (Spring 1986): 10–23.

"Authority of the Future in Feminist Theology," pp. 313–22 in *Gottes Zukunft—Zukunft Der Welt: Festschrift fur Jürgen Moltman zum 60, Geburtstyag*, ed. Gerhard Marcel. Munich: Chr. Kaiser Verlag, 1986.

"Issues in Liberation Theology: A Review Essay." *Reflection* 83 (Winter 1986): 11–15.

"Ordination of Women," pp. 417–19 in *Dictionary of Liturgy and Worship*, ed. J. G. Davies. Philadelphia: Westminster Press, 1986.

"The Power of Partnership in Language." *Theological Markings: A United Theological Seminary Journal* 14 (Winter 1986): 1–8.

1987

Household of Freedom. Philadelphia: Westminster Press, 1987.

"People and the Powers." *Princeton Seminary Bulletin* 8 (1987): 6–8.

"Thirst for Justice." *LUCHA* 11, 1 (1987): 30–33.

Speaking of God. Co-edited with Shannon Clarkson. New York: Church Women United, Wellspring VIII, 1987.

1988

"Crossing Bridges of No Return: Unification, Women, and the Church." *In God's Image* (June 1988): 37–43.

"Feminist Interpretation," pp. 123–25 in *Abingdon Dictionary of Biblical Interpretation*. Nashville: Abingdon Press, 1988.

"How Do We Educate and For What? Reflections on U.S. Graduate Theological Education." *Journal of the Interdenominational Theological Center* (Fall 1987–1988): 35–42.

"Minjung Theology in Women's Perspective." Pp. 75–95 in *An Emerging Theology in World Perspective: Commentary on Korean Minjung Theology*, ed. Jung Young Lee. Mystic, Conn: Twenty-third Publications, 1988.

"Partnership in New Models of Renewed Community." *Ecumenical Review* 40 (January 1988): 16–26.

"Unity and Renewal in Feminist Perspective." *Midstream* 27 (January 1988): 55–66.

"Which Congregations? A Mission Focus for Theological Education," pp. 31–35 in *Beyond Clericalism: The Congregation as a Focus for Theological Education,* ed. Barbara G. Wheeler and Joseph C. Hough. Atlanta: Scholars Press, 1988.

Inheriting Our Mothers' Gardens: Feminist Theology in Third World Perspective. Co-edited with Kwok Pui-lan, Ada María Isasi-Díaz, and Katie Geneva Cannon. Philadelphia: Westminster Press, 1988.

1989

"Consciousness-Raising," pp. 73–75 in *Encyclopedia of Religious Education,* ed. Iris Brubaker Cully and Kendig Brubaker Cully. New York: Harper & Row, 1989.

"The Spirit Is Troubling the Water: Ecumenical Decade." World Council of Churches, *Women in a Changing World* (December 1989): 33–35.

1990

"Good Housekeeping," pp. 225–38 in *Feminist Theology: A Reader,* ed. Ann Loades. Louisville, Ky.: Westminster/John Knox Press, 1990.

"To Have Dominion: Perspectives on Householding." *In God's Image* (December 1990): 49–53.

Editor. *The Church with AIDS: Renewal in the Midst of Crisis.* Louisville, Ky.: Westminster/John Knox Press, 1990.

1991

"Ecumenical Learning in Theological Education: A Woman's Perspective." World Council of Churches, *Ministerial Formation* (July 1991): 15–20.

"Feminism in the Church: A Quest for New Styles of Ministry." World Council of Churches, *Ministerial Formation* (October 1991): 23–29.

"The Many-Layered Look." *In God's Image* (August 1991): 52–59

"Searching for a Round Table in Church and World," pp. 163–78 in *Women and Church: The Challenge of Solidarity in Times of Turmoil,* ed. Melanie A. May. Grand Rapids: Wm. B. Eerdmans Publishing Co., 1991.

1992

"Affirming Cross-Cultural Diversity: A Missiological Issue in Feminist Perspective." *International Review of Missions* 81 (April 1992): 253–58.

"Feminist Theologies," pp. 137–38 in *Encyclopedia of Reformed Faith,* ed. Donald McKim. Louisville, Ky.: Westminster/John Knox Press, 1992.

"Living by the Word." *Christian Century* (Dec. 1991, p. 1131; Dec. 11, p. 1163; Dec. 18–25, p. 1193; Jan. 1–8, 1992, p. 10; Jan. 15, p. 40; Jan. 22, p. 65; Jan. 29, p. 91).

1993

"Authority: A Christian Feminist Perspective." *Creative Change* 2 (1993): 2–4.
Church in the Round: Feminist Interpretation of the Church. Louisville, Ky.: Westminster/John Knox Press, 1993.
"Justice and the Double-Sin of the Church." *Living Pulpit* (November 1993): 13–15.

1994

"Ecumenical Learning in Theological Education: A Women's Perspective," pp. 25–32 in *God Has Called Us: A Report from the Ecumenical Workshop for Women Theological Educators,* ed. Kathy Keay, Linda Katsuno, and Ofelia Ortega. Geneva: WCC Publications, 1994.
"Feministische Theologie heute: Reflexionen aus der Sicht einer weissen Amerikanerin." Pp. 137–45 in *Evangelische Kommentare: Monatsschrift zum Seitgeschehen in Kirche und Gesellschaft.* Stuttgart: Mohringene, 1994.

1995

"Reflections on White Feminist Theology in the United States," pp. 102–11 in *Women's Visions: Theological Reflection, Celebration, Action,* ed. Ofelia Ortega. Geneva: WCC Publications, 1995.
"Searching for Identity around the Pacific Rim." *Journal of Women and Religion* 13 (Spring 1995): 5–14.

1996

"Education as Transformation: Feminist Perspectives on the Viability of Ministerial Formation Today." *Ministerial Formation* (July 1996): 23–30.
"Foreword," pp. xi–xii in *Through the Eyes of Women: Insights for Pastoral Care,* ed. Jeanne Stevenson Moessner. Minneapolis: Fortress Press, 1996.
"The Future of Feminist Hermeneutics." *Semeia* (Winter 1996): 39–55.
"Moving to the Margin." *Dialog* (Fall 1996): 305–10.
"Practicing Hospitality in a Time of Backlash." *Theology Today* 52, 4 (1996): 476–84.
Dictionary of Feminist Theologies. Co-edited with J. Shannon Clarkson. Louisville, Ky.: Westminster John Knox Press, 1996.
Women Resisting Violence: Spirituality for Life. Co-edited with Mary John Mananzan, Mercy Oduyoye, Elsa Tamez, J. Shannon Clarkson, and Mary Grey. Maryknoll, N.Y.: Orbis Books, 1996.

1998

"Education as Transformation: Women in Theological Education," pp. 103–10 in *Community-Unity-Communion: Essays in Honor of Mary Tanner,* ed. Colin Podmore. London: Church House Publishing, 1998.

"Helpmate, Harlot and Hero," pp. 141–45 in *There Were Also Women Looking On from Afar,* ed. Nyambura J. Njoroge and Irja Askola. Geneva: World Alliance of Reformed Churches, 1998.

INDEX

Walker, Alice, 14, 153, 211
welfare, 220–21
Wells, Ida B., 218–20
White, Deborah Gray, 218
White supremacy. *See* racism
Whitehead, Alfred North, 157–58, 168, 169 n. 4
Whyte, M. K., 60
Wilmore, Gayraud, 212–13
Williams, Delores, 149, 161, 211, 223
Wisdom, book of, 181
Wittgenstein, Ludwig, 166
woman, women,
  and Asia, 60–62
  and identity, 107–8

and ministry, *xiii*, 17–18, 20
and moral agency, 77, 84–86, 129–30, 137, 144, 211
and nature, 145–52
and relationality, 235–36
and rights, 16–18
Third World, 10–11
womanhood. *See* gender
womanist. *See* theology: womanist
women's movement. *See* women: and rights
Word of God, 30, 34, 35, 38–40, 42
work, 72
world. *See* creation

Zwingli, Huldrych, 204